WORLDS OF ARTHUR

WORLDS of ARTHUR

Facts & Fictions of the Dark Ages

GUY HALSALL

OXFORD
UNIVERSITY PRESS

OXFORD
UNIVERSITY PRESS

Great Clarendon Street, Oxford, OX2 6DP,
United Kingdom

Oxford University Press is a department of the University of Oxford.
It furthers the University's objective of excellence in research, scholarship,
and education by publishing worldwide. Oxford is a registered trade mark of
Oxford University Press in the UK and in certain other countries

First Edition published in 2013

Impression: 1

British Library Cataloguing in Publication Data
Data available

ISBN 978–0–19–965817–6

Printed in Great Britain by
Clays Ltd, St Ives plc

In Memoriam
Philip Arthur Rahtz
(1921–2011)

PREFACE

It is undeniably ironic that, if asked to name a British medieval king, the so-called 'man in the street' will probably come up with one who may well never have existed, or at least one about whom it is impossible to know anything. Yet 'King Arthur' continues to excite fascination. Again ironically, it is the supposed 'Arthur of History' rather than the 'Arthur of Legend' (about whom one can actually say far more) who inspires this interest.

This volume was conceived on a TGV between Montbard and Paris on 28 September 2009. I was reading the latest populist Arthurian history to hit the shelves. Positive reviews in war-gaming magazines suggested that it presented a plausible, scholarly case. It didn't, and this annoyed me. Almost every bookshop in the UK has at least half a shelf of this sort of book about 'King Arthur'. Written by amateur enthusiasts, each reveals a different 'truth' about the lost king of the Britons. All are mutually incompatible but usually based in whole or part upon the same evidence. Each author fanatically believes his version (and the author *is* usually a he) to be *the* true story, hushed up by horrid academics or by political conspiracies (usually by the English) or sometimes his rivals. Obviously they can't all be right. In fact none of them is, because, as this book will make clear, none of them *can* be. Arthur, if he existed—and he *might* have done—is irretrievably lost.

Such books sell, no doubt. Interest in 'King Arthur' is enormous. Yet they sell not because the 'interested layman' necessarily has a vested interest in the argument that King Arthur was Scottish,

Cornish, Welsh, or from Warwickshire or even, I suspect, in whether or not he existed. They sell because people believe the misleading claims of these books' covers, to reveal the 'truth' or unlock the 'secret'. In other words, they want to know. I could decry the cynicism of publishers who profit from this audience's sincere but ill-informed desire for knowledge and from these authors' dishonesty but I am more troubled by the inactivity of my own, historical profession. Why has it done nothing to help this interested lay audience, by propagating the results of the specialist work that disproves any and all claims to have discovered the real Arthur? Why has it not at least made available some insight into how to judge, and see through, the siren claims of the pseudo-histories, as I will refer to non-academic treatments of this period that ignore recent scholarly analyses?

This book responds to this demand. Before going any further, I should confess to being what might be termed a romantic Arthurian agnostic. That is to say that I wish that Arthur *had* existed but that I must admit that there is no evidence—at any rate none admissible in any serious 'court of history'—that he ever did so. Simultaneously, though, I also concede that it is impossible to prove for sure that he *didn't* exist, that one cannot demonstrate for sure that there is no 'fire' behind the 'smoke' of later myth and legend. If that sounds too wishy-washy, I will argue that this is the *only* attitude that can seriously be held concerning the historicity of the 'once and future king'.

The book is divided into four parts, or 'Worlds' of Arthur. Parts I–III serve as a guide to *why* we do not know anything about Arthur, and to *why* it is impossible to know whether he existed or not. They outline the available evidence and how it has been used and misused. But they are also an introduction to what we *can suggest*, at least, about the world in which Arthur is usually supposed to have lived, that darkest era of the so-called Dark Ages between the fizzling out of Roman imperial rule and the arrival of a different kind of Roman authority, with St Augustine's mission to Kent in 597. These parts of this book explain why you should not waste money on any of the numerous volumes claiming to have 'solved the riddle' of Arthur or which include phrases like 'the true story' or 'the secret revealed' in their titles.

Part I deals with 'Old Worlds', the traditional ideas about what became of Britain after the Roman Empire. Here we will meet all the characters, places, and events of the familiar stories about the world of Arthur. We will encounter the early medieval sources for these stories and the main forms of archaeological evidence that were employed to back them up. This, essentially, remains the 'world of Arthur' encountered in modern 'pseudo-histories'. The second part concerns 'present worlds'. Here I set out how scholars have reassessed the written and archaeological evidence for fifth- and sixth-century Britain, and how specialist academic circles view this period today. We will see that the comforting, familiar story told in Part I can no longer be relied upon. As well as looking at how the written sources have been revealed to be entirely untrustworthy, Part II shows the ways in which excavated data have been reconsidered and are (sometimes at least) used in somewhat different ways from those that were common in the nineteenth and first three quarters of the twentieth centuries. By the end of this part, you will see that in 2012, in many ways, we know far *less* about fifth- and sixth-century British history than we did in 1975. The third part, 'Mad Worlds', rounds off the survey of the current state of play by taking you through some common arguments presented in the 'pseudo-histories' to try and avoid the lessons of modern scholarly criticism. It also contains a not-entirely-serious look at some misleading 'red herrings' about 'the historical Arthur'.

These first three parts, or 'worlds', will give you a grounding in the evidence available for the study of post-imperial Britain, its problems, and how scholars treat it today. They provide a 'tool kit' to help the interested reader evaluate the claims made in the 'pseudo-histories'.

By contrast, in Part IV, 'New Worlds?', I set out my own reading of the evidence. It doesn't claim to represent the truth; it is up front about being a personal view, not currently held by many people, and frequently controversial. It contains precious few 'facts', being about frameworks and interpretations. I hope that this part of the book will be of interest and value to specialists but I firmly believe, too, that new scholarly ideas should be available to the interested audience outside academia. That audience should not have to wait years for those ideas to be accepted, to become the consensus view, and then be filtered down through populist volumes and TV programmes. By the time that happens, the academic view has usually moved on. Therefore, although of necessity quite technical in places, I have endeavoured to make it as accessible as possible to an intelligent non-specialist.

Part IV builds upon the current scholarly consensus in many ways but in others points out some shortcomings of academic interpretations. While very high-quality work has been done on excavating, recording, and analysing the sites and artefacts from this period (we must be clear about that), the readings of this material suffer from several problems. One is a purely British—indeed usually a purely *English*—outlook; we will see that Britain in this period cannot be understood outside its broader European context. Another, less common but persisting nevertheless, is the artificial division between Roman archaeology, which ceases around 400, and Anglo-Saxon archaeology, which starts in the fifth century. A full understanding of the world of 'King Arthur' requires us to look at developments across this divide. Third, possibly the most serious problem of all, is a view of the era which stems ultimately from the legacy of the written sources discussed in Chapters 2 and 4 and which conceives of it in 'binary' terms. That is to say that it sees it simply as a straightforward, two-sided ethnic struggle between *the* Britons and *the* Saxons. My previous research has focused on mainland European history and archaeology between the fourth century and the seventh. This allows me to stand outside these debates and look at them in a different and, I hope, more helpful perspective. I will suggest some—quite radical—directions for future, critically informed work that might, in turn, help us build a new and different 'World of Arthur'.

I have not wanted to bog the non-specialist reader down with footnotes; academic readers will usually know where the information comes from anyway. Instead, I have included a long, chapter-by-chapter essay on further reading, and a bibliography. The further reading essay suggests background reading as well as referring to the technical pieces whence I have taken specific points and arguments. Debts of this kind are acknowledged here rather than in the usual scholarly apparatus.

ACKNOWLEDGEMENTS

That leaves more general debts. In some ways this book is 'my own work' to a greater degree than anything I have written before. Nonetheless, Parts I and II are entirely based upon the work of previous scholars—especially the linguists, the editors, the excavators, and the finds-analysts—who have mastered the era and created the picture of it that we have today, through various technical skills which I lack completely. I cannot do other than express my enormous debt to the work they have produced. Parts I and II do no more than set out the results of all this work for the interested layman or newcomer to the period, and perhaps for specialists in one area who are unfamiliar with the others. The critical lessons of Part III are similarly founded upon what I have learnt from these specialists. Part IV might then seem to turn round and bite the hand that fed me. In some ways this is probably right. However, its bed-rock remains the work of all the specialists just mentioned, and the debt of gratitude remains. I hope this is clear.

I owe most to the Leverhulme Trust, which awarded me a Major Research Fellowship for the years 2009–12 to study the Transformations of the Year 600. The British aspects of this period of profound change across western Europe are much referred to in this book. I am very grateful, too, to Richard Burgess, Kate Forsyth, James Fraser, Fraser Hunter, Charles Insley, Dave Petts, Tom Pickles, Mark Whyman, and Alex Woolf for help with specific areas or research. Charles, Tom, Mark, and Alex read the whole volume in one version or another and provided enormously helpful feedback. Chris Wickham made an important suggestion for Chapter 11 and the Oxford University Press's anonymous readers made a wide range of uniformly useful comments, not least about the book's structure. Luciana O'Flaherty at OUP encouraged me to write a different (and better) book than the one I originally proposed and was continuously enthusiastic about the project thereafter. My thanks also go to all the people who contributed to discussions about particular ideas or sections of the book on the 'After Rome' *Yahoo!* Group and my blog (600transformer.blogspot.com). In particular, my ideas about language change and Anglo-Saxon expansion from the western edge of the villa-zone come directly from a conversation with Stephen Brohan (who also carried out some sterling proofreading). My family and friends always deserve my thanks. So, as ever, does Emma Campbell. In another year, this would have been her book, written (for once) about a topic in which she has a personal interest.

Obviously I owe a huge debt of thanks to the people who taught me early medieval British history and archaeology as an undergraduate: Edward James, Tania Dickinson, Harold Mytum, and Steve Roskams. Above all, though, I thank Philip Rahtz, who passed away while I was writing this volume. I met Philip on the first dig I attended and he was instrumental in my decision to study history and archaeology at York, one I have never regretted. He was a hugely charismatic teacher and a great encouragement in my postgraduate days. I don't know that he would have agreed with, or even liked, everything in this book, but he would have given the ideas space. Philip always had space for ideas; it was one of his many qualities. For what I, personally, and post-imperial (especially 'sub-Roman') British archaeology, in general, owe him, I dedicate this book to Philip's memory with much affection and gratitude.

Half handbook or introduction for the student, non-specialist, or interested layman, and half controversial academic essay, this book will doubtless be seen by many as neither fish nor fowl. That is fair enough. Nevertheless, most animals are neither fish nor fowl and many, I am reliably informed, are quite tasty.

CONTENTS

CONTENTS

ABBREVIATIONS

ASE	*Anglo-Saxon England.*
BAR(B)	British Archaeological Reports (British Series).
BAR(I)	British Archaeological Reports (International Series [originally 'Supplementary Series']).
BBCS	*Bulletin of the Board of Celtic Studies*
EHR	*English Historical Review*
EME	*Early Medieval Europe*
HB	*Historia Brittonum* ('Nennius')
HE	Bede, Ecclesiastical History
JRA	*Journal of Roman Archaeology*
JRGZM	*Jahrbuch des römisch-germanisches Zentralmuseums* Mainz
MGH AA CM	Monumenta Germaniae Historica. Auctores Antiquissimi vol.9, *Chronica Minora saec.* IV. V. VI. VII vol. i, ed. T. Mommsen (Berlin, 1892).
NCMH 1	*The New Cambridge Medieval History*, i *c.500–c.700*, ed. P. Fouracre (Cambridge, 2005).
NMS	*Nottingham Medieval Studies*
P&P	*Past & Present*
PPAS	*Proceedings of the Society of Antiquaries for Scotland*
SzSf	*Studien zur Sachsenforschung*
TRHS	*Transactions of the Royal Historical Society*

LIST OF FIGURES

PART I
Old Worlds

It's all true, or it ought to be,
and more and better besides

WINSTON CHURCHILL

I

The Story of 'King Arthur'

❧❦❧

The 'Arthur story' begins with certainty in the early ninth century. An author writing in Wales, and often known (possibly wrongly) as Nennius, compiled a *History of the Britons* (*Historia Brittonum*). In this jumbled-looking history, which even refers to itself as a 'heap', are included two passages about somebody called Arthur. One of these is better known than the other. The well-known passage is often referred to as the 'Battle-List' of Arthur: a sequence of twelve battles in which this Arthur, described as 'leader of battles' (*dux bellorum*), laid low his enemies. The author evidently places these battles during the fifth or sixth centuries, during the Anglo-Saxon (or English) settlement of Britain. We will return to this list in more detail, as it provides the basis for most modern pseudo-histories of 'King Arthur'. The second Arthurian passage in the *History of the Britons* is less well known simply because it is more inconvenient to fans of 'the historical Arthur'. In this (jointly with the Battle-List) earliest datable reference to Arthur, he is already a legendary figure. The passage alludes to a tale about a great boar-hunt, seemingly a story told in a central medieval Welsh Arthurian romance, saying where in the hills

3

around Builth Wells you can see the footprint of Arthur's giant hound embedded in a stone in a cairn. This can never be stolen but always miraculously returns. In Ergyng, says the *History*, you can also see the grave of Amr, son of 'Arthur the soldier' and slain by Arthur himself. This is never the same length twice, when you measure it. There's no convincing reason to suppose that the two passages refer to different Arthurs. Thus in Gwynedd around 830, some people had heard about an at least semi-legendary character called Arthur.

Possibly around the same time (possibly earlier, possibly later; it's impossible to say for sure) a poet (maybe writing in the same part of the world as the *History of the Britons* was written) composed an elegy about the massacre of a noble, heroic British warband at a place called Catraeth (usually thought to be Catterick in North Yorkshire). In this poem, *Y Gododdin*, the poet (who claimed the name of Aneirin, a poet mentioned in the *History of the Britons*) described the martial feats of one warrior but said that nevertheless 'he was not Arthur'. Sadly our poet, whoever he was, whenever he was writing, does not pause to tell us who *was* Arthur but we can at least say that, like his possible contemporary (and indeed possible neighbour), the author of the *History*, he had heard of someone by that name. It does not, let me stress, imply anything about whether this character was historical or legendary.

The Arthurian story resumes in the tenth century when another anonymous scribe compiled a series of annals (a list of years next to which was written memorable events that happened during them) known to historians as the *Annales Cambriae* (*The Welsh Annals*). Here, two entries give our Arthur character a very precisely dated existence. Under the year 516, we read that Arthur won the battle of Badon, carrying the image of Jesus Christ 'on his shoulders', as he did so. Then, under 537, an entry mentions the 'battle of Camlann, in which Arthur and Medraut [eventually to become better-known as Mordred] perished'. This information is far less precise than many would like.

This, disappointingly, is *the sum total* of *all* the evidence for 'King Arthur' that survives from within five centuries of his supposed existence around AD 500. We might reasonably see this historical silence as the lid on a bubbling kettle of popular tales or legends. The meagre surviving traces represent small puffs of vapour let out when the lid was briefly forced up by the steam, before plopping firmly back down again. It must be said, though, that one might also link these stories together, to some extent, through a purely textual relationship. That is to say that the author of the *Welsh Annals* had read the *History of the Britons*, that the author of the *History of the Britons* had read 'Aneirin's' poetry (or vice versa), which the Welsh annalist might also have read, and that one or more of these writers had read the work of a certain Gildas, whom we shall encounter in the next chapter. No kettle required. Within 200 years of the compilation of the *Welsh Annals*, however, the lid of our 'kettle' had blown right off. Mixing our metaphors somewhat, the steam had turned into a veritable geyser.

Probably behind this explosion was a character called Geoffrey of Monmouth who, in the earlier twelfth century, wrote a *History of the Kings of Britain*, including a long and extraordinarily detailed history of King Arthur and his many exploits. Geoffrey claimed to have based this on a 'very ancient book', whose title or author he omitted to name. It is hardly an unknown strategy among authors who wish to ascribe some form of authority to their own invention, but it has served as a convenient 'get-out clause' for the authors of modern pseudo-history who want to flesh out the details of their stories about Arthur. Even some medieval people thought that Geoffrey was making it up. One, William of Newburgh, wrote:

> it is quite clear that everything this man wrote about Arthur and his successors, or indeed about his predecessors from Vortigern onwards, was made up, partly by himself and partly by others, either from an inordinate love of lying, or for the sake of pleasing the Britons.

But the thing was, and this cannot be emphasized too strongly (even if modern historians sometimes forget it), medieval people did not see the same distinction as their modern descendants do between legend and history. The point of 'history' was moral teaching, not facts about 'how it really was'.

Be that as it may, from about Geoffrey's day onwards the legend of Arthur blooms into myriad tales in numerous different languages, principally French (including Anglo-Norman), and by 1300 or thereabouts all the well-known characters, places, and objects have made their appearance: Lancelot, Guinevere, Galahad, and Gawain, plus Merlin, Excalibur, the Lady in the Lake, the Sword in the Stone, and Camelot, Arthur's capital. These stories, and the characters and events in them, collectively form what was known as 'The Matter of Britain'. A 'matter' in this sense was a specific body of material upon which writers and storytellers could draw. The 'Matter of France', for example, constituted the stories about Charlemagne and the heroic knights of his court (Roland, Olivier, and the rest). The Welsh version of the Arthurian legend also appears in written form from about 1100 onwards, though the relationship between this corpus of stories and the French one is difficult to unravel. Certainly it is by no means certain that the French Arthur derives entirely from the Welsh, rather than vice versa. In the late twelfth century, the monks of Glastonbury Abbey even claimed to have discovered King Arthur's grave in their monastery. If not simply wanting to 'cash in' on the popularity of the Arthur story, it is possible that, as has been suggested, they (perhaps on the instructions of their king, Henry II) wanted to prove to his Welsh enemies that Arthur really was dead and gone and therefore unlikely to come back from his rest to clear the English out of Britain any time soon. The development of this legendary material is not part of this book's remit. There is an enormous body of scholarly literature analysing all aspects of 'the Arthur of Legend' from a wide variety of literary and historical perspectives. For now, all that needs to be stressed is the fact that this legend all comes six centuries, or more, later than the 'historical' Arthur.

After the blossoming of Arthurian romance in the Victorian period, the historical and legendary Arthurs began to separate from each other, unsurprisingly, when the discipline of history established itself as a scientific exercise with its own academic practices, distinct from philosophy or literature. Over time, attitudes towards the claim that there was a figure of this name, alive around 500, divided into two camps. On one side were the Arthurian hard-liners who claimed that the evidence was late and legendary and therefore inadmissible, and thus consigned Arthur wholly to the sphere of legend (by now separable from History), and on the other were the believers in 'no smoke without fire', happy to accept that the Arthur attested in the three first-millennium sources mentioned above had a real existence, giving rise to these tales. Even if most, if not all, cheerily dismissed the legendary writings from Geoffrey of Monmouth onwards, some attempted to weave into the fragmentary first-millennium traces of Arthur the testimony of other indubitably genuine early medieval sources and archaeology. All of these forms of evidence are discussed in the following chapters.

The confrontation came to a head after the publication of John Morris's *The Age of Arthur* in 1973. Morris—who was a very learned and respected scholar, with an awareness of an enormous range of evidence, written and archaeological—claimed that through the consultation of a wide array of neglected 'Celtic' written sources, notably saints' lives, a detailed narrative history of fifth- and sixth-century Britain was possible. All of a sudden this Dark Age was apparently bathed in light. Morris sketched an account of a unified post-imperial British state caught up, first, in a struggle between Vortigern and Ambrosius Aurelianus 'the elder' (for, according to Morris, there were two people by this name—I will introduce these characters more fully in the next chapter), and then subject to Saxon and other barbarian attacks. A revival led by Ambrosius 'the younger' in the later fifth century engendered a period of British triumph under the 'Emperor Arthur' around AD 500, culminating in his great victory at Mount Badon. This stopped the Saxon advance in its tracks for over a generation, during which the British lapsed into civil war and Arthur's 'Empire' fell apart. In the later sixth century, the English resumed their advance against the divided British 'successor states' and by the mid-seventh century the picture of an English lowland and a Welsh highland zone was established.

There are essentially two things that you need to know about Morris's *The Age of Arthur*: one is that it is a marvellous, inspiring read; the other is that very little of it can be relied upon. I sometimes wonder if it wasn't one of the greatest historical hoaxes ever perpetrated. If Morris's intention was to be deliberately provocative and, by proposing an intentionally outrageous theory of post-imperial British history, make people think hard about the problems of the sources for this period, he certainly succeeded. The book received a barrage of criticism, most notably by David Dumville (then of Cambridge University's department of Anglo-Saxon, Norse, and Celtic), who contributed a devastating critique to the journal *History* in 1977 (in an ideal world it would be given away free with every copy of *The Age of Arthur*). Dumville showed that the 'Celtic' sources used by Morris were without evidential value for the fifth and sixth centuries; we will look at why in Chapter 4. A more generous, but still irresistible, discussion of Morris's evidence and interpretation was written by a prominent Oxford Anglo-Saxon historian, James Campbell. From 'Celticist' and 'Anglo-Saxonist' perspectives, then, Morris's book was shown to have more holes than a Swiss cheese.

Morris himself was less than up-front about his evidence. *The Age of Arthur* has one of the most labyrinthine referencing systems you will ever encounter, covering Morris's tracks very efficiently and making it difficult to find the sources for his statements. If you persist you will often find that the evidence cited does not say what he would have us believe it says, or is of extremely dubious worth. Two examples will suffice. In his account of the war (559–60) of the Frankish king Chlothar I against his rebellious son, Chramn, and his Breton allies (*Age of Arthur*, 257–8), Morris plays havoc with the evidence of the contemporary Gaulish bishop-historian Gregory of Tours, reverses events and characters, and uncritically intersperses it with data from late Breton saints' lives. None of this messing about is evident from the text, where it is woven into a seamless narrative. Second, on p. 377 of *The Age of Arthur* you will read how St Finian lost out in a sort of military praying contest to St Columba at the battle of Cuil Dreimhne. If you can track it down, the source for this 'pray-off' is no even vaguely contemporary source but a sixteenth-century collection of O'Neill folklore. In some ways, Morris was the Geoffrey of Monmouth *de nos jours*.

And, like Geoffrey of Monmouth's, Morris's work has mostly remained untouched by the torrent of scholarly critique. It continues in print, available in bookshops across the land, providing the inspiration for droves of writers penning their own half-baked theories about who, where, and when 'King Arthur' was. Meanwhile, though, among the academic community, the sceptics have decisively carried the day. No sane scholar will now argue that there is definitely a 'King Arthur' figure in fifth- or sixth-century history about whom anything solid can be said, so professional historians now tend to leave the issue alone. The old opposition between sceptics and believers has thus, since the debate on Morris's book, been transformed into a division between qualified academic students of the period and enthusiastic, wilfully naive (at best) amateurs respectively. The academics, though, have not attempted to take their argument outside their universities, abandoning the battlefield to the amateurs. Consequently, works like Morris's and his less scholarly imitators continue to lead astray thousands of people with a genuine interest in that mysterious, romantic post-imperial era of British history. This book aims to help this interested audience by acting as a corrective to the shelves of pseudo-historical 'Arthurian' nonsense available in practically every bookshop in Britain.

If you are a firm believer that King Arthur lived, and that he lived in Cornwall, or Scotland, or Warwickshire, or wherever, or even if you want me to tell you—yes or no—whether or not 'King Arthur' ever lived, you will find yourself gnashing your teeth in Part II. If you know anything at all about fifth- and sixth-century Britain you will probably find yourself gnashing your teeth at at least some of Part IV. If you have written one of the pseudo-histories you will find you have little by way of teeth left to grind by the end of Part III. I do not set out simply to shock (or create work for dentists). I hope that the summaries of information and argument set out in Parts I and II are reliable and believe that the case presented in Part IV is better than its currently available alternatives. That does not necessarily make it 'right'. Marc Bloch, perhaps the greatest historian of the twentieth century, once said that right answers were less important than the right questions. The questions asked of the written evidence pertaining to this period were for a long time the wrong ones, as is now generally accepted. I contend that many questions posed of the excavated data continue to be fundamentally mistaken. We will only progress in understanding this fascinating period when that situation changes. This book, then, is principally about asking questions, ones best posed from a vantage point that sees more than just the British 'World of Arthur'. The study of King Arthur has been insular for too long.

2

The Matter of Arthur

The Traditional Narrative

❧❧

Prelude: the ending of Roman Britain

In another ironic twist, the end of imperial authority in Britain is better documented than most periods of Roman rule there. In mid-406, the army in Britain raised to the throne three individuals in rapid succession, usurping the authority of the feeble Emperor Honorius. Two, Marcus and Gratian (the latter at least a civilian), were soon assassinated. The third, a soldier, took (presumably) the most effective elements of the British garrison to Gaul to make good his claim to the throne as 'Constantine III'. This was hardly the first time this had happened. The British army had raised a usurper emperor in the form of Magnus Maximus, who reigned for five years before being defeated and executed by Honorius' father, Theodosius I, in 388. Most famously and successfully, the great Constantine I had been proclaimed emperor in York, and thus had similarly started out as a usurper. This happened exactly 100 years before 'Constantine III's' election, one possible reason for his choice as a candidate; a contemporary writer said they 'took hope from his name'.

Why had the British army taken this well-worn track right now? At about the same time a major barbarian incursion crossed the Rhine into an effectively undefended northern Gaul. It is often said that the Rhine was frozen, allowing the barbarians across, but the earliest source to say so was Edward Gibbon's late eighteenth-century *Decline and Fall of the Roman Empire*! In Zosimus' *New History* (written *c*.500 in the eastern Roman Empire), the invasion is assigned to 31 December of the year we know as 406, placing the invasion *after* the British usurpations. However, it is possible that the event occurred on 31 December 405, *before* the elevation of Gratian, Marcus, and Constantine.

Constantine invaded Gaul during 407. He quickly established himself in Gaul, possibly at Lyon, and his authority was accepted in Spain. With much of the West secure, Constantine marched to Trier, his troops apparently penning the barbarian invaders into the far north of Gaul. By 409 he had tightened his control over Spain, defeating a rebellion there by Honorius' relatives, and even claimed that Honorius had granted him the title of consul. Honorius was hard pressed in Italy by Alaric the Goth and a Gothic-backed usurper, and might have needed Constantine's support. Things then started to unravel for Constantine. The barbarians broke out of northern Gaul and stormed southwards, entering Spain in late 409. In Spain itself, Constantine's general Gerontius rebelled and proclaimed his own usurper emperor, Maximus. Constans, Constantine's son and *caesar* (deputy emperor), fled back to Gaul.

In 410 Constantine 'III' planned a two-pronged counter-offensive. While Constans was sent with another force to retake Spain, he invaded Italy—whether to support Honorius against Alaric or to take advantage of Honorius' plight to seize the western Empire's last remaining components is unknown. It all ended in failure. Constantine's army soon returned to Gaul, possibly after being defeated by Alaric. Constans was hounded back over the Pyrenees by Gerontius and killed at Vienne, south of Lyon. In 411 Emperor Honorius' general Constantius defeated Gerontius, who was by then besieging Constantine 'III' in Arles. Routing a relieving army from the north, Constantius captured Constantine and took him and his other son, Julian, back to Italy, where both were beheaded. Thus ended Constantine's bid for power.

Meanwhile, according to the anonymous *Gallic Chronicle of 452*, Britain was ravaged by the Saxons in 409 or 410. Zosimus says that, after serious barbarian attacks (possibly those mentioned by the *Chronicle of 452*), the Britons took up arms and threw out 'Roman' officials, evidently in 409. They 'installed the government they wanted'. Zosimus also says that Honorius wrote to the cities of *Brittia* (this would be in 410) telling them to look after themselves. It is not certain, it should be said, either that *Brittia* is Britain rather than Bruttium in Italy (which also makes sense in the context of the events of 410) or that Honorius was talking about a high political level of defence.

Post-imperial Britain

After Constantine's defeat, historical darkness descends upon Britain as far as contemporary mainland European sources are concerned. However, the era is described in insular British sources, some of which were mentioned in Chapter 1. The traditional historical narrative is based primarily around four sources: the *De Excidio et Conquestu Britanniae* (*On the Ruin and Conquest of Britain*), by someone called Gildas, usually believed to have been written around 540; the *Ecclesiastical History of the English People*, written by Bede in 731; the *History of the Britons*, of 828–9, ascribed to a writer called Nennius; and the *Anglo-Saxon Chronicle* written in Wessex from the 880s onwards.

The Pictish wars

The relevant part of Gildas' account falls into a 'Northern Section' and an 'Eastern Section'. The former opens with the legions' departure under the *tyrannus* (tyrant) Magnus Maximus. This can be pinned to 383, the year of Maximus' rebellion. Maximus left Britain to endure Pictish and Scottish attacks. The Britons appealed to Rome and a legion was dispatched, building a defensive turf wall before leaving. This did not protect the Britons so a second appeal was made and another force was sent, this time constructing a stone wall and instructing the Britons about military defence before withdrawing. This also failed to have the desired effects. The barbarians took the north of the island and harried Britain from sea to sea. The fifth-century Gaulish *Life of Germanus of Auxerre* mentions that the saint was sent to Britain to adjudicate between orthodox Catholic Christians and Pelagian heretics (on whom, more later). This took place in 429. Whilst in Britain, the bishop took command of local defence against a combined Pictish–Saxon force. Germanus stationed the British army in ambush on both sides of a valley and when the barbarians appeared they rose up shouting 'Alleluia', at which the enemy—unsurprisingly—fled.

Things were clearly looking bleak when the Britons wrote to Aëtius, imperial military commander in Gaul between the later 420s and 454. Gildas cites a passage from their letter, entitled the 'Groans of the Britons'. Aëtius is described as 'thrice consul' (*ter consulus*). His third consulate took place in 446 and he was murdered in 454, giving a date-bracket for the letter. Aëtius was campaigning in northern Gaul in 448, which might provide a more precise context. Aëtius was told how the Britons were driven into the sea by the barbarians and thrown by the sea back to the barbarians, giving them a choice between drowning and having their throats slit. Nevertheless Aëtius sent no help. Bede later explained that Aëtius had his hands full, dealing with the Huns. In Britain things went from bad to worse. Famine broke out, and hunger drove some Britons to surrender to the barbarians. Others fled to remote mountains, heaths, and caves. Some, however, fought back until the barbarians were repelled. In Gildas' view, this victory only led to a period of sin and sexual excess.

The coming of the Saxons

Now Gildas' 'Eastern Section' begins, with rumours of impending barbarian attack. A council, under a 'proud tyrant' (*tyrannus superbus*), invited the Saxons to defend Britain. This tyrant is named by Bede and later sources as a certain 'Vurtigernus'—Vortigern. Vortigern's name means something like 'High Ruler' in Old Welsh and it is thought that Gildas' 'Proud Tyrant' was a pun on this. Alternatively, this might not have been his name at all, but his title: 'over-king'. Bede calculated that this 'Coming of the English' took place under Emperors Valentinian and Marcian (450–5); later narratives narrowed this down to 449.

Bede makes significant additions to earlier versions of the story. He says (*HE* 1.15) the Saxons were commanded by two brothers, Hengist and Horsa, and adds a long, interesting passage about the Anglo-Saxons' origins. The newcomers came, he says, from three mighty peoples: the Angles, Saxons, and Jutes. From the Saxons, says Bede, are (unsurprisingly) descended the West, East, and South Saxon kingdoms, from the Angles stem the East and Middle Angles, Mercians, and Northumbrians, and from the Jutes originate the people of Kent, the Isle of Wight, and of the Hampshire coast opposite Wight. He says that the scale of migration was such that Angeln, whence came the Angles, was depopulated in his day. Elsewhere (*HE* 5.9), Bede gives a much more varied list of people from whom the Anglo-Saxons descend: Frisians, Rugians, Danes, Huns, Old Saxons, and *Boruhware* (seemingly the Rhineland Frankish Bructuari). Bede provides Hengist and Horsa's genealogy, saying that they were the 'sons of Wihtgisl, son of Witta, son of Wecta, son of Woden'.

A century after Bede, 'Nennius' added further details. However, his sources led him to date the coming of the Saxons to the year we think of as 428—the author calculates this in three ways (HB 31, 66). He gives a more elaborate version of the Hengist and Horsa story. As in Bede's account, Vortigern requests their aid in fighting the Picts and Scots, although (says 'Nennius') he was also afraid of a Roman invasion and of Ambrosius (of whom more shortly). 'Nennius' adds five generations to Bede's genealogy, taking the brothers' descent back to Geta 'who they say was son of god but not the god of gods...but an idol they worshipped'. According to 'Nennius', Vortigern gave the Saxons Thanet. 'Nennius' also provides the earliest version of the story of how the Saxon chief contrived to have Vortigern fall in love with his daughter and exploited his infatuation to persuade him to grant all Kent to the Saxons and lands in northern Britain by the Wall to his kinsmen.

The Saxon war

According to Gildas, once invited in, the Saxons fastened their grip on the east of the island and demanded increased supplies and wages. When the Britons withheld these, the Saxons rebelled and ravaged Britain as far as the (presumably Irish) sea. Great slaughter and the destruction of towns ensued. Again, says Gildas, starvation drove some Britons to surrender while others fled to mountains, forests, and cliffs. Possibly confirming this, the anonymous *Gallic Chronicle of 452* says that in 441/2, the British provinces were subjected to Saxon dominion.

The Britons' foes retreated, though, and the Britons, led by a certain Ambrosius Aurelianus, eventually defeated the Saxons. A war culminated in the siege of Mount Badon. Gildas apparently says that this occurred forty-three years and one month before he was writing, in the year of his birth:

From then on, victory went now to our countrymen, now to their enemies: so that in this people the Lord could make trial (as he tends to) of his latter-day Israel to see whether it loves him or not. This lasted right up to the year of the siege of Badon Hill, pretty well the last defeat of the villains, and certainly not the least. That was the year of my birth; as I know one month of the forty-fourth year since then has already elapsed. (*On the Ruin of Britain*, chapter 26.1)

Gildas also gives us another piece of information relative to his own time of writing, which might help us to date this siege or battle. He says that in his own day Ambrosius Aurelianus' grandsons ruled, and he might imply that Ambrosius won at Mount Badon. If Gildas wrote around 540, as is usually said, then this battle should have taken place within a decade either side of 500. However, in Gildas' view, the result of this victory was the wreck of Britain, civil war, sin, and greed.

'Nennius' details Vortigern's other tribulations, apparently occurring during the wars following the Saxon revolt and before Badon. Vortigern begat a son on his own daughter and was cursed by St Germanus. He fled into Snowdonia and later moved to the north, with his supporters. In Kent, meanwhile, 'Nennius' says Vortigern's son Vortimer shut the Saxons into Thanet three times and won four victories (only three are named). At the second of these, Hengist's brother Horsa and Vortigern's son Pascent were killed. Bede says that, in his day, Horsa's monument could still be seen in Kent. On his deathbed, Vortimer told his men to bury him by the sea because that would prevent the English from ever settling in Britain. Of course, fatally they failed to do this, burying him instead, for reasons best known to themselves, in Lincoln. In Kent, the beleaguered Saxons now tricked Vortigern by convening a peace council where, at a pre-arranged signal, each Saxon guest treacherously stabbed the Briton next to him. Vortigern alone survived and had to ransom himself by granting the Saxons Essex, Sussex, and Middlesex. Hated by all and sundry, Vortigern fled from one place to another, pursued by St Germanus for his incest, until he eventually died.

Regional details of the fighting between Saxons and Britons are added, from a Saxon point of view, by the *Anglo-Saxon Chronicle*. This adds four battles in Kent: *Ægelesthrep* (455), where Horsa was killed; *Creacanford* (456), where 4,000 Britons fell and the rest were driven in rout back into London, *Wippedesfleot* (465), where no fewer than twelve British chiefs were slain, including the eponymous Wipped; and finally an unnamed battle where Hengist and Æsc his son took countless spoils 'and the Britons fled from the English as from fire'. After completing the description of the conquest of Kent, between 449 and 473, the *Chronicle* relates the coming of the South Saxons. These arrived, like Hengist, in three ships, under Ælle and his three sons, and between 473 and 491 conquered Sussex. After the foundation of Sussex, the *Chronicle* recounts the foundation of the kingdom of Wessex by Cerdic and his son Cynric. It narrates West Saxon history until 593, with three interruptions (under 547, 560, and 591) mentioning the foundation and royal succession of Northumbria.

Bede gives us one further piece of information to set alongside the *Chronicle*'s account of the wars. He gives a much-discussed list of seven kings who held *imperium* (overlordship) over the English up to 672 (*HE* 2.5). The first three are Ælle of Sussex, Ceawlin of Wessex, and Æthelberht of Kent, all of whom the *Chronicle* mentions. It has been plausibly suggested that Bede drew the first two of these, who otherwise have no place in his *History*, from a Canterbury source, perhaps a list of kings who ruled over Kent.

Arthur and his battles

It will be glaringly obvious that so far we have had no mention of Arthur. Gildas' silence is intriguing and has engendered much medieval and modern speculation. The great war-leader's absence from the English sources, Bede's *Ecclesiastical History* and the *Chronicle*, might not be surprising. Either they had no information about him or they deliberately left him out as an embarrassing 'blip' in their triumphalist English narrative. Thus it might be expected that it is only when we get to 'Nennius' that we hear about Arthur and his wars. 'Nennius' places Arthur's story after the end of his tales about Vortigern. Arthur's battles are recounted in the fifty-sixth chapter of his work. In a book like this, this passage must be quoted in full. Here is my, rather leaden, literal translation:

> In that time the Saxons grew in strength to be a multitude and increased in *Britannia*. Hengist, indeed, having died, Ochta his son crossed from the left part[1] of (or to) Britain to the kingdom of the *Cantii*, and from him stem the kings of the *Cantii*. Then, in those days, Arthur fought against them with the kings of the Britons, but he was the leader of battles. The first battle was at the mouth of the river Glein. The second and the third, and the fourth, and the fifth, were on the river that is called Dubglas, and is in the region of *Linnuis*. The sixth battle was on the river that is called Bassas. The seventh was the battle in the Caledonian Forest, that is *Cat Coit Celidon*. The eighth was the battle in [of?] Castell Guinnion, in which Arthur carried the image of the holy Mary, perpetual virgin, on his shoulders and the pagans were turned over in flight on that day, and a great slaughter was made of them through the power of our lord Jesus Christ and through the power of the holy Virgin Mary his mother. The ninth battle happened in the town of the legion. The tenth battle happened on the bank of the river that is called Tribruit. The eleventh battle was made on the hill that is called Agned. The twelfth was the battle of Mount Badon, in which 960 men were overthrown in one day in a single charge by Arthur, and no one laid them low other than him, and in all battles he was seen to be victor. And they [the Saxons], since they were being

---

[1] The north. 'Nennius' has already said that areas around Hadrian's Wall had been given to Hengist's relatives. If you orient yourself on the east, 'left' would be to the north, 'right' to the south, and these usages seem common in medieval 'Cambro-Latin'. On the other hand, the Romans faced south when swearing oaths, which would make 'the left side' the east. This too would make sense as meaning from across the North Sea.

laid low in all the battles, asked for help from *Germania*, and grew manifold in numbers, without cease, and thenceforth they drew kings from *Germania*, that they might reign over them in *Britannia*, up to the time when Ida reigned, who was the son of Eobba. He was the first king of Beornicia, that is in Berneich.

This fascinating passage has often been suggested to be a fragment of a lost Welsh poem about Arthur. Arthur's evidently non-regal status is noteworthy; some have suggested that his description as 'leader of battles' (*dux bellorum*) refers to a title, possibly a corruption of *dux britanniarum* (Duke of the Britains), one of the late Roman military commanders in Britain.

The late fifth-century date for Arthur implied by 'Nennius'' positioning of his story might be corroborated by three things. We have seen that Mount Badon, the last in the list, can be dated to about 500 from Gildas' account. Bede reckoned it forty-four years after the coming of the English, which he placed in 450–5. Above all, though, concrete-looking dates for Arthur are provided by the *Annales Cambriae* or Welsh Annals. As noted in Chapter 1, this text contains two 'Arthurian' entries:

> Year [516]: The Battle of Badon, in which Arthur carried the cross of our Lord Jesus Christ on his shoulders for three days and three nights and the Britons were the victors.
>
> ...
>
> Year [537]: The battle of Camlann in which Arthur and Medraut fell, and there was a plague in Britain and Ireland.

The latter is the first mention of Arthur's last, climactic battle and of Medraut, the later Mordred.

After Arthur

Bede moves directly from the battle of Mount Badon to the arrival of St Augustine's mission in Canterbury in 597, an event that we can

conveniently take as ending the 'world of Arthur'. Gildas gives us little in terms of straight narrative history but tells us that the period of
sin, decline, and general turmoil, against which his work preaches,
followed the Saxons' defeat.

He writes a tirade against five tyrants reigning in his own day
('Britain has kings, but they are tyrants', he famously says): Constantine
of Dumnonia (Devon); Cuneglasus; Maglocunus, often associated
with a Maelgwn, King of Gwynedd, mentioned in the *Welsh Annals*;
Vortiporius, who seems to have ruled Demetia (Dyfed) in South
Wales; and Aurelius Caninus ('dog-like Aurelius'; 'Aurelius the Dog'),
whose realm is unidentifiable but who might, on the basis of his
name, have been one of Ambrosius Aurelianus' (in Gildas' eyes)
degenerate grandchildren. The *Welsh Annals* say Maelgwn died of
plague in the 540s and it is principally because he was still alive when
Gildas was writing that *On the Ruin and Conquest of Britain* is usually
dated to *c*.540. There are glimpses of previous internecine politics,
with treachery, lust, murder, and incest but unfortunately no concrete
political historical details.

The latter are to some extent provided by the *Anglo-Saxon
Chronicle*'s account of a gradual West Saxon expansion at the Britons'
expense, culminating in their triumph at the battle of Dyrham (577)
(Figure 2.1). Here, three British kings, Condidan, Conmail, and
Farinmail, were slain and the cities of Bath, Cirencester, and
Gloucester fell to the Saxons. Traditionally, this victory drove a strategically fatal wedge between the British kingdoms of the south-
western peninsula (Somerset, Devon, and Cornwall), or West Wales,
and those of modern Wales, or North Wales as it was sometimes
known.

Other sources suggest that the sixth century's last decades were
important. Later Welsh traditions, including the poetry which I shall
shortly discuss, 'Nennius', and the *Welsh Annals*, refer to savage British
internal fighting and serious defeats by the English. Probably the most

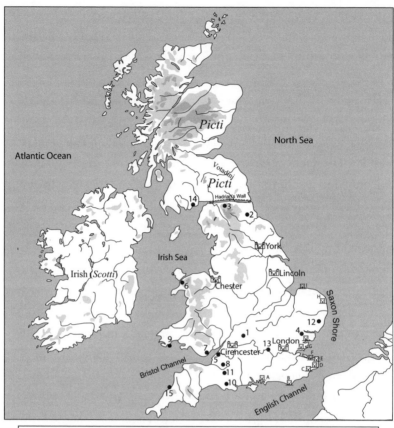

Archaeological Sites mentioned in the Text		Saxon Shore forts mentioned in the *Notitia Dignitatum*	
1. Asthall	8 Glastonbury	A Porchester	F Reculver
2. Binchester	9 Longbury Bank	B Pevensey	G Bradwell
3. Birdoswald	10 Poundbury	C Lympne	H Burgh Castle
4. Broomfield	11 South Cadbury	D Dover	I Brancaster
5. Cadbury Congresbury	12 Sutton Hoo	E Richborough	
6. Cefn Graennog	13 Taplow		
7. Dinas Powys	14 The Mote of Mark		
	15 Tintagel		

Figure 2.1 Roman Britain

famous of the latter was the battle of *Catraeth* (probably Catterick, Yorkshire), where 300 or 360 great warriors, the flower of the army of the kingdom of the Gododdin (based on Edinburgh), fell heroically, leaving only one (or three) survivors. This battle is best known in a long eulogy, the poem known as *Y Gododdin*, attributed to Aneirin. The civil wars also saw the killing of one British king by a coalition of his neighbours at the battle of Arthuret, recorded in the *Welsh Annals*.

This was the era of another British hero, Urien of Rheged, whose kingdom lay somewhere around the Lake District, the western end of Hadrian's Wall or Galloway, or possibly all of these areas and more besides. The deeds of Urien and his valiant son Owain (Eugenius) are celebrated in a series of epic poems attributed to Urien's court poet Taliesin, mentioned alongside Aneirin by 'Nennius'. 'Nennius' tells us that Urien drove the Northumbrian English back until they were besieged on Holy Island off the North Sea coast, but was then murdered out of jealousy by one of his British allies.

This assassination opened the way for further English aggression, especially, Bede tells us, under Æthelfrith of Bernicia (the northern part of Northumbria) who ravaged widely and in 603 destroyed a Scottish army at *Degsastane* (*HE* 1.34), an unknown spot usually identified as near Dawston Burn in Liddesdale. About ten years later Æthelfrith inflicted a crushing defeat on the Britons of Powys and Gwynedd at Chester (*c*.613–16; *HE* 2.2), slaughtering a large crowd of monks from Bangor who had accompanied the British army to pray for its success. This battle is held to have fulfilled the same function in the north as Dyrham had in the south, about forty years previously, dividing the Britons of Wales from those of Cumbria and the Scottish lowlands.

Meanwhile in the south-east, the *Chronicle* tells us that King Æthelberht of Kent beat the then dominant English king, Ceawlin of Wessex (or rather of the Gewissae, as the West Saxons tended to be called at this point), soon afterwards, as Bede also tells us, replacing him as the supreme king. Although Bede describes these kings as having *imperium* or overlordship, the *Chronicle* uses the Old English word *Bretwalda*—'wide ruler'. Not long afterwards, Æthelberht asked the

Bishop of Rome, Gregory I 'the Great', for a bishop. Gregory dispatched a monk called Augustine with a band of followers. These arrived in 597 and the conversion of Anglo-Saxon England began. This is where we leave 'the World of Arthur' and enter the better-documented period of 'middle Saxon' history, stretching from the conversion to the arrival of the Vikings at the end of the eighth century.

There is, however, another reference to Arthur which demands our attention before we look at the archaeology of this period. This comes in Y Gododdin. Most of this poem is an elegy for these dead heroes and one stanza reads as follows (in John T. Koch's translation):

> More than 300 of the finest were slain. He struck them down at both the middle and the extremities. The most generous man was splendid before the host. From the herd he used to distribute horses in winter. He used to bring black crows down in front of the fortified town— though he was not Arthur—amongst men mighty in feats in front of the barrier of alder wood—Gorddur.

This might be the earliest mention of Arthur, as Y Gododdin is often thought to date to c.600. The poet clearly thought that Arthur was a touchstone for military prowess, suggesting that his fame lived on for at least a couple of generations after his death in (according to the Welsh Annals) 537. Indeed, no fewer than three genuinely historical Arthurs are mentioned around the end of the sixth century. One was a son of King Aedan of the Scots, apparently killed in battle. This interesting cluster of three Arthurs appearing close together in the historical record might be proof of the reality of a great Arthur a generation or two before their birth, thus sometime around the early- to mid-sixth century.

Conclusion

This, then, is the basic political historical narrative for Britain between about 400 and about 600 as it emerges from the surviving written sources. Up until the mid-1970s, it was regarded as a broadly reliable account of what happened in *Britannia* between the usurpation of 'Constantine III' and St Augustine's arrival, and it is still widely believed. It introduces the main sources, characters, and events that will be revisited and re-evaluated over the remainder of this book. Before we return to see how this narrative has been altered, we must look at the other principal source of information for 'post-Roman Britain': archaeology.

3

Swords in the Stones

The Archaeology of Post-Imperial Britain

⚜

Cemeteries and sunken huts:
the archaeology of Anglo-Saxon migration

The previous chapter surely illustrated that the written sources give only a vague history of Britain between 400 and 600. From the very end of the eighteenth century, though, the archaeological traces of this period began to be recognized.

The first remains to be identified were 'Saxon' cemeteries. Early Anglo-Saxons buried their dead in fairly distinctive ways. Sometimes they cremated them, gathering up the ashes and burnt bone remains and placing them in hand-made urns, often decorated in particular styles. Other objects, which had not been burnt, could be placed in or near the urn in the pit in which the latter was buried. Otherwise metallic items of the costume in which the deceased had been cremated (further described under inhumation, below) are also found in the urns. Some early Anglo-Saxon cremation cemeteries are very large indeed, with many hundreds of urns. This style of burial and cemetery is most common north of the Thames, but there are examples south of that river as well. Anglo-Saxon cremation was practised until the earlier seventh century, when it generally died out, although there are examples from the second half of that century and occasionally from later still.

The other form of burial was inhumation, frequently 'furnished'—that is the dead were buried with grave-goods (Figure 3.1). The term grave-goods is employed to encompass the objects deposited around the deceased, such as weaponry or ceramics, and those which came from the costume in which she or he was buried: buckles, brooches and other jewellery, and so on, or items which hung from a belt such as knives in their sheaths, or chatelaines (a sort of early medieval key-ring, suspended from the belt with objects like keys and other implements hung from it). Few inhumation cemeteries are as large as the big cremation 'urn-fields', although some nevertheless contain hundreds of graves. These burials are found much more evenly across the 'lowland zone', south-east of a line drawn roughly from the Channel coast in Dorset through to the North Sea coast in east Yorkshire, with some examples extending up the North Sea coast into the Scottish lowlands and a cluster of interesting seventh-century burials in the Derbyshire Peak District. They begin quite early in the fifth century and last roughly to the end of the seventh although, again, later examples are found.

When they were first discovered and recognized as Anglo-Saxon, rather than Roman or 'Celtic' as had earlier been assumed to be the case, the objects in the burials or the pots that served as containers caught the antiquaries' attention (Figure 3.2). Consequently, as elsewhere in Europe, early medieval cemeteries were plundered as a source of artefacts for museum or private collections. Attempts to write history from these sites similarly focused upon the objects. Antiquarians and early generations of academics, who studied the contents of museum collections as well as looking at new discoveries in the field, began to classify the artefacts found in burials according to their form

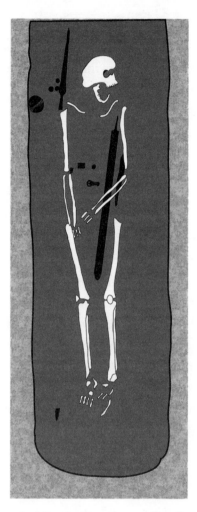

Figure 3.1 A fairly typical 'Anglo-Saxon' masculine furnished inhumation, with weaponry and belt-set, from the cemetery at Dover Buckland (Kent).

and decoration. These could then be plotted geographically and as a result particular groupings emerged. Analogues for the artefacts included in these groups were sought on the European mainland. The end result was that it was felt possible to identify particular objects and combinations of artefacts as 'Saxon', 'Anglian', or even 'Jutish'. Indeed the groupings of artefacts seemingly matched Bede's description of

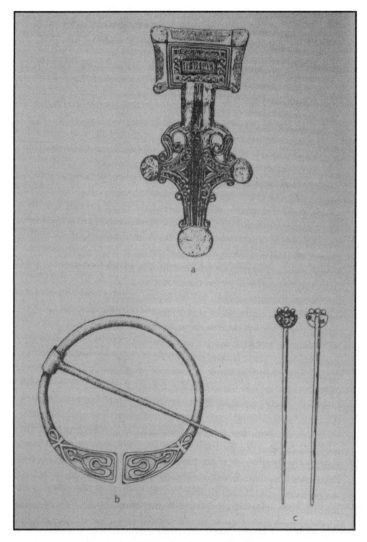

Figure 3.2 The kinds of objects that attracted early antiquarian interest in post-imperial British archaeology: a) a square-headed brooch from Bergh Apton (Norfolk) ('Anglo-Saxon'); b) a penannular brooch from Dinas Powys (British); and c) decorative pins from the Norries Law Hoard ('Pictish'). From Charles-Edwards (ed.) (2003), fig. 2.6.

where these peoples settled after their migration to Britain. One important dividing line lay along the Thames valley, roughly the historical boundary between the 'Saxon' kingdoms of Wessex and Middlesex on the one hand and the 'Anglian' realms of Mercia and the Middle Angles on the other. Another set of objects clustered in Kent, the kingdom of the Jutes. Essex often seems to fit better with the regions south of the Thames than with those to the north as one might expect on the basis of its name. When searching for parallels in the areas from which the 'Anglo-Saxons' migrated, links could be traced between these groups and some regions of northern Germany, southern Denmark, and the northern Netherlands, tallying to some extent with the historical Saxony and 'Angeln'. At the same time the study of the decoration, especially of brooches and other items of jewellery, produced classifications of styles and motifs. These were then placed in chronological sequences, again drawing on similar finds from northern continental Europe. It gradually became possible to assign rough dates to cemeteries and to burials within them.

The principal objective of such research was the construction of a more detailed historical narrative, supporting that constructed from the written sources. It has often been stated that early archaeologists simply shoehorned their evidence into a framework derived from the documentary evidence. More sophisticated recent research shows that in fact they worked alongside the first generations of serious Anglo-Saxon historians to create this narrative.

Writing a history from early Anglo-Saxon cemeteries and the gravegoods they contained entailed a number of important assumptions, which we shall have frequent cause to reconsider. One was that the cremation and furnished inhumation rituals were straightforward introductions from the Saxon homelands and that anyone buried using these rites was therefore either an Anglo-Saxon immigrant or the descendant of one. This was bolstered and refined by the study of artefacts and the costumes they fastened or adorned. These, similarly, were viewed as markers of Anglo-Saxon identity, strictly related to one's geographical origins or those of one's ancestors. It was also thought that, as intimated, Saxons could be distinguished from Angles and Jutes.

Developing these conclusions, a political history was produced, which seemed strikingly to confirm that given in outline by the written sources. A mass Anglo-Saxon migration drove the Romano-Britons into the highland zone: Cornwall and the rest of the south-western peninsula, Wales, and Cumbria. An 'inverse proof' of this idea was found in the absence of 'Anglo-Saxon' material culture (cemeteries and artefacts) from those regions. More detail, apparently matching Gildas' 'doom and gloom' narrative, was furnished by the fact that the well-known Romano-British sites, the villas and the great towns (many of which had been quite thoroughly explored by the early twentieth century), provided no evidence of occupation much beyond about AD 400. To make matters more suggestive still, the last recognizable layers on Romano-British sites often seemed to be marked by fires. This approach could take quite extreme forms, as when the archaeologist E. T. Leeds believed that the political circumstances of specific battles recorded in the *Anglo-Saxon Chronicle* could be revealed by the distribution patterns of particular Anglo-Saxon brooch-types.

All this apparently proved that the Anglo-Saxons had come in force and violently expelled the natives, burning their settlements in the process. The predominance of weaponry in male Anglo-Saxon burials further underlined that this was a 'warrior society'. Assigning dates to cemeteries and burials from the objects in them showed, it was said, the expansion of Anglo-Saxon settlement from east to west. Better than that, it was argued that this spread showed an early sixth-century hiatus, matching Gildas' statement that the British victory at Mount Badon (dated to about AD 500) brought fifty years of peace from 'foreign' wars.

Across the North Sea, confirmation of the Anglo-Saxon migration's scale and importance was found in the fact that 'continental Saxon' settlements and cemeteries were frequently abandoned during the fifth century. Bede had said, after all, that Angeln was still deserted in his day because its inhabitants had moved to Britain. Archaeology seemed to prove this. Other details could be added. Some English pots and brooches, especially from East Anglia, had very close parallels on the North Sea German coast, sometimes seemingly made by the same people. Relationships across the North Sea were therefore traced even down to a communal level.

The other principal aspect of early English history to be illuminated by the cemetery data was religious. Cremation and the burial of grave-goods were held to indicate pagan beliefs. Cremation seemed at odds with early Christian belief—indeed the Church banned cremation during the early Middle Ages. Grave-goods, by contrast, were considered to represent particular beliefs about the afterlife. The weapons in graves tallied, it was thought, with medieval Norse ideas about Valhalla, for example, and some Norse gods were depicted on fifth- and sixth-century artefacts from the North Sea world. Both rites began to die out during the seventh century, which was of course the period of the Anglo-Saxons' conversion to Christianity, beginning with St Augustine's mission to Canterbury in 597. Seventh-century cemeteries differed from their precursors, notably in the provision of fewer grave-goods. This could be attributed to the adoption of Christian belief. After about 700, cremations and burial with grave-goods ceased more or less completely, apparently representing the final working through of the conversion process.

Early Anglo-Saxon history had received important confirmation through the study of the new discipline of archaeology. Thus far, however, contributions had come more or less entirely from the study of cemeteries. Where the earliest Anglo-Saxons had actually *lived* remained elusive because their settlements, unlike high-status Roman dwellings in town or country, had been made of wood rather than stone, leaving traces that were much more difficult to recognize. By the second quarter of the twentieth century, however, techniques had

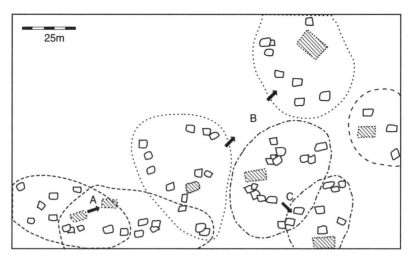

Figure 3.3 Anglo-Saxon settlement plan. The 'Anglo-Saxon' settlement at West Stow (Suffolk) showing its different farmsteads, each with a 'hall' (shaded) and ancillary buildings, and their movement over time. After Charles-Edwards (ed.) (2003), fig. 2.2.

developed sufficiently for excavators to spot the discoloration in the soil caused by the rotting away of timber posts and other constructions. Careful excavation could reconstruct the plans of wooden or wattle structures (Figure 3.3). The first diagnostic form of Anglo-Saxon building to be discovered was the type referred to by archaeologists either as a Sunken-Floored (or Sunken-Featured) Building (SFB), or as a *Grubenhaus* (plural: *Grubenhäuser*)—its German name—or, informally, as a 'grub-hut'. This usually takes the form of a rectangular pit (hence the name)—sometimes floored over; sometimes not—over which was built a simpler structure, usually a simple tent-like roof resting directly on the ground. The ridge of the roof was supported by two or more stout posts. The roughly rectangular sunken pit is comparatively easy to detect in the ground, as an area of somewhat differently coloured soil. Before archaeological techniques advanced sufficiently to identify other building-types, it was thought that the Anglo-Saxons lived in damp and squalid conditions in these

Grubenhäuser. Later, however, other forms of building were defined. The principal dwellings are rectangular, timber-framed buildings whose main structural posts are set in post-holes, which form the major archaeological trace. These are generally referred to as 'halls'. They are surrounded by smaller ancillary buildings, mainly but by no means exclusively *Grubenhäuser*. The uses to which the settlement evidence was put in earlier Anglo-Saxon archaeology were much the same as those for which the cemetery evidence was employed. It revealed where Anglo-Saxon immigrants settled. Further information was sought from these dwelling-places, especially the earlier ones, about what sorts of site were preferred by the newcomers, and perhaps the socio-political circumstances of their initial settlement. Were these sites on marginal land? Perhaps the Romano-British authorities forced 'Germanic' mercenaries and their families onto them. Further deductions were made about the routes taken by the Anglo-Saxon movement across Britain.

Anglo-Saxon archaeology seemed, however, to suggest details additional to those found in the sketchy written record. Some concerned a possible Saxon settlement in later fourth-century Roman Britain, well before the date suggested by Bede and the *Anglo-Saxon Chronicle*. This evidence took two principal forms. One was a body of metalwork in what was called 'chip-carved' style (*Kerbschnitt* in German). Chip-carved metalwork looks as though the pattern has been chipped out of it. If such a technique was used, though, it was in making the model for the mould rather than being used on the object itself. Anyway, it was soon recognized that this metalwork belonged to the late Roman period. It was, however, frequently found in burials with grave-goods in Gaul and, later, in Britain, as well as in cremations in the Saxon homelands. The conclusion was therefore drawn that this metalwork was somehow 'Germanic'. Some barbarians in the military service of the later Roman Empire were called *foederati* or federates: indeed *foedus* [treaty] is used by Gildas in describing Saxon settlement. These buckles and brooches were thus dubbed 'federate uniform'; the evidence seemed to show that there were Saxon federates in fourth-century Britain.

This idea was supported by the recognition of 'Romano-Saxon Ware'. This was wheel-turned pottery in the Roman tradition but decorated with motifs that were also found on the other side of the North Sea on Saxon cremation urns. J. N. L. (Nowell) Myres, an important figure in the development of Anglo-Saxon settlement archaeology, concluded that these wares were manufactured by Romano-British potters to suit the tastes of Anglo-Saxon soldier-settlers (federates) and their families.

These two classes of material, apparently demonstrating a fourth-century Saxon settlement in eastern Britain, produced a reinterpretation of the 'Saxon Shore'. The 'Saxon Shore' (*litus saxonicus*) is a name derived from the late Roman *Notitia Dignitatum* (*The List of Dignities*), an (in its surviving form) incomplete record of the Empire's civil and military offices drawn up around AD 400. The *Notitia* names a Roman military commander in Britain as the Count of the Saxon Shore (*Comes Litoris Saxonicis*) and lists the forts and garrisons he commanded. This tallies with a series of well-known substantial late Roman fortifications stretching from Porchester on Southampton Water to the Wash. It had always been assumed that this *litus saxonicus* defended against the depredations of Saxon pirates and raiders, such as are mentioned or at least alluded to in various late Roman sources. Romano-Saxon archaeology suggested a quite different interpretation to Myres. The Saxon Shore was so-called not because it was the defence *against* the Saxons but because it was the Saxons *who lived there*. In the final and most extreme version of this argument, published in Myres's last book (1986), this Saxon Shore became a vast tract of south-eastern Britain. What should be said now is that this shows that even the readings of traditional Anglo-Saxon archaeologists were not constrained by the documentary sources. Myres's Saxon Shore had no support in any written evidence. For archaeology to propose its own interpretations and its own stories was important, even if, as mentioned, it had always done this to some degree.

Another idea, proposed at about the same time, similarly contradicted the written sources. This was Vera Evison's hypothesis, in her book *The Fifth-Century Invasions South of the Thames*, that the Saxon invasions were coordinated, and indeed led, by the Franks who were establishing themselves at this time in Gaul—eventually of course to become *Francia*: France. Evison claimed that Saxon leadership of these attacks was a later invention. The argument was based on a range of metalwork found in burials in southern England and northern France. Many such items were related to or descended from the 'chip-carved' types mentioned earlier. These artefacts proved, for Evison, Frankish presence among the fifth-century settlers of England. That the graves in which Frankish artefacts were found were often 'rich' (that is, with lots of material in them) showed that these Franks were the leading class of the newcomers.

Neither Myres's notion of the Saxon Shore nor Evison's idea of fifth-century Frankish warlords attracted much support from other archaeologists and for good reason. Nevertheless, they make good examples of the ways in which archaeology was employed to study the Anglo-Saxon migration and settlement up to the late 1970s; they are extreme rather than aberrant. A more mainstream example concerned the famous ship burial, Sutton Hoo Mound 1 (Suffolk), excavated just before the outbreak of the Second World War, re-excavated in the 1960s, and published in detail some time after that. This sumptuously furnished grave was felt to confirm all sorts of aspects of Anglo-Saxon history. The burial's subject was suggested to have been King Rædwald of East Anglia, who died *c.*625, and the nature of the grave was held to confirm what little Bede said about Rædwald. The grave-goods suggested a pagan burial ritual but some of the artefacts, notably a pair of spoons marked 'Saul' and 'Paul' and thus probably a baptism gift, implied that the dead person might have been Christian. Had not Bede (*HE* 2.15) said that Rædwald kept his religious options open after his conversion and kept Christian and pagan altars side by side? The absence of a body is now recognized to result, almost certainly, from the site's acidic soil and its effects on organic material. However, it was originally mooted that the grave was a cenotaph: the convert Rædwald had had a pagan burial monument made for himself but had been buried elsewhere, in a church. Some of the burial's unusual objects, such as the 'standard' and the whetstone, which had never been used and was clearly employed as a kind of sceptre, were held to be the regalia of the *Bretwalda*. The fourth such Anglo-Saxon over-king, according to Bede, was Rædwald.

Sutton Hoo Mound 1 was just the most important of a series of rich mound burials which belonged around the start of the seventh century (other well-known examples being Asthall in Oxfordshire, Broomfield in Essex, and Taplow in Buckinghamshire). That the period around 600 saw important changes in Anglo-Saxon society has already been noted with relationship to the end of cremation and the decline of furnished burial. As archaeological techniques advanced and interests broadened, it was also recognized that the seventh century witnessed the establishment of Anglo-Saxon trading centres (called *emporia* by archaeologists) and more obviously high-status rural settlements. Craft specialization also seemed to increase, manifested, for example, in higher-quality pottery distributed over wider areas. The reappearance of coinage underlined this economic revival. Clearly English history had entered a new phase and this tallied with ideas that historians had long had, and linked to the effects of conversion to Christianity. Overall, then, archaeology up to about 1980 and often beyond was used to create an essentially political history that dwelt on the nature, routes, and chronologies of settlement and political takeover. All this would change importantly, as we shall see in Chapter 6.

Digging for Arthur: the archaeology of the 'sub-Roman Britons'

So far we have only considered the Anglo-Saxons. The remains of their British foes were more difficult to find. Partly this stemmed from the fact that the principal classes of fifth- and sixth-century archaeology across lowland Britain were assumed, more or less automatically, to represent Anglo-Saxons. The Britons were archaeologically invisible by default. The fact that they tended to be referred to as 'sub-Roman' Britons in some ways confirms a rather lowly opinion of post-imperial British culture. In the nineteenth century the idea had been fairly standard that everything good about Great Britain was attributable to the 'Germanic' Anglo-Saxons and their vigorous, martial society, and perhaps to their later taking up of the 'baton of civilization' from the Romans. The English had of course subdued the Welsh and Irish in the later Middle Ages and the politically dominant, English-speaking lowland Scots were considered much superior to highland Gaelic-speakers. 'Celtic' culture, though admired for a sort of romantic, barbaric splendour, was viewed as very much subordinate. After all, even Gildas, their own historian, thought the Britons were a lost cause. Add to this the common idea of the degenerate later Roman Empire and it is not difficult to see why, even if these ideas were rarely held overtly, they had deep roots and profound, if subconscious, effects on the thinking of later generations of scholars. The post-imperial Britons had no culture.

Attempts to find Britons therefore concentrated on identifying forms of metalwork with no Anglo-Saxon associations and 'deviant' burials within 'Anglo-Saxon' cemeteries. Perhaps graves without grave-goods were those of the Anglo-Saxons' British slaves. Didn't the Old English word *wealas* (meaning 'Welsh' or, technically more accurately, 'Roman') come to mean 'slave'? Some radical thinkers proposed that some furnished burials could be Britons 'disguised' as Anglo-Saxons but this interpretation found little support.

The Britons were rescued from this neglect and—to some extent—the negative view of their culture by the recognition of fortified hill-top sites with fifth- and sixth-century occupation. Hill-forts' importance for this period's history was well established. In 1913, one Albany Major published a political history of *The Early Wars of Wessex* that was essentially based around the fact that many hill-forts were located at or near the sites of early battles mentioned in the *Anglo-Saxon Chronicle*. The Anglo-Saxon conquest revolved about the capture of these strongholds. Also before the First World War, an excavation had taken place at The Mote of Mark (Galloway), part of the British kingdom of Strathclyde, as it was usually conceived of at that time. This revealed considerable craft-working, metallurgy, and glass and pottery imported from the European mainland. The excavator had little comparative material but associated this site with some sort of chieftain after the demise of the Roman Empire.

The real growth of interest in post-imperial hill-top settlements is justly associated with the name of Leslie Alcock, who, during a long career in Cardiff and especially in Glasgow, excavated or otherwise surveyed or explored a large number of such sites. The earliest major site studied by Alcock was the fort at Dinas Powys (Glamorgan, South Wales). This Iron Age site was refortified in the post-imperial period, and sheltered a local magnate. The occupants' status was amply demonstrated by finds from the enclosed area, including metalworking debris, imported pottery, glass, and animal bones. The latter suggested a better diet than one would expect for the average fifth- or sixth-century farmer. The site for which Alcock is most famous, though, is South Cadbury (Somerset). Alcock was canny enough to play on a statement by John Leland, sixteenth-century antiquary, that 'by South Cadbury is that Camelot', thus attracting media attention and financial support from especially North American Arthurian fanatics. The South Cadbury or 'Cadbury-Camelot' (as, for a long time, it was often called) excavations turned up what was by now becoming a standard finds inventory for these sites: high-quality artefacts, some imported, evidence of manufacture, and so on. Details of the defences were recovered and a jumble of post-holes rather optimistically reconstructed as a Great Hall. Alcock's work after he took up the chair of archaeology at the University of Glasgow will concern us later.

At about the same time in south-west England, particularly in Somerset, Philip Rahtz developed a similar interest in 'post-Roman' archaeology. With Peter Fowler he excavated another well-known site, also called Cadbury—Cadbury Congresbury (or CadCong to those in the know). This, once more, was a reoccupied Iron Age site and again imported pottery was recovered suggesting long-distance trading connections. Active in the south-west for even longer was Charles Raleigh Radford, who excavated Tintagel, a site—of course—with long-standing Arthurian connections and which was indeed shown to have been important in the fifth and sixth centuries. Rahtz explored another location with mysterious, indeed mystic, 'Arthurian' associations, Glastonbury, both on the famous Tor (hill) itself and elsewhere, but without the startling results that many had hoped for. A bystander informed Rahtz that he would never find anything on the Tor for three reasons: he was digging in the wrong place; he was the wrong person to be doing the digging, and above all he was digging at the wrong *time*!

From these and other excavations four general types of imported pottery from the fifth to seventh centuries were classified: A-, B-, D-, and E-ware (C-ware was later recognized as later medieval). Of these, A-ware is fine red-slipped pottery imported from North Africa (especially) and elsewhere in the Mediterranean; B-ware is a series of amphorae mainly from the eastern Mediterranean; and E-ware is wheel-turned pottery from central France. A- and B-ware belong to the fifth and sixth centuries, whereas E-ware dates mainly to the seventh, though some examples are a little earlier and others slightly later.

The other main category of remains associated with the western, highland zone of post-imperial Britain is the inscribed stone. Many hundreds survive, crudely dressed at best and inscribed with short texts. Heavy concentrations are located in South Wales, Cornwall, and around Snowdonia. In Great Britain (there are large numbers in Ireland) they spread north, through Man, a few round the western end of Hadrian's Wall, to Galloway and the Scottish lowlands and thence up the east coast of Scotland, where some also bear Pictish symbols (to which we will return). Unlike the 'Pictish' symbol stones, this class of inscriptions is also found on the west coast of Scotland, although in smaller numbers. The distribution has an eastern outlier at the Roman town of Silchester. The texts on these stones are basic, usually consisting of someone's name and perhaps title, occasionally with other familial or genealogical information, sometimes accompanied by an inscribed cross. They are usually in the Latin alphabet. Many, however, are in the Ogham alphabet, based on the Latin but composed of lines perpendicular or at an angle to the edge of the stone or to an inscribed vertical line. Given that Ogham looks nothing at all like the Latin alphabet this may sound odd. However, Ogham's symbols represent letters—individual phonetic sounds (vowels and consonants) which can be grouped to form words as they are pronounced—rather than representing the ideas or things themselves (pictograms). Furthermore, Ogham has roughly the same choice and number of such sounds as the Latin alphabet. Put another way, each Ogham symbol translates a Latin 'letter'. This alphabet is generally believed to be an Irish development that took place around the time of the end of the western Roman Empire. The number of Ogham stones, especially in south-western Wales, and the Irish names represented on them are the best evidence for Irish migration into Great Britain during our period. One of the best-known stones comes from Castell Dwyran (Dyfed) and bears the name of a certain Voteporix Protector, whom many have assumed is Gildas' Vortiporius.

This stone has two inscriptions, one in Latin and the other in Ogham. The Ogham inscription has Voteporix's name as Votecorix, the Irish equivalent, demonstrating the most obvious difference between British P-Celtic and Irish/Manx Q-Celtic—that P sounds in the former are often Q sounds in the latter. This would demonstrate a linkage between the Ogham script and Irish identity.

Overall, then, whereas the fifth- and sixth-century Anglo-Saxons were thought to be revealed by their grave-goods and fairly poor rural settlements, the Britons showed themselves through fortified hill-top sites with high-status associations. A binary opposition seemed to be visible archaeologically, just as in the written record. In both types of archaeology, though, political historical concerns predominated. Alcock used the early medieval written record, especially chronicle references, to drive his explorations.

Picts and Scots: the Britons' other foes

Alcock played an important role in furthering the understanding of the archaeology of, according to the written sources, the post-imperial Britons' other enemies: the Picts and the Scots (Figure 3.4). The Picts are best known for the series of carved stones scattered along the east coast of Scotland mainly between the Firth of Forth through to Moray Firth but also further north, as far as Orkney. Otherwise they were long notable mainly for being a 'problem'; an important volume edited by F. T. Wainwright was entitled *The Problem of the Picts*. During most of the twentieth century, archaeological thinking dictated that 'peoples' would be recognizable by particular groups of artefacts and styles of building or burial, frequently found together in particular regions. These typological clusters were known as 'cultures' and the problem of the Picts—essentially—was that they didn't have one. Perhaps the most famous Scottish archaeological sites, the brochs (stone-built towers), did not belong to the right sort of period and nor

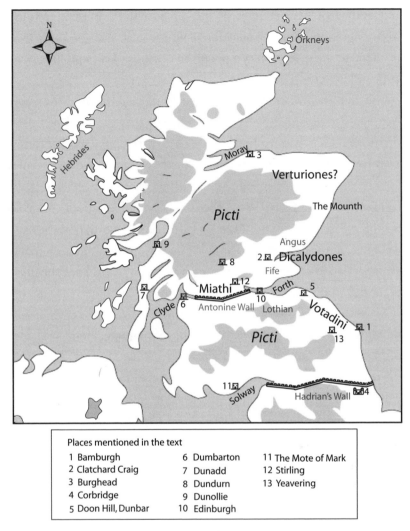

Figure 3.4 Northern Britain

did another well-recognized class of settlement, the 'souterrain': a dwelling with a stone-lined underground cellar and connecting tunnel/passageway, hence the name (French for 'underground'). All seemed (like the prehistoric hill-forts of the lowlands) to have died out before any written sources mentioned Picts. Archaeologists at this time believed that change in the archaeological record and the appearance of new peoples in the documentary sources resulted from migration. Thus the question of where these Picts had appeared from led to the invention of a people in northern Scotland known as 'proto-Picts'.

The Picts had other 'problems'. Their language has left little trace. A story first recorded by Bede (*HE* 1.1) says that the Picts practised matrilineal succession: inheritance passed through the mother rather than from father to son. This and a cluster of late medieval, or later, folktales and legends made the Picts the object of a great deal of romantic nationalism. Wild theories abounded about possible Scythian descent and a pre-Indo-European language. Maybe the Picts were related to the Eskimo. The sole obvious trace of the early medieval Picts, their enigmatic symbols, only served to enhance the mystique and attract a further cluster of fanciful ideas.

Since the Second World War, and especially since the publication of Wainwright's book, the Picts have been the subject of a great deal of high-quality archaeological work, which has dispersed most of the romantic mist surrounding them, or ought to have done. Sadly a widely held but entirely misled belief, fuelled by modern nationalism, remains popular and stubbornly refuses to go away. It is worth remembering that the Romans were not obsessed with conquering every single adjacent territory just for the sake of it. Indeed they (like many subsequent Scottish governments) soon gave up any attempt to control the Scottish highlands, as costing more in manpower, money, and trouble than it could produce in revenue or prestige. This pragmatism is, however, read as the Picts, seen as noble, warpainted savages (think Mel Gibson in *Braveheart*), valiantly maintaining a defiant independence from the Roman Empire (for which read 'the English'). In this chapter, I only describe the earlier phases of modern work.

There are three principal categories of archaeological remains associated with the Picts: symbol stones, hill-forts, and 'long-cist

Figure 3.5 A selection of Pictish symbols

cemeteries'. The first of these are classified into three types but only Class I stones concern us. These are undressed stones (that is, not carved into regular shapes) bearing combinations usually of two or three symbols. The symbols are of various sorts (Figure 3.5). Some are animals, usually naturalistic but sometimes imaginary (most notably the 'Pictish Beast' or 'Swimming Elephant'), and there are some depictions of human beings, but by far the most common are essentially abstract symbols, though some are based on real objects such as mirrors. These stones are fundamentally undatable but on balance current views see them as appearing towards the end of our period, probably in the later sixth century. Some could be earlier. On Class II stones Christian symbols, most obviously crosses, join the others; these are rather more confidently dated from analogies to *c*.700 and later. As there is little or no difference between the Pictish symbols on

Class I and Class II stones the former are unlikely to pre-date the latter by very long. The real pioneer of the study of the symbol stones is Isabel Henderson. Henderson proposed that the stones first appeared north of the Mounth, in the Aberdeen region, and then spread out gradually from that point of origin. This argument was based upon the 'degenerative principle': the idea that the clearest and best examples of particular symbols are the earliest, and that they decline in quality the further in time and place they are removed from the original.

The forts are principally associated with Leslie Alcock's programme of investigation in the 1970s and 1980s, to which we shall return in Chapter 6. Some were known rather earlier, however. A large, early promontory fort, where a line of defences cuts off a promontory from the mainland, was known at Burghead on the coast of Moray, though this has largely been lost in building since the eighteenth century. It produced many symbol stones featuring bulls, which might have originally been placed in the walls. A significant hill-fort at Clatchard Craig (Fife) was destroyed by quarrying in the 1950s. Fortunately, reasonably extensive excavations took place before its destruction. Probably the best-known Pictish fort is Dundurn in Strathearn. This is an example of what has been called a 'nuclear fort': a fort based on an original 'nucleus' with extra enclosures gradually added further down the slope.

The third main category of Pictish remains is their cemeteries. These are known as 'long-cist cemeteries', a long cist being constructed out of stone slabs placed upright, lining the grave itself. Sometimes the floor of the grave is similarly constructed and occasionally there was a stone slab roof as well. The dead were generally buried without accompanying grave-goods and, it would seem, either very simply dressed or wrapped in shrouds. This was the most common burial ritual across post-imperial Britain north of Hadrian's Wall, and lasted for a long time before and after our period, so an exclusive connection with the

Picts cannot be suggested. Without grave-goods the only means of dating burials is through Carbon 14, where samples can be obtained; this is usually imprecise. Nonetheless, the clustering of burials into larger cemeteries of long-cist graves seems to have begun in the fifth century but lasted for some centuries afterwards. In Pictish archaeology, the long-cist cemetery's appearance has generally been linked to a process of Christianization. In the sixth century, barrows and cairns were constructed above some of the graves in these cemeteries. Some of these are found with Class I stones though as yet none has been found with such a stone *in situ*. These developments in memorial custom were presumably linked to changes in Pictish society, although how has not been fully elucidated.

The archaeology of the Picts' neighbours, the Scots, is quite similar. Hill-forts are again the most important class of sites. Probably the best studied is Dunadd, the capital of the early Scots kingdom. This, like Dundurn, was a 'nuclear' site. Its summit enclosure shows traces of what was presumably a royal inauguration site, with suggestive carvings, notably a footprint, in the rock. Imaginative but plausible reconstructions of what the ritual might have been like have been possible. In its earliest phase, again apparently in the crucial period around 600, this fort revealed large quantities of imported French pottery.

Dunadd seems to have been associated with a very interesting site on a crannog (artificial island) at Lough Glashan. Here, there was evidence of specialist leather-working and other craftsmanship. On the whole, this site is rather enigmatic, but the best interpretation sees it as existing primarily for the supply of the royal centre at Dunadd. The other characteristic rural settlement in the Scottish territories is the 'dun' or small fort. The smallest may have been completely roofed over; others were enclosures of buildings. It must be said, though, that 'early historic' Scottish archaeology only really begins in earnest in the seventh century, when imported materials permit means of dating associated indigenous artefacts. For most of our 'world of

Arthur', this region is not especially well understood, archaeologically. One thing that can be said, though, is that the standard form of burial was, as in Pictland and the 'British' kingdoms of the northwest, inhumation in long cists. This is attested as far back as the third and fourth century in areas like the Hebrides. In the Scottish areas, however, burials tend to be clustered in smaller groups than on the east coast, sometimes in enclosed cemeteries. These are often associated with religious foundations (churches or monasteries) and are thus frequently later than the period that concerns us.

Interpretations of northern British, Pictish, and Scottish archaeology have developed steadily over the past four decades. As these interpretations have tended to progress along a single track, rather than taking dramatic new twists as in Anglo-Saxon archaeology, I have limited the discussion here to the description of site-types. The ways in which they are currently understood is set out in Chapter 5.

PART II
Present Worlds

∽҉ఴ

The fact of the matter is that there is no historical
evidence about Arthur. We must reject him from
our histories and, above all, from the
titles of our books.

DAVID DUMVILLE

4

The Antimatter of Arthur

Reassessing the Written Sources

❧❦

Before the 1970s a generally accepted narrative of British history between about 400 and the arrival of Augustine's mission existed, based upon early medieval written sources. From the middle of the 1970s, however, scholars turned their attention to more sophisticated analyses of this evidence, looking at the date, nature, and purposes behind the composition of such writings. This led to fundamental reassessment of the reliability of the traditional Arthurian narrative. This chapter examines the literary evidence again, source by source, in more or less chronological order.

Two extremely important points must be set out at the start. The first is that medieval writers and their audiences (as intimated in Chapter 1) expected different things from 'history'. Unlike 'moderns', medieval people did not have a category of 'factual history' separate from what might today be thought of as 'historical fiction', 'alternative history', or even 'fantasy'. A moral 'truth', a good story with a valuable lesson, was far more important than factual accuracy. Also ahead of 'telling it as it was' came the demonstration of culture and learning, whether biblical, classical, or, later, 'courtly'. Of course, some medieval authors, like William of Newburgh, thought writers like Geoffrey of Monmouth were making things up, but this was not crucial to a 'historical' composition's success or reputation. Moreover, the reasons why William thought Geoffrey was a 'liar' were most likely less 'scientific' than those of modern critics. It's quite possible that William thought Geoffrey was 'lying' because he didn't like the moral 'truth' he was proposing, not because he thought his sources were unreliable.

We know of texts that repeated the words of classical sources because of the 'authority' with which those writings were invested, even when their authors knew that the statements of the classics contradicted what they knew of their own, lived world. We also know that medieval sources told stories that their audiences must have known were 'untrue'. If Jordanes' *Getica* (written around 550 in Constantinople) relays the essence of the lost Gothic history written for the Italian Gothic court by Cassiodorus about a generation earlier, as Jordanes claims,[1] Cassiodorus told a story of recent history that any adult Goth in his audience knew was 'wrong'. This has been solidly demonstrated. Similarly, Frankish sources relate events of Charlemagne's reign, within a generation of that emperor's death, but make huge errors of 'fact'. Even now people regularly 'buy into' very dubious presentations of the recent (let alone the remote) past, for all sorts of reasons (political, nationalist, and so on). What this means is that the modern notion of 'rhetorical plausibility'—that a writer would not make a statement if his audience 'would have known it wasn't true'—carries no weight in assessing medieval accounts.

Closely related to this is the second point: sources must be taken as a whole. You cannot cherry-pick some bits and ignore others according to what you want to believe. You cannot winnow out fact from

---

[1] We know from Cassiodorus himself that he wrote this history. This makes this very different from the 'lost source' claims discussed in Chapter 7.

fiction solely on the basis of modern ideas. The section of Muirchú's eighth-century *Life of Saint Patrick* which adds to Patrick's own account of the background to his mission cannot be accepted on the basis that it looks like sober history and 'he wouldn't say what his audience knew wasn't true'. If it were, what would we do with the section given in some manuscripts, where Patrick turns the British ruler Coroticus into a fox? Must that be factual, too, because the author wouldn't say something his audience knew wasn't true? And if the medieval audience could believe that a saint could turn a king into a fox, in spite of (presumably) never having seen such a thing happen, then why would they not believe as 'true' a history that contradicted what they had previously heard? One must be absolutely consistent in one's treatment of a source's testimony and have good, solid reasons to do so when taking some elements separately from others.

Gildas

The basic building block for the traditional political historical narrative of fifth- and sixth-century Britain is Gildas' *De Excidio et Conquestu Britanniae* (*On the Ruin and Conquest of Britain*). This was certainly composed in Britain during our period but that is about all that can be said with absolute confidence about its date and provenance. We know nothing about Gildas himself. His name is not recognizably British. Many Gothic names incorporate the 'gild' element and many more end in '-a' or '-as'; a Gothic Count Gildilas governed early sixth-century Syracuse. A late fourth-century Moorish prince was called Gildo. Otherwise the name is unique. It is impossible to know *where* Gildas wrote except that it was probably not in a part of Britain controlled, in his day, by 'Saxons'. Nor can we say *when* he was writing. It is frequently claimed that he wrote *c.*540 but this date lacks any solid foundation. Professor David Dumville long ago demolished all the external evidence that might support such a date, principally the

Welsh Annals' reference to the death of King Maelgwn of Gwynedd in the 540s. Gildas railed against a King Maglocunus and Maglocunus is the same *name* as Maelgwn. That, however, does not make Gildas' Maglocunus the same *person* Maelgwn of Gwynedd; an inscribed stone from Nevern (Pembrokeshire) also names a Maglocunus. In any case, at this early date the evidential value of the *Welsh Annals* is very poor, as we shall see. Dumville reinstated a mid-sixth-century date for the *De Excidio*... using Gildas' own narrative of British history after the end of Roman rule. That attempt, though, is based on seeing Gildas' history as a single, unilinear sequence of events, as we did in Chapter 2 and as everyone else has done since the eighth century. Whether this is justified is addressed in Chapter 9.

There is some evidence for an 'early Gildas', writing in the late fifth century. This includes Gildas' rhetorical education, his Latin style, his theological concerns, and a rereading of his historical section and where he places himself within it. I tend towards this interpretation, although it cannot be proven. It is unlikely that Gildas wrote before 480/490 or much after about 550; beyond that we cannot go.

On the Ruin... has three basic elements. One is Gildas' historical section (twenty-five chapters) which everyone who ever opens this work studies, and on which we dwelt almost exclusively in Chapter 2; the second (ten chapters) is his complaint against the kings of Britain, which most people who look at Gildas read; the third is the other seventy-three chapters (70 per cent) of the work, which almost no one ever looks at, in spite of the fact that, as far as Gildas and his immediate audience were concerned, that was the important bit. That is hugely important. Gildas was not writing a history, but a sermon in the late antique tradition of 'speaking truth to power', or *parrhesia*. Had it been written in an age that produced more, or indeed *any*, surviving histories, Gildas' historical section—indeed his whole work—would now only be read by historians of theology and would therefore probably receive fairer treatment. As it is, because part of his short historical section (only about an eighth of the whole tract) is the *only* surviving contemporary British account of fifth-century history, it has been ripped out of context and given an importance that Gildas doubtless never meant it to have. Gildas' own intentions for the passage mean that it is extremely vague and stylized. However, having piously recommended that if you read Gildas you read his whole book, in what follows I will concentrate on the 'historical section', simply because that is the part used most in attempts to unravel the world of King Arthur.

The most significant discussion for present purposes concerns that oft-cited chronological indicator, Gildas' phrase about Mount Badon. It is a commonplace that whenever Gildas has anything important to say his Latin becomes extremely convoluted. Michael Winterbottom's heroic translation of the passage (chapter 26.1) was quoted in full in Chapter 2. This has usually been read simply enough as meaning that the siege took place forty-three years before Gildas was writing, and that Gildas was in his forty-fourth year too. Ian Wood suggested that the Latin *could* mean that Badon took place a month ago in the forty-fourth year of Gildas' age, although this reading has not found much favour. In the eighth century, Bede (*HE* 1.16) thought that Gildas meant that the battle took place in the forty-fourth year after the coming of the English. Some have thought Bede had a different, perhaps better, manuscript of Gildas' book. However, a New Zealand scholar called Wiseman has drawn attention to the confusion caused by modern attempts to make sense of Gildas by punctuating his tortuous Latin. Here is a less stylish, less clear, but more literal rendition of Gildas' single sentence:

> From that time now the citizens now the enemies were victorious so that in this people the Lord could make trial as is His wont of the latter-day Israel to see whether it loves Him or not up to the year of the siege of Mount Badon almost the last defeat of the rascals and by no means the least one month of the forty-forth year as I know having passed which was of my birth.

Wiseman's insight was to ignore modern punctuation and link 'from that time' with 'up to the year'. Simplified, and stripping away the sub-clauses, it says: 'from that time... to the year of the siege of Mount Badon... forty-three years and a month passed, as I know because it was the year of my birth.'

But from *what* time? When is Gildas counting his forty-three years and a month from? Here we must return to the previous paragraph (chapter 25.2–3) where Gildas recounts the Britons rallying under Ambrosius Aurelianus and defeating the Saxons. Forty-three years elapsed between Ambrosius' defeat of the Saxons and the siege of Mount Badon. This was clearly how Bede read the passage when he placed Badon forty-four years after the coming of the Saxons, which he seems to have equated with Gildas' Saxon revolt and subsequent war. It seems to me to be the correct way. It makes it unlikely that Ambrosius won the siege of Badon Hill, but then Gildas never actually said that he did.

Of course we still don't know when Gildas' birth or the siege of Badon Hill were. We'll see that the 'Saxon revolt' might have taken place around 430, dating Badon to *c.*475 and the composition of *On the Ruin*... probably to the start of the sixth century. If pressed, I might plump for the first decade of the century. Naturally, this is a sequence of 'ifs'. If you date the revolt earlier, think the following war was brief, and believe Gildas wrote while still young, you could push the work back possibly to about 490. If you understand the passage to mean that Gildas' birth occurred in the *first*, rather than the *last*, of the forty-three years, you could bring it back further, possibly to *c.*475. If, by contrast, you place the revolt later, think the ensuing war lasted longer, and that Gildas was a wise old bird when he wrote, then the usual date of *c.*540 still applies. We'll never know and that, probably, is the most important thing to say.

Gildas' failure to mention Arthur has produced all sorts of speculation. Later medieval writers invented stories about how Gildas and

Arthur fell out but they were, like us, trying to account for—to them—an inexplicable omission. Was Arthur too well known to need naming? This has often been suggested but it begs serious questions: why was he less necessary to name than Gildas' contemporary tyrants? Gildas doesn't name many people, so perhaps his silence is insignificant. Gildas' account indeed contains few names, but he gives those which matter. Finally, either 'Arthur' is another name for one of Gildas' characters—Ambrosius Aurelianus, 'the proud tyrant', or the Cuneglasus mentioned in the 'complaint to the kings' and addressed as 'bear'[2]—or Arthur belongs chronologically *after* Gildas. The second option might be possible, especially if Gildas is moved back to the very late fifth century. It is, however, obviously a pretty weak, if convenient, argument to explain a silence which, if Arthur never existed, would need no explanation. None of the suggestions for characters who are 'really' Arthur finds any evidential support. Like the first proposal, they spring from a desire to make the data fit an a priori assumption and thus account for the absence of actual evidence.

Gildas tells us much about society, Church, and rulership in the Britain in which he lived and wrote. However, the impossibility of knowing anything certain about Gildas' date and place and the vagueness of his writing make it very difficult to use *On the Ruin...* as the basis for a narrative history. But Gildas never intended it to fulfil that function so it is unfair to judge him on those grounds.

Bede

After Gildas, no insular source describes the 'world of Arthur' until we come to the famous 'Venerable Bede' in early eighth-century Northumbria (in the monastery of Monkwearmouth-Jarrow to be

---

[2] The *arth-* element of Arthur's name means 'bear'.

exact). Bede was a chronographer before he was a historian; he was interested in the measurement of time, essentially for theological purposes: calculating the proper date of Easter; establishing the age of the world, and so on. This led him to popularize the AD system of dating still in use (even if rechristened CE: Common Era); he didn't invent it but he might as well have done. In turn it brought about his two chronicles (the lesser and the greater: *Chronica Minora* and *Chronica Majora*): lists of years and the events that happened in them. At the end of his life his interest in chronology and belief that the contemporary English Church had degenerated from a putative seventh-century golden age led him to compose his most famous work, *The Ecclesiastical History of the English People* (HE), which he completed in 731, shortly before his death (735). We therefore know immensely more about Bede, his life, and circumstances than we do about Gildas.

Bede put his version of British history between the end of Roman rule and St Augustine's arrival in the latter part of Book I of the *Ecclesiastical History* (HE 1.11–1.34). It is a fascinating attempt to put together a coherent narrative from diverse components, almost all of which still survive. In other words, Bede apparently knew as little as we do about the period between *c.*410 and *c.*597. His principal source is Gildas' *On the Ruin* …, which he read as a single narrative of events, probably, as we shall see in Chapter 9, a mistake but one which almost everyone who has read Gildas since has made. Into this he wove information from several other sources. He took information on the end of Roman rule from Orosius' *Seven Books of History against the Pagans*, written by a Spanish Christian in *c.*417, and other facts about fifth-century western political history—especially valuable in assigning dates to events—from the *Chronicles* of Prosper of Aquitaine, from the fifth century, and Marcellinus, from the sixth. As we saw in Chapter 2, Bede explained that Aëtius failed to respond to the 'Groans of the Britons' because he was fighting the Huns under Bleda and Attila. Bede knew, from Marcellinus, that this could not be true. Attila killed Bleda before

Aëtius' third consulship, mentioned by the 'Groans of the Britons' letter. Bede probably, therefore, meant this as a general account of Rome's tribulations at the time, rather than as a precise statement.

Bede placed the Coming of the Saxons (*adventus saxonum*) in the time of the Emperors Valentinian and Marcian (450–5; *HE* 1.15). From Gildas, he knew that the appeal to Aëtius took place after his third consulate, and produced no response. From Prosper and Marcellinus he could date that consulate to the year he calculated as AD 446. He also knew from Gildas of periods of resistance to the barbarians, prosperity, and then famine and plague *after* the appeal. Thus he made an educated guess that the invitation to the Saxons was made five to ten years later, during Valentinian and Marcian's joint reign.

After the Saxon rebellion, Bede copied out Gildas' account of the war up to Mount Badon (*HE* 1.15–16). This, Bede (like most people) thought, was against the Saxons and, as mentioned, he put it forty-four years after the arrival of the English. That, by his reckoning, would have been in the mid- to late 490s. This nevertheless raised problems, which further led Bede to assign crucial significance to the period 450–5. While he knew, from Prosper, the date of St Germanus' first visit to Britain (429), the *Life* of that saint mentioned *Saxons* as Germanus' enemies. That put Saxons in Britain two decades before the date Bede had worked out for their arrival. Therefore, to harmonize his account, Bede moved Germanus' Saxon battle to a point after the *adventus Saxonum* around 450 (indeed after Germanus' death). Quite how he reconciled Gildas' story of the invitation of the Saxons being a response to Pictish attack with the *Life of Germanus'* reference to a combined Saxon–Pictish invasion is another unresolved problem. Nevertheless Bede ironed out the difficulties by recounting both of Germanus' visits, one directly after the other (*HE* 1.17–21), telescoping the time between them, omitting any AD dates, and concluding with Germanus' visit to Valentinian III's court at the end of his life. Adding to that the information, taken from Marcellinus' *Chronicle*, that Valentinian was murdered in the sixth year of Marcian's reign—'and the western Empire fell'—all was superficially brought into harmony in the period 450–5.

We can, therefore, identify Bede's sources—they still survive—and from them we can reconstruct how he calculated his date for what he conceived of as the Saxons' 'arrival'. Bede also added some snippets of geographical information, about where the Picts were from and the limits of the turf wall. Bede first gives us the name 'Vurtigernus' or 'Vertigernus'—Vortigern—for Gildas' 'proud tyrant', and first names the Saxon leaders as Hengist and Horsa.

The status and origins of the information Bede added to Gildas' story are essentially unknowable. Bede uses probably the oldest recorded form of Vortigern's name. Legendary stories were certainly circulating about this ruler in Wales a hundred years later, but his historicity is insecure. Hengist and Horsa's reality is much debated. Brothers with alliterative names often play a part in legends about the origins of a people (think, for example, of Romulus and Remus) and their names mean 'Gelding' and 'Horse', leading some to suppose that they were legendary heroes or lesser gods. One might say that the fact that the Lakota Sioux leaders at The Little Big Horn had names that translate as Crazy Horse and Sitting Bull does not render them mythical, but Anglo-Saxon names that *only* include the name of an animal are rare indeed. Ian Richmond famously—ingeniously—suggested that Horsa's monument, mentioned by Bede (*HE* 1.15), was an old Roman military tombstone in which the remnants of the word [CO]HORS remained visible. Bede, though, doesn't say that the monument was stone or even that it had Horsa's name actually on it, just that it was known by his name. Hengist crops up in another context, the so-called 'Fight at Finsburgh' fragment of the epic poem *Beowulf*. Perhaps he was a real character and only his alliterative 'doublet' Horsa an invention. We'll never know, but scepticism would seem prudent.

Such scepticism would be strengthened by the fact that a place known as *Hengestesdune* (Hengist's Hill) was known in the ninth century at the very opposite end of Wessex, on the border with the Cornish 'west Welsh'; a battle against the Cornish and their Viking allies was fought there in 838. In fact there are two Hingston Downs in the region, one near Callington (Cornwall) and the other near Moretonhampstead (Devon). This suggests a Hengist whom early medieval people associated with landmarks far from Kent. The fact that these places are in an area long contested between the English and the Britons may be significant but does not weaken the possibility that Hengist was a more widely known legendary hero, rather than a historical individual who received lands in Kent. Let's repeat, though, that Bede's story of Vortigern, Hengist, and Horsa is simply Gildas', but with names added.

We need to emphasize that Bede's is a significant mutation of Gildas' story. For Gildas, the arrival of these Saxons was only one political event, which he fastened on as lying at the root of later wars and trouble; he does not imply that this was the first arrival of the Saxons or even that it was the only such *foedus*. Only from Bede's time does Gildas' account become the focus of the story of *the* (singular) Coming of the English. That became ever more underlined as later sources placed layer upon layer of detail and legend on the bare bones of Gildas' story until the early twentieth-century schoolchild would learn that the English came to England in 449, a date as evidently precise and important as 1066.

Hengist and Horsa's genealogy is entirely suspect. Wihtgisl, Witta, and Wecta are all versions of the name of the Isle of Wight. Bede said that Wight's inhabitants, like those of Kent, were Jutes, so this probably represents a claim to Wight by the seventh-century Kentish kings. Early medieval genealogies were often used to further political agendas. After Gildas' narrative expires, with the period of sin after Mount Badon, Bede skips straight to the very end of the sixth century, with St Augustine's mission to Kent (597) and the Northumbrian king Æthelfrith's victory over the Scots at Degsastane (603). The one possible trace of independent information is the postulated Canterbury source for the first part of Bede's list of kings with *imperium*, mentioned in Chapter 2. This neatly underlines how Bede knew almost nothing about the 200 or so years before Augustine's arrival independently of sources we still have. Thus his account has flimsy and unreliable foundations, and can bear little weight. For Bede that was irrelevant. The point of the *Ecclesiastical History* was that the Britons had lost control of Britain's green and pleasant land, driven out by the Saxons, chosen by God to be His scourge of a sinful people. Bede felt that the Anglo-Saxons could go the same way if they didn't mend their ways. When the Vikings turned up sixty years after his death, Bede's standing as a scholar and prophet was further enhanced. He might therefore not have been unduly bothered by moving Germanus' visit out of its proper place and could even have been aware that he was doing violence to Gildas' account by straightening it out into a single sequence of events.

Note, though, that neither Bede, nor any of his sources, oral, legendary, or written, says anything about 'Arthur'. For this the most straightforward and, given that we still have almost all of Bede's sources, unsurprising explanation is simply that he (and they) didn't know anything about him. It doesn't necessarily imply that Arthur never existed; a perfectly acceptable and consistent qualification of the explanation just given is 'or, if they had heard of him, he didn't matter to their story'.

The *History of the Britons*

So we come to the first datable source to mention Arthur, the *History of the Britons* (HB), written in 828/9, in North Wales. The name Nennius (or Nemnius) was only attached to a later manuscript of this source.

Although there was a Nennius about at the right sort of time and place (rather an interesting figure too), that doesn't mean he actually wrote it, so henceforth we will refer to the source simply by its title. By now, we are over 300 years from Arthur's putative existence and that is a *long* time for legends to grow and for details to intrude into basic and anonymous stories. This cannot be overemphasized.

The *HB* shows just how elaborate legends about the fifth century had become by the early eighth. Structurally the work looks like a mess. It is a mix of genealogies, legendary accounts of the Britons' origins and history under the Romans (*HB* 7–30), an at least semi-legendary tale of the foundation of Kent, featuring Vortigern, his son Vortimer, Hengist, and Horsa. This is mixed with a much revised story of St Germanus' visit to Britain (also featuring Vortigern and Ambrosius; *HB* 31–49), and a potted history of St Patrick (*HB* 50–5). Then we come to the 'Battle List of Arthur' (*HB* 56), which serves as a linking passage introducing the *History*'s account of northern Britain, mainly in the seventh century (*HB* 57–66). A list of the 'Wonders of Britain', including the second passage about Arthur (mentioned in Chapter 1), is appended to the end of the *History* (*HB* 67–75).

The author of the *HB* dated the coming of the Saxons to the year we think of as 428. From this and a comparison with the 449 date given by the *Anglo-Saxon Chronicle* for the Anglo-Saxons' arrival, John Morris proposed that all the *Chronicle*'s dates could be moved back by a standard twenty-one years. Alas, as we shall see, the *Chronicle*'s fifth-century dates are historically worthless, so this was a mistake. In particular, the *Chronicle*'s date for the coming of the English is simply a rationalization of Bede's educated but much vaguer guess about the date of that event.

However, in chapter 66 the writer says that the Saxon *adventus* occurred 429 years before the fourth year of King Merfyn of Gwynedd, which would be in AD 400/1. In chapter 31 he puts it even earlier in the Year of the Passion (AP) 347. In his source, Prosper's *Chronicle*, this would have been AD 374, during the reign of Emperor Gratian, who nominally ruled the western Empire with his father Valentinian I from 367 to 375 and then jointly with his brother Valentinian II (though to all intents and purposes alone) until 383, when he was killed by Magnus Maximus, the usurper from Britain. It is difficult to know what to make of this. In Chapter 9, we will discuss the *HB*'s chronology in more detail and examine its reliability. For now all that needs to be said is that the scholarly consensus is that it is unreliable.

The account given in Chapter 2 did not include all of the elements of the *HB*'s tale. After its version of the Hengist and Horsa story, it presents us with strange tales of St Germanus, who confronts a tyrant called Benlli and foretells the origin and power of the kings of Powys. Another digression about Vortigern follows the account of his infatuation with Hengist's daughter. In this, after his incest with his daughter and cursing by St Germanus, Vortigern fled into Snowdonia and attempted without success to build a fortress. Having been told by his 'wizards' that this failure could only be rectified by the sacrifice of a boy with no father, he manages to find such a child. The boy, however, reveals that the fortress cannot be built because of a lake under its foundations. He then produces a miraculous portent in which two worms, one white, one red, fight for the control of a piece of cloth, with the red worm, after difficulties, eventually driving the white one off the cloth altogether. This, says the child, foretells the weakness and tribulations of the Britons (the red worm, or dragon) who will eventually rally and drive the Saxons (the white worm) out of Britain. Understandably impressed, Vortigern grants the western regions of Britain to the boy, who turns out to be Emrys or Ambrosius 'the overlord', son of a Roman consul (the fact that his mother previously avowed that he had no father is now mysteriously forgotten). Vortigern moves north with his supporters. In the end, hated by all and sundry, he fled from one place to another, pursued by St Germanus for his sin of incest, until he eventually died, either in divine fire that consumed his fortress, or of a broken heart, or because the earth opened and swallowed him up.

There is, you might have realized, scant cause to take any of this seriously. There is no compelling reason to extract the tale of Vortimer's battles as more historical than the worms fighting on the cloth, as Arthurian pseudo-historians are wont to. The *HB* assembles material from a string of sources, some of which can be identified but almost none of which has any claim to reliability. We will examine these in more detail in Chapter 9. Much of the story is woven from Bede's and thus, behind that, Gildas' accounts; part of chapter 43 ultimately derives from Gildas' statement about one side and then the other being victorious. The references to Horsa's death and, probably, to the inscribed stone in the third battle in Kent (see Chapter 2) are elaborations of Bede's tale of Horsa and his monument.

The four-battle story of Vortimer's wars seems to come from a common legendary stock, as we shall see. The outlines of the story of Vortimer's siege of the Saxons on Thanet are repeated later in the *HB* with regard to Urien of Rheged and the establishment of the Saxons in the north. This north/south parallelism appears elsewhere in the *HB*'s structure. The author also takes a certain amount of information from royal genealogies and might draw upon English myth. Hengist uses the English word '*saxa*' (*seax*: dagger) when he tells the English to draw their knives at the conference with Vortigern's elders. Clearly the material about Germanus and Emrys is legend pure and simple. What is interesting is how St Germanus' visit has lost any reference to British heresy and how his moralizing against Vortigern is supported by the British Church.

The commonly available translation of the *HB* muddies the waters by naming the Kentish sections 'The Kentish Chronicle'. This comes from John Morris's supposition that these entries originated in a lost set of Kentish annals, which, if true, would increase their historicity. However, there is no reason to suppose such an origin; the text does not read like a chronicle and as far as I can see the manuscripts of the *HB* provide no basis for these headings. In the Latin text given by Morris himself, the heading is only '*in Cantia*' ('in Kent'; one might prefer 'meanwhile, in Kent...').

And so we return to Arthur's battles (chapter 56). As was mentioned in Chapter 2, it is often supposed to represent a fragment of a lost poem celebrating Arthur's achievements. The battles themselves have engendered any number of pseudo-histories, purporting to reconstruct King Arthur's campaigns. Their locations are suggested and a putative military context invented, within the traditionally supposed overall situation of a war between defending Britons and invading Anglo-Saxons (for which see Chapter 8). Of course the locations are usually chosen with the context in mind, so it is almost invariably a circular argument. On the other hand, sceptics counter by saying that, whether this is a poem or not, we have no way of knowing whether it gives any sort of historical account. By 830 there had been at least 300 years for poems to be composed and elaborated, for characters to be invented, battles made up, for real battles from various contexts to be brought together and ascribed to a mighty, legendary war-leader.

The battle in the city of the legion might actually be the battle of Chester (*c*.613–16). In some manuscripts, 'Mount Agned' is replaced by 'Bregoin', a battle associated with that other semi-legendary British war-leader Urien of Rheged. *Tribruit* appears as *Tryfrwyd* in a later Welsh poem, with no connection to Arthur; the poem might have taken the battle from the *HB*, or both might have taken it from a common source. Badon is mentioned by Gildas and Bede, both known to the *HB*'s author, as the last significant battle in a war supposed by Bede at least to be between Britons and Saxons. Gildas and Bede associated it with Ambrosius Aurelianus. Anyone familiar with Gildas and Bede would know that Badon ought to come last in the list. These objections are impossible to refute; not that that has stopped people from trying. Nonetheless, one might also point out that, though it is possible, it is not *certain* that the *HB*'s 'battle of the town of the legion' *is* Bede's battle of Chester. As we have seen, it seems unlikely that Gildas *does* say that Badon was won by Ambrosius Aurelianus. The other five locations are found nowhere else in surviving literature, making it at least 'not proven' that they are a diverse medley of famous battles assembled and connected with Arthur.

One other point must be stressed. With the exception of the 'Battle of the Caledonian Forest', which ought to be somewhere north of Hadrian's Wall, and *Linnuis*, which *might* be Lindsey (Lincolnshire), the locations of all of these battles are unknown and unknowable. This is of supreme importance if reading modern pseudo-histories so I'll say it again:

THE LOCATIONS OF ALL OF THESE BATTLES ARE UNKNOWN AND UNKNOWABLE

The *Historia Brittonum* is a fascinating, infuriating source. It still holds many secrets, doubtless including ones that no one will ever uncover. Most of them, however, relate to politics and history-writing in early ninth-century Wales. That topic is no less important or interesting than fifth-century history. Let's be clear about that. As with Gildas and Bede, we must identify the questions which the source *does* address rather than hammering it to fit those which it doesn't.

In this connection, it is important to say something about the context within which the *HB* was written (in 828/9). The *Welsh Annals* record a 'Saxon' conquest of Powys in 822. Indeed, their account of the late eighth and early ninth centuries is one of repeated English attacks. This period begins roughly with the construction of Offa's Dyke, believed to have been a response to a phase of Welsh inroads into Mercia. Perhaps this was a time when a Welsh historian might have felt the need to invent a great figure from the past who smote the Saxons left, right, and centre, to rally his countrymen in a difficult period. Its author had heard of a legendary 'Arthur the soldier', and he seemed to fit the bill. We will return to this theme in Chapter 8. It is significant that he placed Arthur's story here rather than somewhere else in his history, but we must not forget that his history of post-imperial Britain included a lot of indubitably legendary, unhistorical names and other material (Horsa, and Emrys/ Ambrosius and his prophecies, for example) or that even the Arthur he knew about was associated with the bizarre, miraculous, and legendary.

It is salutary to think about the *HB*'s figure of Emrys/Ambrosius as a possible comparison with its treatment of Arthur. If Gildas' writings had not survived his lifetime, we would doubtless dismiss the possibility that there was a real Ambrosius behind the crazy tales of the boy prophet. Yet, because *On the Ruin...* did survive, we know that Ambrosius was a really existing historical personage. By the same token, though, everything that the *HB does* tell us about Ambrosius is surely fictitious. On this analogy, the dubious nature of the *HB* as a source for Arthur does not mean that no such person ever lived during the fifth or sixth centuries. In the end, the *Historia Brittonum* provides no decisive grounds for accepting or rejecting 'the historical Arthur'; 'you pays your money and takes your choice'. However, it cannot be stressed too strongly that the *HB does not* provide *any* reliable information about *any* historical figure of that name.

None of this makes the *HB* any less fascinating. It tells us enormously interesting things about the tales circulating in early ninth-century Wales, about how they could be woven together to tell a particular story about the past and thus about the compiler's political agendas. None of it, though, can be taken even remotely on trust as a reliable account of the fifth century. Elements of fact might lie within it but there is now no way to identify them or to know whether they have been correctly placed in the sequence.

The *Anglo-Saxon Chronicle*

Our final major source, much used in Arthurian pseudo-histories, is the *Anglo-Saxon Chronicle*, first composed at or near King Alfred's court in the 880s and continued in various different manuscripts down to the reign of King Stephen (1135–54). The *Chronicle*'s account of the fifth century is extremely dubious and it is staggering that people took it literally for so long. I have played a game with my first-year undergraduates wherein I give them selections from Gildas, Bede, and the *Chronicle* dealing with the fifth century, but with no information about the sources' titles or where they come from; I simply label them, out of chronological order, A, B, and C and ask them to put them in order of composition and justify their sequence. Interestingly, they often put the *Anglo-Saxon Chronicle* first, because it looks like a bald record of facts, later expanded and elaborated, as they see it, by the other sources. Something like this reasoning might have driven earlier generations of historians to believe that there had to be a reliable, older source behind the *Chronicle*.

The *Chronicle*'s account begins with what is essentially Bede's story of Hengist and Horsa and the settlement of Kent, but padded out and with a few details of battles added. Being a chronicle it adds precise dates to these events. It moves Bede's loose 'in the days of Valentinian and Marcian' for *the* coming of the Saxons to 449 exactly, but mangles the names of the two emperors (to Mauritius and Valentinus): a testimony to the decline in learning in ninth-century Wessex that King Alfred himself decried. This completes the transformation of Gildas' tale into England's point of origin. The *Chronicle* then adds details of other Saxon arrivals in Sussex and Wessex, as we saw in Chapter 2. The structure of the *Chronicle*'s account of the fifth and early sixth centuries ought, by itself, to have given pause for thought. Obviously artificially, the account moves from east to west. The English settlements build up to their climax: the foundation of Alfred's own kingdom, Wessex, by his putative ancestors. When the *Chronicle* was composed, Kent and Sussex were sub-kingdoms of Wessex and thus clearly to be subordinated historically. Of the three Northumbrian dates inserted into the account of West Saxon history, the first comes directly, and the second implicitly, from Bede's *History*.

The *Chronicle*'s sources were Bede, whom we've already discussed and dismissed as a reliable independent witness for the fifth century, and a range of genealogical and other legendary sources. Exactly the same problems occur with this evidence as were mentioned with reference to Bede. However, although they might have lacked a certain scholarly ability, the *Chronicle*'s compilers were no fools. Barbara Yorke showed that their account of Wessex's foundation is, in its structure and overall narrative, *exactly* the same as their version of the foundation of Kent, but with the names of people and places changed. Wessex didn't have a foundation legend which could compare with that of its subordinate kingdom, Kent. This would never do, so the compilers adapted the Kentish story to fit Wessex and the West Saxon royal genealogy. A different version may have been incorporated, about Stuf and Wihtgar, the latter of whom is clearly intended (and invented) to lay claim to the Isle of Wight—also, we have seen, claimed by Kentish tradition.

Other problems arise. Nicholas Brooks plausibly argued that the account of the conquest of Kent drew upon the same legendary stock as the *History of the Britons*. As there, we are given four battles, only three of which are named, of steadily increasing severity, culminating in a catastrophic defeat for the enemies of those writing the history. In the *HB* the battles move from west to east and climax with the Saxons driven in flight to their ships, 'like women'. In the *Chronicle*, the battles move from east to west and end with the Britons fleeing from the English 'as from fire'. One version might have been copied from and 'corrected' or 'improved' the other, or neither version might be 'true'; they could be different versions of standard folklore. We have no way of knowing.

Another problem concerns Sussex's foundation by King Ælle. We have seen that this account is artificially placed between Kent and Wessex in a narrative that proceeds from east to west. Moreover, Bede knew about a King Ælle of Sussex who seems to have ruled over Kent. In Bede's list, Ælle was succeeded as the king with *imperium* by Ceawlin of Wessex. Ceawlin appears in the *Chronicle* at the very end of the sixth century; he fought, and was beaten by, Æthelberht of Kent, the next king with *imperium* in Bede's list. Æthelberht is indubitably historical and, though the date of the start of his reign is uncertain, that of his death around 616 is fairly secure. So is that of his reign's most important event, St Augustine's mission in 597. We can therefore assume that the *Chronicle*'s account of Æthelberht fighting Ceawlin and throwing off his domination is likely to be broadly reliable. We can at least say with some certainty that Ceawlin was a genuine late sixth-century southern English ruler. That, however, makes it much more likely that his predecessor in Bede's list, Ælle, reigned immediately before him, around the middle quarters of the sixth century, perhaps slightly later. The *Chronicle* has thus moved Ælle back in time by a century. Taking his name from Bede, it has invented an account of the foundation of Sussex to place chronologically and geographically between the origins of Kent and the creation of Wessex.

Many people mentioned in the *Chronicle* were invented to justify land claims. This is most obvious with 'Port' who landed, according to the *Chronicle*, at Portsmouth in 501. We can also spot Ælle's sons, Cissa, Cymen, and Wlencing: Cymen gives his name to *Cymenes ora*, where the South Saxons landed, later called The Owers, south of Selsey Bill; Wlencing derives his name from the place Lancing; and Cissa is the eponymous founder of Cissa's *ceastre* (fort)—Chichester. In the West Saxon royal genealogy, Wihtgar takes his name from *Wihtgarsbyrig*, the *burh* (fort) of Wight, and various battle-sites provide names for defeated Britons: 'Wipped' from *Wippedesfleot*, and 'Natanleod' from Netley (conquered after his death in 508, according to the *Chronicle*). For all we know, this punning might have been uproariously amusing in late ninth-century Winchester but it is hardly the stuff of sober history.

Several sixth-century battles are employed similarly to argue that Wessex had always owned particular territories because it conquered them from the Welsh. Many such battles are in the upper Thames/ lower Severn region, disputed between Wessex and Mercia between the seventh and ninth centuries. The four towns of Limbury, Aylesbury, Bensington, and Eynsham, for example, were conquered after the battle of *Biedcanford* (possibly Bedford, possibly not) in the *Chronicle*'s year 571. Gloucester, Cirencester, and Bath were captured after the battle of Dyrham in '577'. The *Chronicle*'s authors were thus doing something rather similar to what in Chapter 8 I will suggest the author of the *Historia Brittonum* might have been doing a couple of generations previously. This does not mean that none of these sixth-century battles occurred, or that they did not involve any of the personages named. Some or all of the Welsh kings named by the *Chronicle* (Conmail, Farinmail, and Candidan) may indeed have fought at Dyrham. We have no way of being sure, though, and it remains much more unlikely that they ruled the three cities named as falling to the West Saxons afterwards, which lie in the territory disputed by Wessex and Mercia. Nor can we ascertain when, if ever, these battles took place.

There could be snippets of sixth-century fact in the *Chronicle* but it is impossible now to disentangle them from the narrative and structure of its authors' propaganda, or from the huge dose of myth, legend, and pun with which they injected it.

The Welsh Annals

The last insular narrative to consider is the *Annales Cambriae* (*Welsh Annals*). As noted in Chapter 2, this contains two 'Arthurian' entries, one concerning Badon, the other Arthur's death at Camlann. The source itself probably belongs to the later tenth century; its last entry is 954 and the last year counted 977. The earliest manuscript dates to around 1100 (the *Annals* are appended to a text of the *HB*), though, and the two other variants belong to the thirteenth century. Immediately, therefore, we note how much later it is than Arthur's alleged existence. It has been argued that the *Annals* draw upon lost chronicle sources, in particular Irish annalistic accounts. Even so, it is difficult to find anything very reliable for the sixth century, even in the most trustworthy of the surviving Irish annals. Few scholarly analyses claim that contemporary records were being maintained in Wales much before about 800. There is no persuasive reason to presume that the *Welsh Annals* simply transmit earlier more contemporary records in unmodified form. A closer look confirms these suspicions.

The second obvious point to remark upon is the similarity between its account of Badon and the *HB*'s description of *Castell Guinnion*. The image of Mary has been replaced with the cross of the Lord, however. It seems that the author of the *Annals* has merged the *Historia*'s account of *Guinnion* with his information about Arthur's heroic exploits at Badon. He has probably chosen Badon as the focus because that was the one mentioned by other sources like Gildas and Bede, whereas *Castell Guinnion* is otherwise unknown. It is also possible, however, that he had access to different traditions about Badon. Whether or not that is the case, there is no prima facie reason to take the account very seriously. Like the *HB*'s story it is clearly legendary. The entry before the discussion of Badon reads: 'Bishop Ebur rests in Christ in the 350th year of his age'. Anyone wishing to see the Badon entry as historical has to find some reason why we should take it and its biblical-sounding 'three days and three nights' more seriously than the nonsense that comes directly before it.

The Camlann entry must come from somewhere else, however. This is the first mention of Arthur's last, climactic battle and of

Medraut. Note, though, that our source does not say that these two were on different sides. They might just as easily have been two leaders killed in a great defeat. All the material about Arthur's incest, with Mordred as both his son and his nephew, comes later, though it might owe something to the tradition recorded by the *HB* that 'Arthur the soldier' had killed his own son. Whereas the Badon entry is entirely Latin in form (*bellum Badonis*), the Camlann annal must have had a Welsh source; it is called *gueith Camlann*. Whether this tradition was any more trustworthy than those used by the *Historia* in its miraculous accounts of Arthur's hound's footprint and Amr's grave is unknowable. There is no good reason to suppose that it was.

As with the *HB*, the political context for the *Annales Cambriae*'s discussion of Arthur is important. The tenth century saw the creation of the unified kingdom of England under the House of Wessex (Alfred's descendants). This kingdom was at its apogee between the reigns of Æthelstan (924–39) and his nephew Edgar (954–72), the period of the *Annals*' composition. These years saw many submissions of the Welsh rulers to their powerful neighbours. Edgar even forced a number of his subject kings, including Welsh princes, to row him in a boat on the river Dee. These tribute-takings and submissions, with their humiliating rituals, were clearly resented. A Welsh poem composed at this time, the *Armes Prydein* (the *Great Prophecy of Britain*), makes this very apparent. It foresees a time when all the non-English peoples of Britain, 'Celtic' and 'Viking', will unify and drive the English back into the sea whence they came. Interestingly, though, in spite of its message and of being what one might have thought was the ideal place for the deployment of this heroic anti-English figure, the *Armes Prydein* nowhere alludes to Arthur. Its silence is not evidence that Arthur never existed but it is eloquent testimony to the fact that, if he did, in the mid-tenth century his story was still a long way from being well known or politically significant. One can see the other side of this 'ideological war' in the triumphalist Old English poem *The Battle of*

Brunanburh, which celebrates Æthelstan's great victory over such a non-English coalition in 937. This battle is hailed as the greatest triumph of the English since they came from over the sea, 'as books tell us', and 'won a kingdom by the sword's edge'. In other words, the history put to ideological service by both sides in this period of English unification and conquest was one which saw the fifth-century past as one in which the English, one 'people', fought, conquered, and expelled the Welsh, another. This is not unlike the situation that might have produced the similar historical vision of the fifth century in the *HB* in earlier ninth-century North Wales.

The *Welsh Annals* remain a dubious source for 'the historical Arthur'. Their author possibly had access to *some* Arthurian tradition otherwise lost, different from the account handed down from Gildas via Bede and the *HB* (an argument, in other words, for the 'bubbling kettle' reading, described in Chapter 1), but it is impossible to argue that these traditions had any better claim to historical reliability.

Welsh 'heroic' poetry

The other source possibly from before AD 1000 to mention Arthur is the poem Y *Gododdin*. It has recently been suggested that, as the references to the British army's annihilation seem to appear in the later traditions incorporated in this poem, the original battle of *Catraeth* might have been a bloody draw—although the questions of why anyone would write a great poem about a draw or why that might later be emended to make it into a *defeat* are unanswered. Be that as it may, some suppose Y *Gododdin*'s stanza about Gorddur to be the earliest mention of Arthur. The poem, however, is not clearly datable. The events it describes are generally supposed to relate to the period around 600. Some historians have suggested a half century earlier but on no good grounds. The poetry need not, however, be contemporary with them. It cannot entirely be later than about 1100, when the Welsh language adopted forms different from some of those attested in the poetry. The manuscript tradition provides no clues, as it belongs to the thirteenth century. Indeed much of the poem is itself written in language entirely consistent with twelfth- or thirteenth-century composition. Close analysis reveals a complex textual 'archaeology', with different versions and layers of traditions super-imposed upon and merged with each other at various dates. Currently the most optimistic argument is John Koch's, based upon scholarly discussion of linguistic forms. He sees the earliest *stratum* of this 'archaeology' as belonging to the earlier seventh century and pins the oldest version precisely to *c*.638.

However, as we have no Welsh texts from such early dates, the lin-guistic argument is—indeed it can only be—highly speculative. Koch's argument, whilst very learned, begs questions at every turn. He makes, for instance, serial assumptions about the close chrono-logical relationship between a verse and a historical referent. Thus the mention of the battle of Strath Carron (642) means that linguistic characteristics present in the 'stratum' of the text below that contain-ing that stanza must date before *c*.643. Yet the mention of Strath Carron only gives us what in archaeology is called a *terminus post quem*—a 'point after which'. Clearly it can't belong *before* that battle but equally it might, for all we know, date to a hundred years or more *after* it. Even Koch admits that his oldest linguistic stratum might date from as late as the eighth century. Into this are woven inferences from archaeology and political history which can seriously be questioned (see, above all, Chapters 8 and 11), so Koch's argument has not con-vinced everyone.

If, nevertheless, we accept Koch's rough date, we are still left with important problems in thinking about the 'World of Arthur'. A great deal happened around 600, involving social, political, and economic upheavals. One outcome seems, as we shall see in Chapter 12, to have been a shift in the balance of power from the highland kingdoms to those of the Anglo-Saxon lowlands. In the sphere of military history, moreover, the period around 600 was one of profound change, in weaponry, tactics, and organization. This raises two issues. First, it is difficult to project information in seventh-century sources into the period before 600. Second, the 'heroic' warfare described in these verses is not merely *not* that of the poet's own time, but possibly *not* even that of the period described in the poem. In other words, it might be wishful thinking: a harking back to a heroic 'golden age', which never actually existed, even if the events described did. The very production of these poems might result from the important social changes just mentioned.

So where does this leave Gorddur, who 'was not Arthur'? It is certainly odd that 'pro-Arthurians' argue that the decisive evidence for Arthur's historical existence is a source saying that someone *wasn't* Arthur. Stating that someone was or was not 'Arthur' implies nothing about Arthur's existence. In the mid-sixth century, Procopius, the eastern Roman ('Byzantine') historian, refers to one warrior who in his view actually *was* 'the Achilles of the Vandals'. This does not mean there ever was a real Achilles.

Koch says that scepticism about deducing Arthur's existence from this stanza depends on one or both of two suppositions that he calls 'problematical':

1. 'The poets of dark-age Britain had invented a fictional military superhero and placed his career within the sphere of living memory (*c.*500).'
2. 'the battle-list synchronism of *HB* ch. 56 and the Badon and Camlann entries of [*Welsh Annals*] 516 and 537 reflect a radical and unhistorical chronology for Arthur, devised between *c.*638 and 829.'

The first supposition is by no means inherent, as the text no more implies that this 'Arthur' existed within living memory than Procopius' reference to Achilles as a military touchstone means that Achilles must have died within a lifetime of his writing. In the second supposition, it is Koch's hypotheses that are 'problematical'. The date of *c*.638 for Y *Gododdin* cannot be regarded as certain. Moreover, the precise date of the stanza mentioning Arthur is a matter of debate. Koch argues coherently that it belongs to the original text, thus to sometime between the mid-seventh century and the middle of the eighth. Others, though, have presented scholarly arguments for this stanza being a *late* insertion into the poem, possibly later than, say, the *HB*'s discussions of Arthur.

It could belong to more or less the same period and thus the same milieu as the *HB*, and we've seen why a Welsh author in that context might have invented a post-Roman Arthur using a legendary figure as a basis. A mighty warrior defeating the Anglo-Saxons at all points *might* have been an attractive fictional figure when the *HB* was written, when the English were threatening the Welsh militarily. From this and Bede, it would not be difficult—certainly not 'radical'—for a tenth-century Welsh scholar to concoct dates around 500 for this Arthur. There is not very much synchronism between *HB* 56 and the *Annales Cambriae*; such as there is probably comes at least in part from the likely dependence of one source on the other.

We cannot rule out Arthur's existence on the basis of these doubts, but it is equally impossible to use this stanza from Y *Gododdin* as evidence that he *did* exist. All we can say is that, by whatever date this stanza was composed, the poet knew of an Arthur figure who could be used as a benchmark for military prowess. Whether that Arthur was a really existing leader or a mythic figure cannot be deduced.

The issues just discussed apply to the rest of Welsh 'heroic' verse, including the works of 'Taliesin' about other legendary northern British military heroes like Urien and Owain of Rheged, which—highly significantly—does not otherwise mention Arthur.

Odds and ends

The foregoing list encompasses pretty much all of the written material deemed to be of relevance to reconstructing the 'World of King Arthur'. A little more needs to be said about one or two additional sources.

The Life of St Germanus

Constantius of Lyon's late fifth-century *Life* says that Germanus twice went to Britain (once, we can establish, in 429 and once in the 440s) and on his first visit defeated a Pictish–Saxon force in the 'Alleluia Victory'. The *Life* was composed about thirty years after Germanus' death but its author knew people who had known the saint, including Bishop Lupus of Troyes who accompanied Germanus to Britain. That said, it is a work of hagiography (writing about saints), filled with miracles. Telling a sober history as a repository of facts for later scholars was no part of its purpose. It has been argued—at one extreme—that the entire *Life* is a patchwork of hagiographical commonplaces intended as a teaching instrument about proper theological beliefs and the correct role of a bishop. One cannot simply take the *Life*, ignore the miraculous elements, and sift out the rest as 'proper' history; one must take it as a whole. Nonetheless, this is not as damaging to the *Life* as a historical source as might be expected. Recent work has shed much light on how miracles worked in the early medieval mind-set. Most miracles concern the curing of afflictions that have psychosomatic (or, one historian suggests, 'sociosomatic') causes.

There seems little reason to doubt the broad outlines of Germanus' first visit. It sheds important light on the very end of Roman Britain. It is interesting that religion had a part in local politics, as elsewhere in the Empire. Accusations of heresy played a significant role in denigrating one's enemies. Equally, it is interesting that an outsider from Gaul was invited in to resolve the dispute; this too has many parallels.

The Holy Man's role as an 'outsider' was an important part of his mystique. Gildas' narrative shows a series of appeals to outsiders and, at the end of the fourth century, Bishop Victricius of Rouen was invited to Britain to resolve an unspecified theological dispute.

The Pelagian heresy, with which Germanus had to contend, concerned 'good works' and was propagated by a Briton called Pelagius (hence the name). In suggesting that one could earn a passage to heaven by good works, it was clearly heretical, as it denied God any role in deciding who got into heaven and who did not. St Augustine's riposte, stressing divine Grace, strayed close to predestination, however. This did not please everyone, especially in Gaul, so the controversy rumbled on. Even if true Pelagianists dropped out of the picture quite soon, the accusation could still be used to insinuate that one's opponents were not orthodox. Note though that there is no evidence that Pelagianism had ever really had a hold in Britain; Gildas does not mention it at all, in spite of his concern with heresy and backsliding. All of Pelagius' writing and the debate on his ideas took place in the Mediterranean. Once declared heretical, though (in 418–19), it became a politically useful accusation and its association with Britain might have made it particularly effective there. Other aspects of the account of Germanus' first visit suggest, as elsewhere in the West, a hotbed of local rivalry and at least the trappings of traditional Roman civilization. Whether the details of the Alleluia Victory are trustworthy is difficult to say. Take the alliance of Picts and Saxons, for example: any Gaulish writer would 'know' that barbarians in Britain 'ought' to be Picts and Saxons.

St Germanus' second visit (of the later 440s) has been doubted. The events so closely parallel those of the first that suspicions are immediately aroused that it is a simple stylistic duplication (see the discussion of Gildas in Chapter 9). The chronology of Germanus' life leaves little time for such a visit; indeed it can be argued that there is no place for it at all. It is difficult to take this account as seriously as the first.

The Gallic Chronicle of 452

The other contemporary mainland European source for British events is the *Gallic Chronicle of 452*. This anonymous work was apparently composed somewhere in south-east Gaul (Valence or Marseille have been suggested). It can hardly be called detailed and, like most fifth-century sources, its principal interest is doctrinal controversy. It is a series of fairly terse annalistic entries that stops in 452, hence the name: the whole text seems to have been written at about that date. Amongst these are two British entries. The first mentions that the British provinces were 'laid waste by Saxon invasion'. The second says that the British provinces were 'subjected to the authority of the Saxons'. It was once suggested that these entries were added in the ninth century by a scribe familiar with Bede's *History*; the earliest manuscript of the *Chronicle* belongs to the late ninth or early tenth century. This proposal has been rejected.

The *Chronicle* is organized by 'Olympiads' (four-year units) and then by the year of the current emperor's (or joint emperors') reign. However, for all that it is set out as a list of events, the *Chronicle's* organization is almost certainly not exclusively chronological. The first British entry comes in the 16th year of Arcadius and Honorius (410–11). Yet it precedes events datable to 409, and comes after at least one dated to 408. Sometimes the *Chronicle's* entries seem to be misplaced by four years or more; the Gothic settlement of Aquitaine in 418–19, for instance, is placed under the year we think of as 414. The section including the first British entry begins with a general comment about Rome's enemies growing in number and the strength of the Romans falling away. A list of calamities follows: Britain ravaged by Saxons, Gaul by Vandals, Alans, and the usurper Constantine, and Spain by the Sueves, before the list reaches its culmination in the sack of Rome. This passage was obviously organized for rhetorical and stylistic effect. The list moves from north to south. Furthermore, the

Sueves crossed into Gaul with the Vandals and Alans (in 405–7) well before the date suggested by the event's placing within the *Chronicle*. The Vandals and Alans, in turn, were still with the Sueves when the latter invaded Spain (409). So the Saxon raid on Britain, if not a purely rhetorical invention (after all, all the other events at least happened, even if not at quite the time or in the way suggested), might not have occurred then or have been of great significance. In the *Chronicle's* defence, Zosimus' *New History* also refers to barbarian attack around the time of the collapse of Constantine 'III's' regime in 409–11.

The *Chronicle's* second British entry occurs in the 18th year of Theodosius II, which it places around 440–1.[3] It has been suggested that it is placed in a series culminating in the Vandal sack of Carthage (439), but this is far less clear than the more obviously stylistic 410 passage. Although, within the western Empire, Carthage was second in importance only to Rome, its loss was not accorded the same importance as Alaric's sack of Rome. That said, the *Chronicle* places its capture out of chronological order by no fewer than five years, in spite of its occurrence only thirteen years before the *Chronicle's* composition. This section appears to be a melancholy list of barbarians overrunning the Roman provinces, culminating, when the chronicler starts discussing the reign of Valentinian and Marcian, with a comment on the miserable state of the 'Republic', as Romans still referred to the Empire. Hardly any province, it says, was by then not being farmed by barbarians. The reality of the event seems reasonable enough but its precise dating is unreliable. More importantly, quite what the chronicler (in south-eastern Gaul) or his informants meant when they said that Britain had been subjected to Saxon authority is unknown. We cannot determine whether this and the other Saxon attack were the only British events the chronicler knew of, or whether

---

[3] Although Theodosius II had been emperor since 408, he became senior *Augustus* in 423.

they were selected for rhetorical or stylistic effect from a more general 'background noise' of tales of Saxon attacks. This makes it impossible to evaluate these events' significance. The evidence of the *Gallic Chronicle of 452* cannot bear much weight.

Welsh sources

Most of the relevant Welsh sources have been discussed already. There are other traditions and legends, which appear in later medieval Welsh and Breton saints' lives and in more Welsh poetry. This material was that upon which John Morris drew heavily in *The Age of Arthur*. It does not require detailed analysis. Suffice it to say that these sources are all very late and postdate the florescence of Arthurian legend discussed briefly in Chapter 1. The extent of influence from the other Arthurian traditions flourishing by then cannot be assessed. Nor can we identify what might be separate traditions or evaluate the extent to which they might preserve earlier tales. Thus these stories cannot reliably be projected back into the fifth and sixth centuries.

Names

Finally, we have encountered three genuinely historical Arthurs living in the late sixth century, which some have seen as arguing that a real Arthur existed not long before. This is quite an attractive suggestion although it is, of course, not the only factor that could produce three minor royals sharing an unusual name at about the same time. To other writers, one of them actually *is* our 'King Arthur', the son of Aedan being the most popular candidate. After all, the earliest possible (or, alternatively, most optimistic) date for the stanza referring to Arthur in Y *Gododdin* would be within a generation of the lives of these three. Sadly we know little or nothing about them. None of them appears to have been particularly noteworthy. This has usually been the basis of attempts to dismiss the idea that one or other of them might be 'King Arthur', the mighty warrior of lore. This is a weak argument, given the scarcity of references to Arthur in the 400 years after their deaths and the failure (evident from the *Armes Prydein's* silence) of the *Historia Brittonum* to make a heroic national figure out of its Arthur, at least until Geoffrey of Monmouth took up the cause 300 years later. The fact that even John Morris had to acknowledge that no one else was known to have called their son Arthur for another 500 years or so, until the mid-eleventh century—in other words until about the time of the explosion of Arthurian legend—is further, weighty evidence against any historical Arthur being at all well known, even in legend, in the second half of the first millennium. That the next, eleventh-century, Arthurs we know about are all Normans or Bretons, rather than Welshmen or Scots, supports the notion mentioned in Chapter 1, that the Arthur legend was largely reintroduced into Great Britain at the Norman Conquest. The possibility that one of the late sixth-century Arthurs might, for whatever reason now lost to us, be the reality behind the Arthur legend might very well be the simplest and most prosaic—but also (if I'm honest) slightly disappointing—solution to the whole Arthurian conundrum.

Place-names

Britain abounds with 'Arthur' place-names, from Scotland to Cornwall. Most of these lie in the highland areas of the island but there is little or no use that the historian can make of this fact. These names are not recorded until well after the explosion of the Arthurian legend in the eleventh century. That the legendary corpus frequently associated Arthur with the highlands, perhaps through his leadership of the Britons, is reason enough for the popularity of Arthur names in those areas. What is more, landscape features very often have personal names attached to them without there being any historical basis to the association. Restricting the discussion to indubitably historical persons, the frequency of 'Caesar's Camp' as a name for hill-forts located far from anywhere Julius Caesar ever trod makes the case fairly well. Much more recently, Oliver Cromwell has been associated with slighted castles and countless other buildings and locations, regardless of any actual visit by 'Old Noll' himself to the place in question. Some places in fact acquired names and associations precisely because of the activities of older generations of scholars and antiquaries. South Cadbury's 'Camelot' associations may well have grown considerably after John Leland's visit in the sixteenth century. The river Adur in Sussex (just west of Brighton) was in fact only so called after a local landowner and gentleman-antiquary decided that *Portus Adurni*, a site named in the *Notitia Dignitatum* (now generally recognized to be Porchester Castle in Hampshire), was located at its mouth.

Conclusion

If you want to believe in a real 'King Arthur', the analysis of the written sources for fifth- and sixth-century Britain makes depressing reading. With the exception of Gildas (and restricting Gildas' testimony mainly to its 'non-historical' elements) and probably the *Life of Germanus*' account of the bishop's first visit, there is no reliable written source for this period. Unless some important new written sources are discovered, which is unlikely, the construction of a detailed narrative political historical account is quite out of the question and always will be. The claim of any book that purports to present such a history should be rejected immediately and out of hand. Such attempts represent fiction, no more and no less. Some of the 'old chestnuts' by which modern pseudo-histories try to circumvent this unpalatable but ineluctable conclusion are dealt with in Chapter 7. The sources are interesting and useful if pressed into service in the exploration of other questions—questions they can answer—such as about the idea of history in ninth-century England

and Wales. For British political history between 410 and 597 they are quite useless. Shadows of real events and people might survive in the material compiled between the early eighth and the late tenth century but we cannot now identify them. However, if our written evidence is absolutely incapable of proving that Arthur existed, and certainly of telling us anything reliable about him, its faults do not prove that he did not exist. Now, having more or less swept away all the written sources once thought useful for the history of fifth- and sixth-century Britain, we must return to the archaeological evidence and examine whether it makes up for this documentary shortfall.

5

Continuity or Collapse?
The End of Roman Britain

℞

In determining how we should see post-imperial Britain—the
'World of Arthur'—we must discuss what remained of Roman
social and economic structures in the fifth century. Traditionally,
'King Arthur' fights to preserve a world of Roman civilization—
towns, villas, baths, mosaics—against the onrush of Saxon barba-
rism. It is a tragic, heroic sunset before the 'Dark Ages'.

I have already mentioned that in early British archaeological
research it was thought that the excavated record confirmed all the
bleakest aspects of Gildas' picture in *De Excidio*… Towns and villas
throughout the land were destroyed, the last levels of occupation
being covered by layers of ash and general destruction. As archaeological techniques improved, and with them the interpretations of
the evidence, it emerged that this picture was some way wide of the
mark. Fires need not have been caused by invading Picts or Saxons.
They are fairly regular occurrences, especially in buildings heated
fundamentally by setting light to branches and other pieces of wood
underneath the house. Kitchens, then as now, were frequently the
source of blazes, often even more dramatic in structures largely built

of, and roofed with, wood. Such fires punctuate the occupation of Roman sites throughout the Empire. What required explanation was why there was no rebuilding after the last fires. It was difficult to invoke Saxon or Pictish marauders to explain this. Some ashy 'destruction levels' were probably instances of the 'dark earth' that overlies the latest Roman occupation on many British sites, and to which we shall return. Other evidence of destruction, on re-examination, simply represented collapse after a period of dereliction. Bodies in the ruins, rather than being dramatic examples of civilized Roman Britons hewn down in their homes by ravening sea-wolves, turned out to be the subjects of burials. Buried using crude and unusual methods and in straitened circumstances, to be sure, but buried nevertheless. Pillaging marauders tend not to bother burying their victims. And so on. As time passed a chronological dislocation between the last period of Roman occupation and the Saxon settlement also became apparent. The 'fire and slaughter' interpretation of late Roman archaeology had to be abandoned.

Advances in interpretation also showed that the Roman period was not one of constant 'Romanized' prosperity, beginning with the pacification of Boudicca's revolt and the construction of the cities and lasting until 'the withdrawal of the legions': the picture given in much traditional school or children's history.[1] There were periods of crisis and change. The towns, for example, were fortified around the end of the second century. There were shifts in the nature and spread of settlement.

An especially important stage in the development of these ideas came with the 1980 publication of Richard Reece's article 'Town and Country: The End of Roman Britain'. In this piece, originally

---

[1] A particularly nice example can be found in the last two-page spread of the Ladybird 'Adventures in History' book *Julius Caesar and Roman Britain* by L. Du Garde Peach and J. Tenney (Loughborough, 1959). This book shaped my own early ideas of Roman Britain.

scheduled to appear as part of the proceedings of a conference on the end of Roman Britain but refused by the publishers as too radical, Reece argued that Roman Britain effectively came to an end in the third century. His argument essentially ran like this. The things that made Britain Roman, such as towns on the classical model, ceased to receive much by the way of new building and investment from around the third century. People instead put their money into their rural dwellings: villas. One could read this information as showing that, after the third century, the Romano-British elite were no longer interested in participating in traditional Roman municipal life. Roman towns declined and, in terms of governmental structures, the people who mattered no longer cared. Thus, regardless of political history, to all intents and purposes Roman Britain ended in the third century. In another paper, published a year later, Reece developed the theme by considering the 'third-century crisis', proposing that by the third century the economic situation had changed. The production of Roman goods that had taken place in the heart of the Empire had moved out to the provinces. Instead of a unified system exporting Roman goods from the core to the periphery in return for raw materials flowing from the periphery to the core, a more fragmented system now existed. Production and consumption took place within provincial units. Reece saw this regionalization as explaining the elite's move away from towns and municipal government and concentration on their landed estates.

There is much that works about Reece's argument and it is still descriptively adequate. However, as one might expect after thirty years, as an explanation it is less satisfactory. Nevertheless, this was an important stage in moving the debate forward. The obvious problem was that the argument assumed that 'being Roman' was a constant set of values and attitudes. Roman-ness might have meant something rather different around 300 from what it had meant in c.100; at any given time it meant different things to different sorts of people. Yet, Britons need not have been any less politically committed to the Roman Empire, or seen themselves as any less Roman. Such changes in ideas might be visible archaeologically in a switch from investment in towns to investment in private buildings.

To understand the problem we must go back to the Roman conquest of Britain. The imperial government organized the provinces by creating new administrative units based on the pre-conquest British tribes. Each was focused on a town, sometimes a pre-Roman centre (such as Silchester) but often a new centre deliberately sited in low-lying country to prevent it from being used as a centre of resistance. A good example is the tribal centre of *Viriconium*, moved down from the Wrekin hill-fort (which still preserves traces of its original name) to the now abandoned town of Wroxeter (also a corruption of *Viriconium*). The tribal units were called *civitates* and the towns are referred to as the *civitas*-capitals; the Romans unhelpfully used the same word—*civitas* (plural: *civitates*)—for the town and the administrative unit focused on it. The tribal aristocracy, generally a warrior elite, was pacified, partly by encouraging them to form regular auxiliary regiments in the army and then by promoting competition not in warlike matters but in civic politics. An important aspect of this was the provision of public buildings (temples, baths, etc.). Spending private money on such projects brought important political rewards. It might bring support in the competition to control the *curia* (town-council) of the *civitas*. The *curia* was responsible for tax-collection, and this could be an important source of patronage (or, if you prefer, bribery and corruption, but such things oiled the political cogs of the Roman world). Success here could be a platform for advancement on a broader political stage, the acquisition of Roman citizenship, and perhaps even promotion to highest orders of Roman society. Thus the early Roman Empire needed minimal central bureaucracy. Such was the importance of 'becoming Roman' in local and regional politics that the provincial aristocracies did most of the governmental work themselves, binding their communities closely into the overall edifice of the Roman Empire.

Goods produced in the Roman Mediterranean had been much in demand in Britain before the Roman conquest—control over their distribution had been an important way by which late pre-conquest tribal leaders had bolstered their position. We shall see a similar dynamic among barbarians in the late Roman world. By the early second century the *civitas*-capitals had become a network of markets through which such imports passed, giving them an important economic function to add to their political and cultural importance. Roman London was a somewhat unusual case. It boomed in the immediately post-conquest period as the port through which the all-important Roman goods flowed into the new provinces. By the second century, when the other *civitas*-capitals were established with their markets, it declined, although it would be fairer to say that it fell back from an unusual period of prosperity to a status closer to those of the other towns.

Some change took place in the late second century, but across the Roman Empire, especially in its western portion, the crucial moment came in the third century. By this time it was clear that the exceptional circumstances behind the unified Empire of the first century no longer pertained. They might have stopped pertaining some time earlier but by the third century the disjuncture between what we might (guardedly) call socio-economic 'reality' and political ideology and organization were clear. Put another way, the system was out of step with what people wanted from it. People were playing by a different set of social and political rules from that which was supposed to govern their behaviour. By now, the artefacts that were held to denote cultural membership of the Roman commonwealth were being produced in the provinces. The earlier, unified economy was replaced by a series of regional economies with little linkage between them. Even the Mediterranean trade network was often quite separate from the economies of areas away from the coast. At the same time involvement in local government and the expenditure of private money on public projects yielded far less significant results than before. When, in 212, every free person born inside the Empire was legally declared to be a citizen, the competition to obtain the benefits of citizenship was ended at a stroke. Local elites no longer saw active involvement in the Empire as necessary for their social and cultural standing. In pre-industrial societies (and in industrial ones too), states have enormous difficulties existing without the active participation of the locally and regionally powerful.

Other factors emphasized this regionalization. Significant inflation and debasement of the coinage led to economies based heavily around barter and other forms of exchange (such as in 'gifts'). This— obviously—was possible only within limited areas wherein people knew and trusted each other. Whether or not the third-century economic 'crisis' should be seen, as was once the case, primarily in terms of economic 'decline' is questionable. In Britain it does not seem to have had very much effect on towns and rural settlements, although a restriction in the amount of surplus accumulating in local aristocratic hands is visible in other areas of the West. There, economic contraction seems more plausible. Increased economic regionalization appears to be more important.

Political instability and civil war heightened these problems, as separatist empires were formed in Gaul and in Palmyra, in the East. The idea of a unified Empire came seriously under threat. When political stability was restored by a series of soldier-emperors culminating in Diocletian (284–305), a new means of binding the Empire together evolved. This almost certainly did not result from a single overarching 'plan'. It was a development and perhaps systematization of ad hoc responses. Put very simply, the attractions provided in the first century by municipal government were now furnished by service in a hugely expanded imperial bureaucracy. The emperors had

had to make up for the increasing shortcomings of local government by sending in their own men to do the job, often seconded from the army. This was now formalized into a 25,000–35,000-man civil service. In part because of its origins, this was, like the army, referred to as a *militia* and used similar badges of rank. Its different offices provided social status, privilege, and formal precedence. They brought exemption from unpopular duties as well, and a pathway towards involvement in imperial politics on the wider scale as well as new means of cementing local patronage networks. In the bureaucracy, moreover, one could indulge in public benefaction (usually, at this period, by restoring public buildings) without actually dipping into one's own fortune. One might have to give first place in claiming the credit to the Emperor but nevertheless one's own involvement could still be trumpeted. Taxation was reformed, and was often levied in kind (in cloth, or food supplies, for example). The mechanisms of this system need not concern us but the fact that, however it operated, the system must have involved collecting supplies and money at nodal points of the imperial administration is significant. The 'new empire' of the fourth century was mapped onto the settlement pattern right across the West.

With all this set out, we can return to late Romano-British archaeology, as it makes the observable changes much easier to understand. Fourth-century British towns were rather different from their second-century precursors. Where there had been shops, larger town-houses appeared. On the whole, inhabited areas shrank. Space in some public buildings was given over to manufacturing, like metalworking. New public buildings such as bath-houses ceased to be built, on the whole. Some became derelict. Simultaneously, a shift occurred, away from the relative importance of the economic functions of towns, probably linked to the rise of what archaeologists call the 'small towns'. These settlements were generally more 'organic' than central planned centres, like the *civitas*-capitals, and they grew, essentially, as markets. As the network of such centres increased in density the role of the *civitas*-capital as the central market for its dependent territory was eroded.

The way in which larger, more lavish town-houses replaced earlier shop-frontages illustrates how the late Roman town was, even more than its predecessor, a political centre. The local elite had to reside there for at least some of the time in order to maintain its position and, in the fourth-century socio-political system, compete with each other for imperial patronage and advancement. The reuse of public buildings for manufacturing or processing—something that can be detected in Rome itself—is, I would say, indicative of how urban centres were used by the administration to convert raw materials levied as tax into usable products. These could be supplied to the army, the court, and the bureaucracy, or sold to provide coin for taxation.

The fourth century was a prosperous period. Villas—often lavish ones—were built, especially in a band of territory running from the East Yorkshire Wolds and the Channel coast in Dorset (a zone that we will have cause to revisit). Indeed much of the prosperity of Roman Britain shifted towards the west. Mosaic industries were located in these areas and towns continued to flourish. Nonetheless, the Romano-British elite does not seem to have been super-wealthy, by comparison with the aristocracy of the rest of the Empire (as manifested by its archaeology and by the written sources), with the principal exception of that in the north of Gaul. Yet archaeology gives us a picture of social stability.

In the cemeteries of this period, burial ritual was not a focus for competitive displays of wealth within communities, although within its peer-group the aristocracy may have competed in the provision of lavish above-ground monuments. A good example is the cemetery of Poundbury (Dorset). Here, the bulk of late Roman graves were simple inhumations, with few or no grave-goods, carefully arranged in rows. This is not untypical of ordinary late Roman burials and here it suggests that the community took an important role in determining the position and the nature of the burial, hence the rows, rather than familial plots. However, excavation also revealed the presence of a series of *mausolea*. These, very importantly, were aligned slightly differently from the other graves of the cemetery, breaking the rules. There was evidence suggesting the provision for repeated visiting of graves. Alongside the building of an above-ground monument, this was a quite different, permanent statement from the temporary rituals of the usual unmarked inhumations. This is a characteristic indication of a secure local aristocracy. There is a fair amount of diversity in late Romano-British cemeteries, in town and countryside, but the overall picture drawn from Poundbury does not seem untypical. It is also, it is worth stressing, quite different from the image presented by the burial customs of the *fifth* century.

Late Roman Britain's prosperity has been plausibly linked to its importance within the late Roman state. A key element of the Empire's rebuilding after the 'Third-Century Crisis' was the emperors' relocation of their chief residences to the frontier. York occasionally had this function, but more important were Trier on the Moselle, behind the Rhine frontier, *Sirmium* (Sremska Mitrovica, Serbia) near the Danube border, Constantinople (Istanbul, Turkey) after the 320s—another crucial strategic point—and Antioch (Antakya, Turkey), strategically close to the Persian frontier. Large concentrations of administrators and other court functionaries were therefore resident in northern Gaul, as, possibly, were even larger numbers of troops than before. In the late Empire, as mentioned, taxes were often raised in kind and state employees (military and other) were often paid in kind too. To ease this they were spread over a deeper belt of territory than had been the case earlier. A chance reference in a contemporary history by Ammianus Marcellinus tells us that British grain was important in feeding the Roman army on the Rhine. The location of the prosperous zone of late Roman Britain, on the frontier between the arable lowlands and pastoral uplands, leads one to wonder whether other commodities such as meat, leather, and wool were equally significant. Another reason might be that this band was where two fundamentally different economies, ecologies, and social structures came together. The highland pastoralists produced things wanted by the more settled arable farmers of the lowlands, and vice versa. The territorial zone from Dorset and the Yorkshire Wolds would surely have been important for such trade and exchange, and its social elite could have based its economic success on controlling these interactions.

In northern Gaul, probably the most plausible explanation for the changes in the settlement pattern there is that most of the land in that region was taken over by, and harnessed to the supply of, the state. In Britain, however, the local aristocrats were able to control and keep some of the proceeds from the surplus they raised and converted into the *annona* or 'tax-in-supplies'. Similar situations, where the local aristocracy was able to control the system of tax-collection and retain wealth in their locality for their own use, can be found in late Roman North Africa and in Italy. At the same time, the importance of imperial service meant that local elites competed for posts within the bureaucracy. The effective distribution and redistribution of such offices (many of which were only held for a restricted period) was more effective in Britain because of the relative proximity of the imperial centre. This prevented any one aristocratic group from becoming completely dominant. Such service and the possibilities it presented cemented the Romano-British elite's position above the remainder of the free population (as witnessed at Poundbury, for example), and the arms of the Roman state protected that status. Thus we have the social structure of late Roman Britain, lacking the sharp divisions in wealth and power visible in other, more Mediterranean areas of the Empire but nevertheless prosperous and stable.

And yet, late Romano-British archaeology seems fairly unambiguous in portraying dramatic collapse around AD 400. At the very end of the fourth century, the British towns entered a period of decay and dereliction, resulting in their more or less complete abandonment by about 425, especially in the south-east of the island. Similarly, British villas are abandoned during the first quarter of the fifth century. The last phases of occupation on such sites are difficult to date conclusively. This is because the supply of coin from the rest of the Empire dried up in the fifth century's first decade, and coins provide one of the best means of dating Roman habitation. Similarly, it is clear that the organized manufacture of pottery in Britain went into profound recession and in some areas might have died out completely at the start of the fifth century. Something similar happened in northern Gaul, which had provided Britain with most of its fourth-century ceramic imports. Roman pottery was produced by specialists manufacturing a wide range of forms with varying decoration, making it almost as good an indication of the date of a site or phase of occupation as coins are. This resource too disappears by c.425. This all suggests a serious economic collapse, but it makes the duration of the last periods of Roman sites' use very difficult to pin down. Even generous estimates, though, have difficulty pushing occupation into the second third of the fifth century.

This reading of the data suggests probably the most dramatic period of social and economic collapse in British history. Someone born in 375 entered a world of long-distance trade, a heavily monetized economy with widely available, finely produced pottery, a world of towns with the old Roman urban facilities, of elite, stone-built, tile-roofed villas with under-floor heating and mosaics, and so on. If she died aged 60 in 435, she left a world without towns, villas, or organized, specialist crafts and industry, where the economy was local and small-scale, relying on barter and gift rather than on the medium of coinage, and where people universally lived in thatch- or shingle-roofed timber buildings. As mentioned earlier in this chapter, this collapse began long before we have any significant archaeological trace of a meaningful 'Saxon' political identity in Britain. If (if!) 'Arthur' lived in the late fifth century and fought against Saxons, he was certainly not struggling to preserve the Roman world of civilized villas and towns; that had long gone and its demise had had nothing to do with Saxons.

Dissenting voices have been raised against this picture. The 'black earth' layers overlying the last Roman occupation levels on many British and mainland European towns have been claimed to represent not abandonment and dereliction, as usually supposed, but continued, dense inhabitation in wattle-walled, thatch-roofed buildings. The argument is partly based upon a comparison with a site called Birka in Sweden, an important town of the Viking period. Here, archaeologists found the occupied area manifested by a deep layer of black earth. Using this analogy, it is argued that Roman cities continued through the fifth century.

This tallies with the suggestion made by the excavators of Wroxeter (Shropshire) that this Roman town survived until the seventh century. Here the evidence is not black earth but ephemeral traces of post-imperial occupation, revealed by meticulous excavation over decades, using trowels alone. Wroxeter has mostly not been inhabited since its abandonment at some point after the end of the Roman Empire; it was claimed that the fragile evidence found there would have been destroyed on more continuously used sites. Furthermore, most urban excavation is 'keyhole' archaeology— investigating very small sites unlike the large area uncovered at Wroxeter. Crucial areas of occupation might therefore be missed. On more continuously occupied sites, the upper layers of Roman occupation could have been sheared away or otherwise damaged by later building. Buildings have been occasionally located on the sites of Roman towns whose occupation clearly went on into the fifth century, and there are increasing traces, especially in towns towards the west of the diocese, of some buildings and public areas being used into that century.

The absence of recognizably fifth-century evidence has been explained by arguing that old pottery was used and repaired much later than its actual period of manufacture. New coins were not minted or imported but older issues could still have been used. These proposals would account for the difficulty in recognizing and dating fifth-century occupation. In this reading, then, town life would continue, even if in a rather different form from that which existed earlier. Roger White, an authority on the western half of Roman Britain, has suggested that, rather than manifesting the steep and dramatic decline suggested earlier, the pattern of survival would be more like that seen in Italian and African towns.

Such continuity would bring Roman Britain more into line with the image of mainland Europe in late antiquity. An 'industry standard' set of dates for 'late antiquity' has never really been established. To define it as the period between the third century and the seventh would be a reasonable average, though some scholars put the opening date earlier and others place the closing date later. Be that as it may, since Peter Brown's classic *The World of Late Antiquity* (1971), it has been widely accepted that we should see this era as characterized more by a persistence of specifically late antique features of society and culture, neither truly classical nor medieval, than by the dramatic rupture espoused by old notions of 'the Fall of the Roman Empire'. Late antique scholarship has tended to be Mediterranean, and particularly eastern Mediterranean, in its focus; Britain, with its seemingly stark end to Roman settlements, society, and economy, has not seemed to belong in this world. If we accept the arguments against a drastic decline in her towns, *Britannia* is drawn into the world of late antiquity.

Arguments have been put forward for rural sites which would point in the same general direction. The abandonment of villas, not just in Britain but in Gaul and elsewhere, has been argued to result from a change of fashion, perhaps a rejection of Roman civilization, rather than from economic hardship. The processes whereby the imperial provinces became Roman are now rightly seen as ones in which local elites actively chose to adopt Roman culture, rather than having it imposed upon them in a 'civilizing process'. Now, it is thought, the descendants of those same aristocrats similarly chose not to subscribe to Roman culture any longer. It was 'Romanization' in reverse: an active 'de-Romanization'. Other features, in this way of seeing the post-imperial world, were more important than old-style towns and villas: Christianity, the Church, military retinues. Long-term continuity or gradual evolution would characterize these features, rather than sharp breaks, harmonizing this reading of the rural settlement evidence, to some extent, with the more optimistic interpretation of the evidence from towns. In western Roman Britain, in particular, this line of argument has been maintained. Here local elites seemingly transferred their dwellings from villas to hill-forts and, as with the towns, the more meaningful traces of fifth-century occupation do seem to gravitate towards this side of the island.

A different twist on the 'continuity thesis' has been proposed, with points of contact with the suggestion that Britain was not really Romanized at all and did not feel itself to be part of the Empire. In this vision, the tribes of Roman Britain never lost their mutually antagonistic identities. The Empire never welded them together into a new 'Roman' identity. The study of metalwork and other small-finds suggests that objects still circulated within *civitas*-units (the administrative districts based on the pre-conquest tribal kingdoms). At the Empire's demise, it is argued, *Britannia* underwent a process like that in the former Yugoslavia: it was a 'failed state'. Old tribal loyalties rose to the surface and conflict tore the former diocese apart. To support this argument some of the regionally distributed items of metalwork, such as belt-sets and brooches, are given a specifically military reading. This argument might be seen in conjunction with other research from the 1990s which assembled evidence suggesting that the *civitas*-unit was the basic framework for post-imperial kingdoms.

Another argument turns on the cost of maintaining a military retinue in the changing fifth-century world. Rather than the villas, bathhouses, and so on being abandoned purely as a matter of free choice, it is claimed that the expense involved in the upkeep of an armed following left little remaining for the maintenance of old-style country- and town-houses. A different 'fashion' argument suggests a shift from the civic to the military as the dominant expression of aristocratic status. Like other suggested developments, this could be seen in terms of a long-term, gradual process. In many late Roman forts there does not seem to be very clear evidence of investment in the large officers' headquarters of earlier periods. If army officers were not especially bothered by their living quarters then perhaps a militarized aristocracy had a similarly blasé attitude towards villas, mosaics, and the rest.

I evaluate these different interpretations in more detail in Chapter 8. For now they must be left to stand as a guide to the range of current thinking about the end of Roman Britain.

6

Beyond Brooches
and Brochs

*Rethinking Early Medieval British
Archaeology*

❧❦❧

Chapter 3 briefly described the archaeology of post-imperial Britain, taking the story up to about 1980. Since then, as well as advances in excavation techniques and the scientific analysis of finds, methods have been developed which allow the non-destructive investigation of archaeological sites: ground investigating radar, resistometer surveys, and so on—the 'geo-phys' familiar from TV archaeology programmes; field-walking; aerial survey and other forms of landscape study. Without doubt one of the most important developments has been the establishment of good working relationships with metal-detector enthusiasts (many of whom are extremely skilled), producing the Portable Antiquities Scheme. Here the chance finds of small artefacts, principally metalwork, are studied and recorded before usually being returned to the finder. The ensuing distribution maps have altered our understanding of much of early medieval Britain quite considerably. The volume of material that can be studied has also been multiplied several times over. As well as new finds, sites, and techniques, though, the archaeology of post-imperial Britain has changed considerably in its interpretations. This has been clearest in early Anglo-Saxon archaeology, and it is with this that we will begin. As in the previous chapter, no pretence is made that the coverage is complete. I will concentrate on the areas of greatest thematic relevance to this book.

The debate on the Anglo-Saxon migration and ethnicity

In the standard Arthurian narrative, whether in academic accounts, fiction, or pseudo-history, we find 'King Arthur' defending Britain against the invading Anglo-Saxons. Earlier, we saw that archaeology was generally pressed into service in support of this story. Particular types of object and sites (cremation and furnished inhumation cemeteries; settlements with post-built 'halls' and 'sunken-featured buildings') were used to plot the spread of the Anglo-Saxons across the British lowlands. In the 1960s, the idea that migration could explain change in the material cultural record came under serious scrutiny. Anglo-Saxon archaeology tended to lag behind these theoretical debates so it was really only in the 1980s that the extent of the Anglo-Saxon migration began to be questioned.

This rethinking of the evidence also stemmed from British archaeology's reluctance to have its data used to 'prove history' and answer questions driven by the written sources. Chapter 4 described the reassessment of the written sources that was carried out by historians from the 1970s and 1980s. These developments were eagerly seized upon by archaeologists to argue that historical evidence was of no use and that therefore archaeology should be the driving force in understanding post-imperial Britain. In most regards this was (and is) absolutely correct. The problem was that often the excavated evidence was not used as rigorously as it might have been. Archaeologists have in fact often been more reluctant than historians to abandon the great narrative outline bequeathed by the early medieval written sources. But one important outcome was that the Anglo-Saxon migration was closely scrutinized, in terms of its scale and even—sometimes—in terms of its reality. In its extreme form, this argument claims, or at least implies, that the Anglo-Saxon migration was invented by Bede and the rest in the eighth century and afterwards.

This contention is not worth spending much time on. The cremation custom which appeared in eastern England is—in its ritual and in the form and design of the urns used—entirely analogous to that employed for some centuries in north-western Germany, the Anglo-Saxon homelands (Figure 6.1). Its introduction, its popularity, its precise nature, and the suddenness of its appearance are incapable of satisfactory explanation without invoking the movement of people into Britain from northern Germany. Simultaneously, from about 430, many objects—chiefly jewellery—appear in the same regions, with typological origins similarly in the coastal regions of northern Germany, Denmark, and Scandinavia. Once again, a complete explanation will never be entirely satisfactory without acknowledging at least some migration of people.

Above all, moving outside the archaeological realm, by the seventh century at the latest the language of lowland Britain became English, a west Germanic tongue. It has recently been argued that the Germanic language of lowland Britain pre-dates the Roman invasion, but this hypothesis lacks any scholarly basis. We will return to the issue of language but, ultimately, there is no way of explaining this shift without invoking population movement, even if it does not *necessarily* imply a particular *scale* to this movement.

Nonetheless, more moderate versions of the minimalist view deserve attention. As far as the archaeological material has been concerned, a principal locus for debate was the new types of rural settlement discussed in Chapter 3. As we saw there, it was initially thought that these were simply enough the places where the Anglo-Saxon incomers, as opposed to native Britons, lived. In the 1980s the

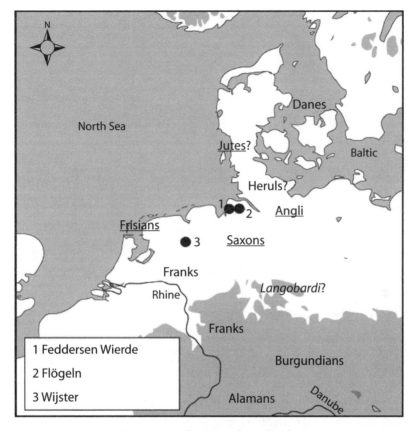

Figure 6.1 The Saxon homelands

connection with migration was called into question. It became unfashionable to assume that any change in structures was to be explained by a migration of new people, so the material was looked at afresh. Some Anglo-Saxon halls have the same rough proportions (length to width) as many rectangular Romano-British buildings, but are built of timber and wattle rather than of stone. This suggested that the 'Anglo-Saxon' long-house might be an insular British adaptation of Roman buildings, responding to the economic constraints that accompanied the collapse of Roman rule. Nevertheless it was rarely suggested that these buildings had nothing at all to do with the

Saxons. Instead it was proposed that the 'halls' could be hybrids, with cultural input from Britons as well as Saxons. Other differences between early Anglo-Saxon settlements and those in the Saxon homelands were pointed out. English sites lacked the organization that one can see on some fourth-century continental Saxon settlements like Feddersen Wierde (for which see Chapter 10). Furthermore, the *Wohnstallhäuser* (long-houses containing cattle byres at one end and human living spaces at the other; singular: *Wohnstallhaus*) characteristic of northern Germany were absent from rural settlements in Anglo-Saxon England. In the north of Anglo-Saxon England, the earliest phase of the celebrated high-status site at Yeavering was suggested to have possibly been a British palace, later taken over as a 'going concern' by Northumbrian rulers (Bede refers to it as a Northumbrian royal site).

These were important points in furthering the debate, but they were not decisive. As we will see in Chapter 10, the *Wohnstallhaus* disappeared from the fifth-century settlements of the Saxon homelands, too. What is more, continental Saxon settlements acquired a more disorganized-looking appearance in the fifth century, like that of the English sites. Those invoking migration as an explanation furthered their argument by using such features as the width of doorways, which are, it is claimed, roughly the same in English sites as in those on the Continent. In other cases (as in the counters to the 'British' reading of Yeavering's early phase) the argument has essentially proceeded on the basis of totting up the number of observable parallels between the early Anglo-Saxon period's structures and those either of Roman Britain or the Saxon homelands, and finding more in the latter area than in the former.

All this makes the role of incomers from the east coast of the North Sea fairly clear, but one can legitimately ask how much more than that it does. After all, some 'revisionist' considerations of the 'halls' had never excluded the 'Saxons' from having a role in the development of new building forms. One might suspect that, for all its (perhaps greater) foundations in a solid knowledge of the data, the 'counter-revisionist' position can look like the more extreme, less nuanced, interpretation. We are entitled to wonder whether the measurement of doorways really represents a fundamental theoretical advance—in detecting the ethnicity of a site's occupants—from the measurement of skulls that took place a century ago. We should ponder whether or not the geographical origins of a site's inhabitants can reliably be inferred from a process of adding up the respective parallels for the architectural features of their dwellings. We may consider whether the role of migration in explaining the observed changes in the nature of rural settlements might be somewhat more subtle. The extreme argument that the settlements of early Anglo-Saxon England are indigenous developments of Roman models, thus requiring no Anglo-Saxon migration, seems unconvincing. But so too does the counter-argument that these sites are of continental inspiration, and therefore their inhabitants must be Saxon immigrants.

The discussion so far should have raised the issue of how we think about early medieval ethnicity. In the discussion above it is implied essentially that if one can determine where material cultural traits originate, geographically (or where most of them do), then that will tell you the geographical and biological roots of the people concerned. That in turn, runs the implication, will lead you to the ethnic identity of those people: Saxons or Britons. The same assumptions lie behind the readings of the funerary and artefact evidence discussed in Chapter 3. Some fifth-century political groupings might be revealed by the study of the metalwork placed in graves. In the earlier days of Anglo-Saxon archaeology these were seen as simple reflections of the ethnic identity of the people in the graves, understood as their geographical and biological origins. So a 'Jutish' brooch indicated a Jutish woman and a Jutish woman was one who came from, or whose family had come from, Jutland; an 'Anglian' wrist-clasp indicated an

'Angle' whose kin originated in 'Angeln', neighbouring the Saxon homeland in northern Germany; and so on. Ideas like these have not entirely disappeared and, as will be discussed in Chapter 10, they relate to what seem to be real distributions of material. One must always remember that, even if interpretations have moved on, traditionalist archaeological views were very often based upon knowledge of the material that was and is second to none.

As migration correctly declined in popularity as an *explanation* (though the complete removal of the notion as a contributory factor, or even a descriptive element, is less welcome), ideas of ethnicity developed. From the 1960s, early medieval historians adapted ideas from social anthropology about how ethnic identities are mutable and not a fixed 'given'. Analysis of ethnicity revealed that there is no fixed element that defines an ethnic group. For every case where such a grouping was said to be defined by a belief in common descent, or shared religion, or language, or whatever, there was another where the opposite was the case. The only constant appears to be that ethnicity is a matter of belief. People think of themselves as belonging to one group and think of other groups as different. Trying to find an innate (or 'primordial') factor, to allow us to identify past people as members of an ethnic group, other than what they said they were (at particular times), is a quite pointless task. The implications of this for post-imperial British archaeology are, or should be, obvious. Furthermore, anthropological studies of ethnic groups in Africa and south-east Asia revealed quite clearly that the links between material culture and ethnic identity were very vague. Sometimes they were the diametric opposite of those assumed in traditional archaeology; artefacts associated with one group were actually used in another to stress other types of social difference, such as age-grades. What people *said* were the distinctive traits of their ethnic group ran contrary to what could actually be observed in practice. These are problems which must be borne in mind when reading archaeological interpretations of 'Britons' and 'Saxons'. They are not just theoretical. They raise obstacles to accepting such identifications which are all but insurmountable.

The other crucial lesson taught by modern social anthropology and by a closer study of mainland European written evidence was that ethnicity can be *changed*. In other words, over time, a family that at one point thought of itself as, say, Icenian (a British tribe) could come to see itself as Roman. That same family might, with the passing of further centuries, eventually consider itself as East Anglian or English. The reasons why people change their identity are complex, but political and social advantage are important. It is thus not difficult to envisage how Britons in the post-imperial world might adopt a Saxon identity in order to maintain or improve their social standing in a world dominated by Anglo-Saxon warrior elites. Similar processes could be seen at work in fifth- to seventh-century mainland Europe.

Putting all these ideas together, we can conclude that even if we can identify the geographical origins of a custom, type of object, or feature of a building, this would not necessarily provide a sure guide to the ethnic identity of the people who used them. Even if we *could* plausibly link a material cultural feature to an ethnic identity, it would not necessarily mean that all such people came, originally, from the same area. 'Saxons' could include immigrants from all over the Saxon homelands of north-west Germany, people of native Romano-British descent, and perhaps folk of other origins too. These conclusions are vital.

One result of these discussions has been the idea that what took place in lowland Britain during the fifth and sixth centuries was not a mass migration, driving out the Britons and seizing their lands, but an 'elite takeover'. That is to say that a small number of Saxon warriors arrived in post-imperial Britain and came to dominate the region politically and militarily. This dominance led others to adopt their ethnicity and the cultural traits that marked such an identity. The spread of furnished inhumation cemeteries did not mark the expansion of the territory controlled by immigrant communities of Saxons but rather the spread of Saxon political dominance. This idea had been proposed somewhat earlier for the spread of such customs in Frankish northern Gaul, and had gained widespread support. Similar factors could account for other material cultural features, such as costume (clothing being a common means of marking an ethnic identity) and the related artefacts, cremation, and possibly even settlement- and building-type.

This conclusion has not gone unchallenged. It has been objected (rightly) that people cannot just pick and choose whatever identity they want. There are constraints on this, such as whether the group into which membership is sought will accept them. Furthermore, ethnic identity is not just a matter of political advantage; even minority identities can exert a powerful affective force, holding back change. Simple 'straight swaps' are in fact not very clearly attested in the evidence from this period.

The archaeological evidence has sometimes been claimed to support this latter reading. Analysis of inhumations with weapons has suggested that men interred with weaponry were on average taller and sturdier than those without. This point is used in turn to make the slightly more subtle argument that, although a furnished inhumation cemetery might not necessarily be the sign of an immigrant Saxon community, the families of incoming Anglo-Saxon stock distinguished themselves within it through the use of weapons in the graves of their menfolk. Some data suggest differences in diet between the 'weapon-bearing' and non-weapon-bearing groups within cemeteries. Another argument against 'elite takeover' has been that the inhumation cemeteries of early Anglo-Saxon England are not on the whole very well furnished, when compared with sites in various parts of mainland Europe. This might suggest that the subjects of

'Anglo-Saxon' cemeteries were not a wealthy elite but perhaps more like communities of free peasants.

Those explaining change through migration have also deployed what they call 'migration theory'. This is a set of analytical observations about migrations in better documented periods, especially the twentieth century. The use of these observations, it is claimed, helps us understand how a fifth-century migration across the North Sea of larger numbers of Anglo-Saxons might have been possible.

Two other important areas seem to support the argument for large-scale migration. The first is language. By the time we can examine the issue, during the seventh century, the inhabitants of lowland Britain seem to have spoken English as a matter of course. Furthermore, there are very few British loan-words in Old English. Two initial points must be made: one is that widespread language change can be brought about by proportionately small migrations. The other is that the period between the Anglo-Saxon settlers' rebellion (whenever that was) and the point at which we can see that English was the dominant language is a long one—at least 200 years. English, for example, exercised a huge linguistic influence upon the south Asian subcontinent, although in its full form the Raj lasted only about a century. That was with an English settlement that was, proportionately, minimal. Had British rule lasted longer, one can imagine an even greater dominance of English at the important social and political levels in India. These are important points. However, the second point about language change in Britain, mentioned above, counters them. Even with the British Empire's political and military dominance, modern English is filled with borrowings from South Asian languages: bungalow, pyjamas, gymkhanas, and so on. The lack of borrowings from British into Old English has been argued to suggest minimal contact between speakers of these languages. This circumstance is difficult to imagine if linguistic replacement was a slow but steady, gradual shift to the language of a politically dominant group. These arguments all point convincingly towards a large-scale migration. There are other ways of seeing this evidence, however. The lack of borrowings might suggest that the two societies—post-imperial British and immigrant Anglo-Saxon—were similar enough to be able to communicate concepts to each other without borrowing terms. Another argument is that although it is a 'Germanic' language, many Old English grammatical structures have something more in common with Latin and the Celtic languages. This might suggest closer contact.

The second form of evidence adduced more recently to support large-scale immigration is genetic, particularly the study of the DNA of modern populations. This has attracted a great deal of media interest—indeed it is not unduly cynical to see this as one of the approach's attractions. In one important case study, samples of DNA were taken from the modern population of particular areas of England, as well as from Wales, northern Germany, and parts of Scandinavia. The analysis showed closer similarities with modern populations in Germany than with inhabitants of North Wales or Norway. It was further claimed that the point at which the northern German and English populations began to show these similarities was fifty to sixty generations ago (between 1,800 and 1,250 years, depending on how you measure a generation). This DNA evidence is argued to show an 'apartheid-like' structure in early Anglo-Saxon England, something claimed (wrongly, as it happens) to find analogies in fifth- to seventh-century texts from the European mainland. Unfortunately, the proponents of this argument do not seem to have thought this analogy through. Their case suggests a process of inter-marriage between British and English over two or three centuries, something that would be explicitly discouraged in an 'apartheid-like' social structure. Be that as it may, this genetic evidence might support the notion of substantial population movement between northern Germany and lowland Britain during our period.

More sophisticated analyses of skeletal data have also shed light on the migration. These include the analysis of the stable isotopes in the tooth enamel of excavated skeletons from this period, which can suggest (from comparison with isotopic analysis of the water and geology of different regions) where the deceased was born and raised. Then there is 'ancient DNA', DNA evidence extracted from bone samples from early medieval cemeteries. The difficulties in extracting usable samples were once feared to be insurmountable but techniques have now advanced to a stage where this data is considered capable of furnishing usable conclusions.

Currently, the majority opinion on the scale of the Anglo-Saxon migration would seem to tend (as it probably always has done) towards the 'mass folk movement' rather than the 'elite takeover' model, but the subject is far from closed. We shall return to it in Chapter 10. The rejection of minimalist readings appears to me to result at least as much from the silliness of some of the arguments proposed in their support (especially at the extreme 'no migration' end of the scale) as from the scholarly weight of the arguments for large-scale movement.

Social analyses of cemeteries

One reason for questioning the older 'ethnic' readings of the cemetery evidence was that researchers started to look more closely at burials and their contents and to ask different questions of them. These were often inspired by analyses of prehistoric evidence. This in turn was driven by the desire to see the post-imperial era in Britain as a sort of prehistoric period. This it effectively is, although it more accurately lies *between* historic periods than *before* them (interhistoric?), raising subtly different problems. It was, and is, undoubtedly 'a good thing' to consider these data on their own terms, and to try and find patterning within them, rather than using them to flesh out the image of the fifth and sixth centuries presented in eighth-century and later written sources. Archaeological theorists, using anthropological analogy, had argued that the layout and furnishing of a burial in pre-industrial societies was a means of presenting the deceased's social status. Whether this was an *accurate* portrayal, rather than an idealized image, that the bereaved family wished to present, was another matter. It was proposed that the furnishing of burials could be an interesting and useful gauge of past social complexity.

A well-excavated furnished inhumation cemetery, or at least one with large enough numbers of intact burials in soil conditions that allow the preservation of skeletal material, has a vitally important advantage. Correlations can be made between the age and sex of the deceased and the artefacts (their type, decoration, construction material, and numbers) deposited with them. Other variables and correlations can be observed, such as the grave's construction and dimensions, the arrangement of the body and layout of the grave-goods. Thus, in good conditions, cemetery archaeology provides an excellent, voluminous 'archive' for community-level early medieval 'social history'. Indeed an important lesson of newer studies was just how much variability existed in early Anglo-Saxon funeral customs. The basic unit of analysis would have to be the individual site. Grouping together data from larger areas, although showing important patterns and answering other questions, could seriously blur issues such as the treatment of the dead of particular ages and sexes. Similarly, change within the period has been observed. Researchers had always noted the difference between later, seventh-century, cemeteries and those of the preceding period, in which we are primarily interested. These ideas have been further refined. This variety, through space and time and between people of different ages and sexes, has been vitally important in making early Anglo-Saxon England a much more diverse and interesting place.

Some of the most important conclusions have related to gender and age. These factors, taken together, played a very important role in determining what sorts of grave-goods (if any) were deposited with the dead. Differences have been noted between older and younger women, in the forms of brooches used to fasten their clothes, for example. Full sets of weapons only appear to have been buried with males over the age of about 20, even though single weapons, such as spears, were often deposited even with young children (presumably male children, although skeletons cannot be sexed anthropologically before puberty without DNA). Although some general features look similar, important differences exist between the furnished burial custom in England and that practised in Gaul at the same time. In Gaul, males generally received more lavish grave assemblages than females, whereas the opposite was frequently the case in England; amongst the Franks, children were almost never interred with weapons, but we have just noticed that this was far from the case with the Anglo-Saxons. Shields quite commonly accompany adult Anglo-Saxon males, but these items only appear in lavish masculine burials in Gaul. And so on.

On the other hand, in both areas the display of the deceased's identity during the funerary ritual concentrated, especially in the sixth century, on their gender and position in the life cycle rather than on simple matters of wealth or social rank. The links between diversity in burial display and gender and the life cycle question the extent to which funerary display had much (or anything) to do with ethnicity. Similar factors have been identified in cremation cemeteries, although obviously the burnt bone evidence from these sites can be more problematic. This picture is still sometimes read, from a rather crude observation that some of the dead went to their graves with more objects than others, as indicating a 'ranked society'. This is then held to represent a puzzling contrast with sixth-century settlements, which do not suggest clear differences of wealth and power. But this need not be a contradiction; in my view it definitely isn't. Even in the 1960s, archaeological theorists had proposed that a society which expressed difference in funeral remains largely in terms of gender and age was likely to be more egalitarian in its structure. Another (as I see it) more plausible reading of the funerary data sees the emphasis on age and gender in funeral display as revealing a society where, at a local level, no family had acquired an established dominance. It is a sign of competition for local power; the opposite of the situation at Poundbury described in Chapter 5. Position in society was dependent upon connections and the performance of roles associated with gender and position in the life cycle. Marriage and other kinship-creating links formed a web of alliances within a community. When an individual died a certain stress was produced within local politics. If, for example, a man died before his male children had established their own social position, this could cause tension as the heirs attempted to inherit his status. Similarly, the death of a young adult woman dissolved a marriage alliance between families, and added problems might be caused if there were young children.

The archaeological remains of a grave are likely to be only one aspect of a long ritual process. This may well have included other features renewing or recreating bonds between the deceased's family and its neighbours, allies, and competitors (or at least trying to), such as feasting and gift-giving. The items in a burial might have been 'gifts to the dead' and the food offerings frequently found in graves the deceased's share of the funerary feast. We cannot be sure, but these are reasonable suppositions. When we note that the furnished inhumation cemeteries are essentially found in the same, lowland part of Britain as the villas, and that the social hierarchy represented by the villas collapsed during the fifth century, the idea that these cemeteries reveal competition for local power when authority and status were very much up for grabs gains extra plausibility. On cremation cemeteries, it seems that the dead were often laid out publicly, before the pyre was constructed, in a similar fashion to that in which they were placed in the grave in inhumation cemeteries. It is likely, therefore, that similar factors were at work on those sites too, although the precise details doubtless differed. None of this implies that early Anglo-Saxon societies were 'egalitarian' communities of freemen; it simply means that local power and authority were not inherited automatically and were subject to rivalry and competition.

The implications of newer readings of the cemetery data have not, it seems to me, been fully worked through. They call into serious doubt many of the ethnic ('Anglo-Saxon') and religious (pagan) readings of these sites, which are still commonly espoused, more often implicitly than explicitly. Nevertheless, we can underline the importance that these analyses have for understanding post-imperial British politics.

Archaeology and the early Anglo-Saxon kingdoms: the end of an 'Arthurian context'?

What might fifth- or sixth-century realms in lowland Britain have been like? Currently the most common hypothesis is that immediately post-imperial kingdoms were myriad and tiny, perhaps encompassing single valleys. In archaeological circles it is not infrequently argued that kingship itself did not exist, only being introduced around 600.

This line of thought is based upon archaeological evidence, close study of place-names and other features of landscape history, and a method of extrapolating backwards from later historical sources. We have just discussed the social analysis of cemeteries, with their demonstration of age and gender's importance in governing the deposition of grave-goods. In this context, it becomes very difficult to find individuals or groups of burials which might convincingly relate to an established elite (unless you think, for example, that this was a society governed by young adult women, a suggestion probably best left to middle-aged male fantasy). One possible conclusion is that a vertical social hierarchy did not really exist. This is assumed to indicate a society organized more in terms of small, local 'chiefdoms' with an emphasis on kin-group rather than wealth or class. The lack of a secure elite is also evident from the rural settlements with groupings of buildings, plausibly associated with individual kindreds, all of about the same size. Such settlements are quite ephemeral in their archaeological traces, indicating that the idea of making a more permanent or elaborate mark on the landscape either did not exist or, with perhaps more likelihood, was simply not feasible. Wealth instead seems to have been invested in costume and other transient displays.

The study of place-names and the landscape, especially as revealed in later Anglo-Saxon charters (documents recording land-grants, usually to churches), has suggested small territories, in particular valleys or other geographically coherent units. Sometimes these later fragmented into more than one parish, but retained links through their names. Finally there is the study of other historical documents. One, the *Tribal Hidage*, lists political units, at least some of which are known to have been kingdoms, and evaluates them in terms of the number of *hides* they contained, a *hide* being the amount of land needed to support a family. The document probably dates to c.700 (though the manuscripts are much later), but other details of its origin and purpose are matters of discussion. For our purposes these debates concern us less than the general, and reasonable, assumption that this document relates to the payment of dues or tribute. The *Tribal Hidage* names, as well as the known kingdoms (Wessex, Sussex, Kent, and the rest), a large number of smaller units, mostly otherwise unattested (Figure 6.2). The *Gyrwe* of the Fens are mentioned in an eighth-century saint's Life, the *Arosaetna* presumably lived around the river Arrow, near Redditch (Worcestershire); others cannot confidently be located. The argument runs that these are lost kingdoms, tributary components of the greater kingdom of Mercia by the time the *Tribal Hidage* was composed, but shortly to vanish from the record. If these ephemeral realms had lasted to *c*.700, then surely it is plausible that there were once still others, subsumed into, say, Wessex or East Anglia in the *Tribal Hidage* or which had been swallowed up at an even earlier date by the smaller kingdoms listed. This model can be extended to encompass Wessex's gradual elimination of all its rivals

Figure 6.2 Anglo-Saxon kingdoms and provinces in the seventh century (according to the *Tribal Hidage* and other sources.)

and the creation of the kingdom of England. The idea of the steady elimination of some kingdoms by others until only one was left has, because of the similarities with a sporting knock-out competition, led to this being referred to as the 'FA Cup Model'.

One important implication of this model is the lack of any 'Arthurian context' it provides. It is difficult to see how a warlord leading a realm no larger than a few modern parishes clustered in a river valley could lie behind the legend of the great war-king, even in the fairly limited form in which it circulated in the early Middle Ages. If this model is correct, we would have to consider very seriously the possibility that the Arthur figure of the *History of the Britons* was either a total fabrication of the early ninth century or perhaps slightly earlier, or a newly created manifestation of an archaic, folkloric 'bear-man' hero. The latter alternative has been suggested, for example, in the one sustained academic attempt to disprove the existence of 'King Arthur' written in recent years, Nick Higham's interesting *King Arthur: History and Mythmaking*. This interpretation is impossible to dismiss even if it cannot be proven either.

The Britons and Welsh

The archaeology of the non-English groups of post-imperial Britain has taken fewer and less dramatic twists than that of the Anglo-Saxons, in terms of its interpretations. In the western regions, developments have principally involved the recognition and excavation of new types of site and the identification of particular classes of material.

The investigation of the fortified hill-top sites has continued apace, with new campaigns of investigation into famous sites like Tintagel, where the discovery in the 1990s of a slate inscribed with the name 'Artognou' led to much Arthurian hysteria, in spite of the fact that the name is nothing like Arthur, Artorius, or Arturus. Leslie Alcock's excavations at South Cadbury and Dinas Powys received full publication. Alcock's investigations of princely forts in what is now Scotland (conducted in the 1970s and 1980s and published in the 1990s), to which we shall return, also encompassed the British fort at Dumbarton. This fort was mentioned by contemporaries as *Alt Clut* (the Rock of the Clyde) and described as a great fortress of the British kingdom of Strathclyde. Alcock's exploration confirmed early medieval occupation and fortification and, as at the other sites he examined, its high status.

Other sites of this type have been recognized and excavated and slightly different categories of settlement have been identified. For example, on the South Welsh coast at Longbury Bank, what seems to be a trading site has been excavated. The control of such places would be important for Welsh rulers in ensuring that access to prestigious imports could only be obtained through them, and that their acquisition was linked to political service and obedience. The quantity and distribution of imported pottery and other goods has been more extensively studied. This evidence is now generally held to represent regular trade with the Mediterranean—even if not on an enormous scale. For a long time, it had also been able to be read as revealing only a few scattered visits.[1] A leading archaeologist of west and north Britain once said, provocatively, that all the imported pottery from Britain could have arrived on a single ship. This no longer looks plausible.

Excavation of Roman sites has produced new interpretations. Perhaps most importantly, since the 1980s and excavations at Birdoswald fort, the later use of the Hadrian's Wall forts has been significantly reconsidered. Although occupation of the traditional, official military sort falters in the late fourth century, habitation persisted. At Birdoswald itself, the fort's buildings were renovated and

---

[1] Philip Rahtz used to tell what might loosely be termed a joke, in which a Briton asks his local pottery-seller when he is expecting the next delivery of amphorae. The merchant replies, 'B-Ware? The Ides of March'.

reused, culminating in the construction of a large timber hall within the old fort. This suggested that the site had become a high-status site in many ways akin to the hill-forts of the western highlands. A survey of the available data implied that this might not be unusual. It was at first suggested that a 'sub-Roman' authority might have refortified the Wall but it now seems more likely that some forts gradually 'morphed' into the centres of lordships.

The Wroxeter excavations and the 'maximalist' interpretation of the evidence they produced were mentioned in the previous chapter. Here it should be pointed out that not everyone has accepted this reading and that another possible interpretation of the data is of a site similar in some ways to the post-imperial occupation of the Wall forts. That is to say that a local chieftain reworked some of the public buildings within the fortified area into a high-status centre. We should also repeat the point made in Chapter 5 that similarly nebulous but nonetheless incontrovertible traces of very late and post-imperial use of urban public spaces and buildings have been observed on other western sites, such as Chester and Exeter.

The debate on the high-status site at Yeavering has already been mentioned. Since then other 'palaces' from the late sixth century and early seventh, the very end of the period which concerns us, have been recognized between Hadrian's Wall and the Antonine Wall. Some have been excavated. One such is at Doon Hill near Dunbar. An important feature of these sites is large halls, similar to that at Birdoswald. Currently the most common reading of these settlements is similar to that once proposed for Yeavering. They are high-status British sites later taken over by Anglian rulers. The change in ethnic/ political affiliation is often deduced from a change in the nature of the buildings. The 'Birdoswald type' hall at Doon Hill was overlain by a 'Yeavering type' hall in the seventh century. The discussion of ethnicity and migration in Anglo-Saxon archaeology earlier in this chapter highlighted some possible reservations about this kind of reading.

A growing number of more mundane rural settlements has been excavated, such as at Cefn Graennog in the Lleyn peninsula. These apparently show, in line with the investigation of other classes of evidence, a greater degree of continuity from the Roman period into the early Middle Ages. This trajectory of development is, unsurprisingly, much closer to that seen in the west of the lowlands than in the rest of the former civil zone.

More recent, systematic study has also explored late and post-imperial British Christianity and compiled a more impressive list of Christian traces than had once been thought to exist. This continues work by one of the pioneers of post-imperial British archaeology, Charles Thomas. Not all of this evidence is entirely convincing but it seems difficult to avoid the conclusion that Roman Britain was significantly Christianized. This is what we should expect, given the importance that Britain's connection with the Roman Empire had in underpinning and stabilizing its social organization. With the devout Christianity of the Empire's rulers from 312 (with brief intervals in 359–61 and possibly 392–4) and their well-documented favouritism towards Christians, we ought to expect the new religion to be drawn quite deeply into Romano-British society along the links of imperial patronage. That Christianity should have spread into the highlands by the time that Gildas was writing should not astonish us either; as mentioned, non-Christian religion does not seem to have been something that worried him. This is especially so when we remember the greater Roman to post-imperial continuity in these areas and how they were probably home to the more politically powerful realms. Archaeological traces of Christianity go hand in hand with this.

Highland cemeteries have received growing attention and interest. The absence of grave-goods from burials in this region, continuing a late Roman trend, had meant that they were under-explored by comparison with 'Anglo-Saxon' sites. Indeed, they were difficult to find and date until techniques advanced to a particular level. Unfortunately,

Welsh soil-types often mean that the bones of the dead are no longer preserved, necessitating even greater skill in excavation. In the north of the British realms, between the Hadrianic and Antonine Walls, burials were usually placed in stone-lined cists, as was the custom in Pictish and Scottish areas too. At the Catstane cemetery now under Edinburgh airport, burials were focused on an inscribed stone, the Catstane itself. Throughout the British regions a key variable concerns earthworks in and around cemeteries. Enclosure is often interpreted as showing the presence of an organized church, which is plausible but not the only reading of this feature. Within sites, such banks and ditches around graves seem to continue the Roman tradition of delineating out special burials with permanent markers. If we had more inscribed stones *in situ* we might find these in association with such features. These burials' 'special' nature could be social (belonging to the elite) or religious (shrines of holy men, or similar).

Detailed recent work has further illuminated the material cultural productions of the post-imperial British areas. This has become more possible with better recognition and excavation of settlement sites. Most of the highland zone, not being arable farmland, lends itself less well to metal-detector work than the 'Anglo-Saxon' lowlands and, as repeatedly stated, burials do not tend to yield artefacts. For these reasons this work has had to proceed on the basis of excavation, the close analysis of the objects themselves, and the study of material found in other contexts such as 'Saxon' cemeteries. Classes of metalwork are now recognized—especially types of penannular brooch—which apparently originate around the Severn Estuary. We now have a much better, although still very partial, idea of what post-imperial highland material culture was like.

Irish immigration into the western highlands has attracted rather less attention than that of the Anglo-Saxons into the lowlands or Irish migration to western Scotland. Partly this is because diagnostic evidence is lacking. Some forms of pottery were once thought to be imports from Ireland but this is no longer believed to be the case. That apart, the best evidence is the Ogham inscriptions. The presence of Irish names or versions of names on the stones is difficult to explain away, although whether such evidence manifests a large-scale movement or an elite takeover is impossible to decide. Some Welsh political and historical traditions certainly thought that an Irish migration and conquest had taken place, but the weight that we can place on such evidence is limited. The links between Ireland and Roman Britain had—strangely—never been very extensive. In the late Roman period they may have increased in density but, at the same time, been more socially restricted. With massive social change taking place in Ireland between the fourth and seventh centuries, comparison with the political dynamics on Rome's other frontiers suggests that some emigration from Ireland would have been very likely. In the seventh century the sort of high-status exiles that this model envisages are visible, crossing the Irish Sea in both directions. What is odd is that (within our period) the Irish Sea only really becomes visible as an important zone of cultural interaction in the seventh century. The Mediterranean pottery imported onto high-status sites in Cornwall and Wales is rarely found in Ireland. In the seventh century, in newer trading patterns established around the end of the period covered by this book (see Chapter 12), imported French pottery is more evenly distributed around the Irish Sea. It might, of course, be the case that Ireland did not produce whatever it was that Mediterranean traders wanted in return for their wares whereas it did produce things of value to Frankish merchants. On the whole, though, it seems that before the end of the sixth century the Roman situation was continued, whereby the eastern shores of the Irish Sea seem to have been culturally dominant. This itself might have been a reason for Irish noble warriors, losing out in political struggles at home, to want to move to Great Britain. The same sort of dynamic can be seen on other frontiers of the old Empire.

Important work has also been done on the inscribed stones introduced in Chapter 3. This culminated in the Celtic Inscribed Stones
Project (CISP) at University College London, which catalogued all of
the non-runic inscriptions of the British Isles and Brittany. This
immensely useful catalogue is freely available online. The function of
these upright stone markers, very few of which are still in their original location, has been the subject of discussion. Are they grave markers or stones proclaiming landownership, or both? A shift in function
has been proposed from simple funerary memorials to the markers
of landownership. The date and origin of the Ogham script have also
been discussed. The outlying Silchester Ogham stone has been of
some importance. Re-examination of the find's context (the stone
was discovered in 1893) has led to a return to an old idea that it is one
of the very early stones in the corpus, possibly even fourth century.
Although the Silchester stone commemorates someone with an Irish
name it has been mooted that Ogham might have originated in
Britain and been exported to Ireland, probably in connection with
the Christianization of the island. The idea that these inscriptions
represent a custom introduced from Gaul has also been rejected.
More extensive examination of early medieval inscriptions shows
that the formulas employed on the British stones are not limited
to Gaul but are found across the late and post-imperial West. This
suggests—as, increasingly, do other data—that post-imperial Britain
was not a backwater that went its own way between 410 and 597.
It was fully incorporated in the currents of European historical
development.

The Picts and Scots

As with that of the Britons, Pictish and Scottish archaeology can be
described more in terms of development and refinement than in
terms of frequent and dramatic shifts of paradigm. The main exception

to this rule would concern the migration of the Scots from Ireland, whether or not it can be detected archaeologically and thus whether or not it actually took place in our period (or indeed at all). The spurs for this debate will be familiar from the discussion of the Anglo-Saxon migration. In Scottish archaeology, however, the influence of Scottish nationalism can also be felt and is, as with all nationalism, rarely a blessing for sophisticated readings of the data.

Amongst the Picts, the investigation of hill-forts has generally confirmed the outlines of earlier ideas. Alcock conducted a programme of investigation of 'royal sites' between 1975 and 1984, published between 1986 and 1992. He excavated Dundurn and revealed that, like the British forts, it showed similar traces of high-status occupation (although there was little imported pottery). There was evidence of bronze working and a great deal of glass. Here and at Clatchard Craig, the excavation of which was also published in the 1980s, it was suggested that the Pictish forts generally owed their origins to the late sixth or early seventh century, at the very end of our 'world of Arthur'. Some, like Burghead, were earlier, reaching back to the fourth century. In the current state of play it is difficult to know what these forts represent, or which sort of site is the more typical, the smaller cellular 'nuclear fort' or the larger sites like Burghead and Clatchard Craig. It is possible that early, large sites like Burghead represent an earlier phase of large, but perhaps quite weak, kingdoms and that the small sites represent the domination of smaller areas. It seems more common to place these smaller and more numerous sites in the context of the steadily growing power of the Pictish kingdom. In this reading they manifest a tighter, more intensive, and more localized authority over regional societies. At their fullest extent a hierarchy of hill-forts possibly existed, representing different levels of power from king down to local aristocrat.

Other levels of Pictish settlement have proved more elusive, although good archaeological work is beginning to put together a picture of rural farmsteads. Probably the best studied and published to date are those in Orkney, such as at the Brough of Birsay, Bucquoy, and elsewhere. These settlements show interesting developments in the middle of the first millennium AD, with change at the start and at the end of our period. Circular and cellular buildings were established, often within the remains of earlier brochs, reusing earlier stone walls. Dwellings are sometimes grouped around small yards. On the whole, settlement seems dispersed although population might have been growing. Gradual re-nucleation on the Orkney sites between c.400 and c.600 seems plausible from recent excavations. These sites have also produced evidence of crafts and much more pottery than was, in the past, thought used by the Picts. Further south, in Perthshire, Pictish settlements have been manifested by 'Pitcarmick houses', long-houses with a central 'soak-away'. Elsewhere sub-rectangular buildings replaced roundhouses in the mid-first millennium. It nevertheless often seems to be the case that the fifth century is part of a 'gap' in the occupation of settlement sites. Coming out of this 'gap' appears to have been one of the changes taking place in Pictland during the era that concerns us.

Changes are also visible on Pictish cemeteries. In the fifth century a change appears to occur, towards a greater concentration of burials into communal cemeteries. The graves are stone-lined cists, as are earlier more isolated burials. The appearance of the cist cemetery has been associated with the arrival of Christianity. This is unlikely as they are known from as early as the third century and before, and from areas as remote from Christian influence as the Hebrides. Instead it has been proposed, possibly more plausibly, that the increased use of this burial rite stems from the influence of the Roman Empire, in which inhumation became the norm from the third century. In the sixth century, perhaps later within that century, aboveground monuments appear on cist cemeteries in Fife and other areas in the south-east of the Pictish regions. These include barrows and stone cairns and probably the earlier Pictish symbol stones, although none of the latter has yet been found indubitably in connection with a cist or barrow. Like the roughly contemporary appearance of the smaller hill-forts, this development has been read as revealing the increasing complexity of Pictish social organization.

Pictish symbol stones have continued to undergo analysis and interpretation. As before, some attempts have been more scholarly than others. The patterning and associations of the different symbols have been studied with different results. One suggestion was that the combinations represented names, made up of two elements which could be reversed. This would be like the Germanic naming system where, for instance, the elements 'here' (army) and 'wulf'/'ulf' (wolf, unsurprisingly enough) could theoretically be combined into the names Wulfhere or Herewulf. Substituting 'berht' or 'bryht' (bright) for 'here', you could have Berhtwulf/Bryhtwulf or Wulfberht/ Ulfberht. One could take an element from each parent's name, so that (using a Frankish example) a Brunechild and a Sigebert could have a son called Childebert. Elements could be used repeatedly within a family, acting like a 'surname'. Rival Northumbrian dynasties used different 'leading names' for example. Similarly, King Æthelwulf of Wessex had sons called Æthelstan, Æthelbald, Æthelberht, and Æthelræd (Noble Stone, Bold Noble, Shining Noble, and Noble Counsel)…and of course Ælfræd (Elf Counsel), although, given his surfeit of elder brothers, Alfred might never have been expected to become king. The Pictish symbol combinations suggested a pattern similar to that demonstrated for Anglo-Saxon 'dithematic' names. The problem with this alluring idea is that we do not know that the Picts had names like this; indeed the names we do have do not seem to fit this model. It must be said, though, that we know rather few Pictish names and the ones we do know are almost entirely royal. On balance this is a nice idea but not entirely convincing.

Another, more subtle, proposition is that the symbols represent a kind of language. The number, variations upon, relative frequency, and combinations can be plausibly presented as a set of abbreviated and formulaic words. This is not suggested to apply to all the symbols, some of which might be pictograms rather than letters as we would understand them (that is to say as in the Latin and Ogham alphabets). This would make the 'language' of the symbols akin to that of ancient Egyptian hieroglyphics: a similar mix of pictograms and phonetic letters. This is a beguiling possibility although it is impossible to reconstruct the alphabet or language and therefore to progress very far with it. Another proposal has been that, on anthropological analogy, the symbols mark particular kindreds or lineages. This is possible although it has not caught on among specialists.

The date and function of the symbols remain unclear. The discovery of a stone carved with a symbol at Pool in Orkney, knocked face-down in a sixth-century settlement context, suggests that these symbols might have begun earlier and perhaps further north than had hitherto generally been thought. It has been suggested that the symbols' resemblance to surviving Roman artefacts might make them as early as the fourth century but this proposal has not been popular. That the flourishing of the early 'class I' stones began in the late sixth or seventh century remains the most common reading. Symbol stones have been located in connection with burials under cairns and barrows but to date none has been found in its original position, making its function as a burial marker unproven. Nevertheless a funerary connection is very likely. As with the inscribed stones discussed earlier, we should probably not assume that there was a single function or that there can have been no shift from one function to another, through time.

Since the late 1980s, the idea of the Picts as a complex society, rather than the wild and woolly savages envisaged in early studies, has rightly gained ground, although the popular notion of 'the mysterious Picts' stubbornly refuses to die. A common framework within which the Pictish evidence is understood is that of the development of 'the Pictish state'. I have already mentioned how changes around 600—the early phases of the more common, smaller forts, the appearance of grave markers and the 'class I' stones—have been seen as a stage in the development of the Pictish kingdom. The later phases of this development lie outside our remit but we should raise the questions of whether this is the only way to read these changes and whether political change must follow a single, straight line (questions that should also be asked of the 'FA Cup Model' of the Anglo-Saxon kingdoms' growth). That Pictish society and politics were complex and probably to be conceived of alongside those of other 'barbarian' groups, within the British Isles and outside, seems however to be firmly established and is an important conclusion that must be remembered.

The archaeology of the early Scottish kingdoms has perhaps been a more interesting focus for archaeological debate over recent decades. In some ways the Scots suffer as they lack the Picts' 'mysterious' credentials, their symbol stones and so on. On the other hand, as the eventual 'winners' in traditional Scottish historical narratives, they also lose out to the Picts in not being the 'voiceless' underdogs. As is common in archaeology, having what is widely thought to be an established historical narrative—in this case, migration from Ireland, conversion to Christianity by St Columba, the gradual conquest of the western regions, and eventually, under 'Kenneth MacAlpine', the defeat of the Picts and creation of the Kingdom of the Scots—can act as a brake on interest in what the excavated evidence can say, whether or not the historical narrative is well founded. Unfortunately, most of the really diagnostic features of early medieval Scottish archaeology only really develop in the seventh century and thus after the close of our period.

The forts of the Scots, like those of the other northern British peoples, have been one focus for investigation. Alcock's investigations took in the fort at Dunollie (Argyll), which appears to have been established at around the time of the end of our 'world of Arthur'. This revealed many of the typical features of a northern British fortified high-status site: craft-working, weaponry, and imported pottery (in this case 'E-Ware' from south-west France). The best-known Scottish fort is Dunadd, mentioned in Chapter 3. This site began as a *dun* in the fifth century, before, at about the same time as the first phase at Dunollie, it became a fully-fledged high-status site. It has revealed plentiful evidence of trading connections, with one of the highest concentrations of continental pottery and glassware. There is botanical evidence of the importation of madder dye (producing a deep red) from France, as well as coriander and dill. Dunadd was also the site of bronze working. The contemporaneity of this site and Dunollie has led to the reasonable suggestion that the two sites might have developed in competition with each other, as centres of competing early Scottish dynasties. At Loch Glashan excavation produced evidence of substantial leatherworking activity. The site looks very unusual when one compares its general nature with the activities that went on there. The plausible conclusion has been drawn that this craft-working centre was provided with raw materials by the nearby high-status centre at Dunadd. Other settlements also reveal changes around the end of our period. Metalworking appeared around 600 at Eilean Olabhat on North Uist.

Investigation of post-imperial Scottish cemeteries and burials has proceeded along similar lines to those seen for the northern Britons and Picts. The standard burial rite is, as in neighbouring areas, inhumation in stone cists, although rarely grouped into large cemeteries as further east, until perhaps the seventh century. Then such cemeteries are frequently enclosed and possibly associated with churches. Seemingly at about the same time, stone grave monuments appear, although it seems to me that some examples might be somewhat (or even considerably) earlier. One stone at Cladh a'Bhile (Mid-Argyll), for example, has a six-leafed design which looks very much like those on fourth- and fifth-century Roman metalwork.

Recent decades have seen a debate about the extent and reality of Irish migration into western Scotland, traditionally believed to have occurred around 500. The classic features of early medieval Irish archaeology (ring-forts etc.) are not found in Scotland, and the frontier between the Goidelic (Irish) Q-Celtic and the Brythonic (British) P-Celtic language might always have lain along the edge of Argyll. These arguments do not seem especially convincing. For one thing, the features deemed characteristic of early medieval Irish archaeology do not really develop in Ireland until the seventh century. For another, there is fairly good evidence that the people of Argyll and the western Isles were P-Celtic-speakers in the Roman period. Their tribal name—Epidii (horse people), giving rise to the Hebrides—suggests a P-Celtic language and there is some evidence that this remained the case in the early Middle Ages. It is not fanciful to suggest that the attempts to reject an Irish migration and to instate Q-Celtic Gaelic as always present in Scotland are linked with nationalist efforts to promote Gaelic-speaking as an official language, against 'Scots', which is of course a dialect of English. The unpalatable fact (to nationalists) is that Scots was widely spoken in what is now Scotland from at least as early a date as Gaelic. As one historian of early medieval Scotland has commented (though not published), if a return to the ancestral language of Scotland was really sought, then Scottish schoolchildren should be taught Welsh.

Post-imperial Scottish society was, like Pictish, complex, diverse, and dynamic. This is important. The Scots were not locked into some timeless, mystic pan-Celtic heroic age. Yet we should not overestimate this. Like attempts to promote the idea of a 'precocious' Pictish 'state', arguments that the realms of the Scots were unusually advanced, made on the basis of the *Senchus Fer nAlban*, a (possibly) mid-seventh-century list of ships and rowers to be provided by the different areas of the Scottish kingdom, suffer from a lack of awareness of the evidence from other early medieval kingdoms. A list does not a state make. Nonetheless it is evidence of aspirations to complexity and political organization that cannot be ignored. Attempts to posit the Scottish regions of the north as a 'crossroads' of the early medieval world seem to misunderstand the nature of a crossroads, even if we might rightly want to reject the use of the rather demeaning word 'fringe' to describe the region. A T-Junction is a more appropriate analogy.... Nonetheless, Scottish early medieval studies do not have a monopoly on the malign influence of nationalism. Arguments for the early development of a complex and efficient early English state suffer from analogous motivations. Similar distortions appear in the archaeology of Gaul and elsewhere.

Conclusion

The archaeology of the various 'peoples' who inhabited post-imperial Britain is thus a vibrant and interesting sphere of research with new excavation, the recognition of new classes of materials, new techniques, and the constant confrontation of interpretations. It has come a long way since the 1970s, let alone the earlier twentieth century. Yet in some regards it remains locked within certain frameworks which, in my view, are not necessarily very helpful.

PART III
MAD WORLDS

❧❦

What a fool believes he sees
No wise man has the power to reason away

THE DOOBIE BROTHERS

7

Red Herrings and Old Chestnuts

✢

To round off the survey of current views of the 'world of Arthur', in this chapter I discuss some arguments frequently used in modern Arthurian pseudo-histories to attempt to circumvent the lack of reliable written evidence for this period of British history and some commonly encountered theories. A unifying feature of all is that the essential points about using medieval sources, made at the start of Chapter 4, are completely ignored.

Red herrings

Oral tradition and folk memory

A common attempt to circumvent the problems of the written record involves arguing that, although late, our sources are based upon oral tradition and folk memory. Such sources accurately preserve the details of the distant past and its events, because of the supposed nature of 'oral' societies. In non-literate societies stories undoubtedly circulate for a long time and preserve the general outlines of their plot. There is no doubt, either, that stories, songs, and poems circulated in early medieval Britain without being written down. The *Historia Brittonum*, for example, refers to Arthur's dog Cabal leaving a footprint in a stone near Builth during the hunt for the boar Troynt. Many believe that this refers to a story written down half a millennium later as a major element of the Welsh tale *Culhwch and Olwen*, in which Arthur and his men hunt the boar Twrch Trwyth. Sure enough, Arthur's dog Cavall appears there too, led by Bedwyr (later the Sir Bedevere who, in Malory's *Morte d'Arthur*, throws Excalibur back into the lake, replacing Girflet, who played this role in earlier versions). Yet this does not mean that the tale's elements were the same in both stories. Many details could have changed. The region of Builth is not mentioned in the later account, for example. This story could be a version of a common 'great boar-hunt' folktale (compare, for example, the mythical Greek hunt for the Great Boar of Calydon). Studies of such tales reveal that quite significant details can change according to the demands and expectations of particular audiences even while the story's general outline remains. Claims to have shown the astonishing perseverance of oral tradition over centuries are almost always (naturally enough) based upon examples where a written version exists, which naturally renders the case doubtful.

Stories might well therefore have been told and retold for generations, centuries even, but we cannot use this point to argue that the versions eventually written down faithfully preserve the details of an original composed in the 'world of Arthur'. Indeed, by the very nature of the argument, they cannot even be used to claim that the original is not older than the fifth century, with the name Arthur added later. The tale of the boar Troynt/Twrch Trwyth might have been very old indeed, have always featured Culhwch and Olwen and only had Arthur appended later; or it might always have involved Arthur and only subsequently have acquired Culhwch and Olwen. These are only two of many possibilities, all of which have significantly different implications for Arthur's historicity, none of which can now be chosen as more likely than the others on the basis of the evidence we have. Oral tradition allows us to suggest that some of the people and events mentioned in our sources really existed during the fifth and sixth centuries. It does not permit us to decide *which* characters and battles contained in later documents are 'real', whether they are correctly associated with each other, or even if they have been placed in the right order.

Lost sources

A variant on this argument postulates lost *written* sources, from the fifth and sixth centuries, behind the accounts found in the eighth- to tenth-century histories. Lost annals are a favourite contender. Again the case is superficially attractive. Many documents must have been written in Britain between *c*.400 and *c*.600. It would be odd indeed if, while the three surviving sources composed during these 200 years all presuppose a literate audience, they were the *only* ones written (other than inscriptions on stone) and, furthermore, that we have a 100 per cent document survival rate, attested nowhere else in the Middle Ages. The most common form of post-imperial historical writing was, moreover, the 'Minor Chronicle', the terse list of years and associated events. The general subject matter of the Minor Chronicle was—essentially—high politics: kings, emperors, and battles, precisely the things we would need to write a political history of the 'world of Arthur'. Unfortunately it is impossible to convert these reasonable points into an argument that will sustain the use of our surviving histories to construct a narrative account of the fifth and sixth centuries.

There are several reasons why this is so. Most importantly of all, we can identify the sources used by the authors of the extant histories for almost all of their accounts; in nearly all cases they still survive. Thus there is not in fact much room for the 'lost source'. An argument was made, over a century ago, on the basis of a change in the quality of Bede's Latin, that his account of St Alban's martyrdom was based on a lost 'Passion' of the saint. Remarkably a copy of this very source was later discovered. Unfortunately, similarly sound arguments have not been made for other lost post-imperial accounts. The old argument that contemporary annals lay behind the *Anglo-Saxon Chronicle*'s narrative of the fifth and sixth centuries has not survived the detailed critical work done on that source since the late 1970s. In Chapter 4, we also saw that John Morris's attempt to invent a 'Kentish Chronicle' in the *Historia Brittonum* is entirely unconvincing.

Where we *can* plausibly suggest lost sources, they are usually of the type just discussed: oral traditions and legends. Otherwise they are things like royal genealogies, which can be written or transmitted orally but which are notoriously susceptible to later corruption and distortion. The most sustainable cases for lost 'historical' sources concern the Kentish list of overlords suggested as a source for Bede's account of kings with *imperium* and the Minor Chronicle consulted by the author of the *Historia Brittonum*. Unfortunately the uses of the former are limited indeed (though not unimportant). It is impossible to be sure that the chronicle used by the *HB* is not the surviving one written by Prosper of Aquitaine. It is impossible either to extract those elements of the *HB* which come from this source or to know what, if anything, the *HB*'s author has done to them. In Chapter 9 I discuss the way that that writer artfully moulded his information into the 'Battle-List of Arthur', in such a way as to make it impossible to see beyond his composition to the sources behind it. Indeed the analysis of that passage, once viewed as a fragment of a poem, illustrates how modern criticism has destroyed earlier, more hopeful claims to see lost sources faithfully preserved in later historical texts.

To be convincing, any argument postulating a lost source must demonstrate several things. First of all it must show, through analysis, that the supposedly preserved fragment is discrete. It must have clear stylistic or linguistic differences from the rest of the source. This would remove the suspicion that it is the composition of the later author, or at least distorted by him. If a source is changed in transmission, it becomes impossible to winnow out the original elements from later additions or alterations. Second, it must make a convincing case for the type of source the transmitted passage represents, so that we can examine its worth within that context. Something from a saint's Life, for example, needs to be treated within the rules of hagiographical composition, which are different from those of, let's say, a Minor Chronicle. This might affect the reliability that we could attribute to the source in question. Finally, a persuasive case would have to be presented that the transmitted source was from our 'world of King Arthur' and not later. If not, it would be subject to the same problems as any other later source. Suffice it to say that no argument for lost historical sources has passed these stringent but necessary tests.

Geoffrey of Monmouth's 'ancient book'

The best-known example of a 'lost source' is Geoffrey of Monmouth's claim to have based his account on an 'ancient book' about the history of the Britons. Modern writers wanting to use Geoffrey's detailed and elaborate history of King Arthur to pad out their stories often shelter behind this claim. Appealing to a lost book to add authority to an account was far from unknown in the early Middle Ages. Sometimes it might have been more than a conceit. Geoffrey's contemporary William of Malmesbury said he used a now lost poem for his account of the tenth-century King Æthelstan, and stylistic analysis of the Latin in the relevant sections of his history suggests that he might have been telling the truth. This is unusual. Geoffrey, however, makes his claim three times, names the man who had lent him the volume (Walter, archdeacon of Oxford), and says that Walter brought the volume out of Brittany and that it was in the British language.

This makes his statement more difficult to dismiss out of hand, which in turn makes denser the smoke-screen he laid down by claiming to have derived his history of Arthur from an ancient book. The screen can nevertheless be dispersed.

No specific passages are tied to the volume (unlike the case of William of Malmesbury), which is used as a general authenticating claim and a warning to other historians to stay away from Geoffrey's patch because they don't have a copy of this book. At one point Geoffrey says he got his detailed story from the book *and* from what Walter of Oxford told him. His most specific reference says that the book tells the story of the Britons from Brutus to Cadwalladr, a description which would fit the *History of the Britons* perfectly. Even if not—the *Historia Brittonum* is not in the Welsh language, as Geoffrey claimed *his* book was—and even if we believe Geoffrey's claims to have such a book which *was* in Welsh, it would still seem likely that his putative source was either a Welsh version of the *HB* or some other work later than and based upon that volume. By the 1070s there was certainly an Irish translation of the *HB*. As we have seen, the *Historia* is itself of dubious historical worth. The fact that the 'ancient' book's account is said to have begun with Brutus, the legendary Trojan founder of Britain, would hardly dispose us to trust it if it *did* exist. In other words, there is scant reason to suppose either that Geoffrey of Monmouth knew of a now lost, reliable contemporary or near-contemporary Arthurian source or that he was not, as William of Newburgh alleged, making the whole thing up.

Bias and 'forensics'

Scholarly analyses of the extant sources, as outlined in Chapters 4 and 9, have recently been dismissed by a non-academic writer about Arthur as examples of 'bias'. What this alleged bias is in favour of is not spelled out but the claim's author argues that instead we should adopt a 'forensic' approach, treating the sources as a criminal investigation would deal with witnesses and constructing a story by comparing their accounts. Once again, this sounds like a good point. However, the supposedly forensic line of argument raises two insurmountable problems. One is that it requires precisely the sort of detailed examination of a witness's reliability as are represented by modern scholarly dissections of the written sources. A jury is unlikely to accept the testimony of a demonstrable liar, even if some of his lies seem to tally with other witnesses' accounts. Believing a witness without further questioning, because one is predisposed to believe his story, really *is* bias. The second problem with this approach is that it assumes that the 'witnesses' are independent. A court shown that all the witnesses called by the defence (or the prosecution) had colluded to tell the same story would reject (or be told by the judge to reject) their testimony out of hand. Yet, as we have seen, Bede's dependence upon Gildas and the *Anglo-Saxon Chronicle*'s upon Bede are clear, as is that of the *HB* on Bede and Gildas. We can also identify shared sources even where our writers are not copying directly from one another. These are *not* independent witnesses and no weight can be placed upon the fact that they sometimes tell exactly the same story. The 'forensic' argument is flimsy indeed.

Old chestnuts

We can now move on to the 'old chestnuts': theories, some more commonly held than others, on which modern accounts of the historical Arthur have been based. I have not covered them all for reasons of space and the inevitable repetition that would ensue. In addition to those made above and in Chapter 4, there is one key point that you should always bear in mind when evaluating the latest claim to have revealed the 'truth' about King Arthur. Does the author present prima facie evidence? In other words, does a tombstone, for example, actually say that someone called Arthur, Artorius, or

Arturus was buried there? Does a source actually mention Arthur? If not, if the author has to resort to convoluted explanations as to why a person referred to by another name (or anonymously) is 'really' Arthur, then you can dismiss the argument straight away. It means that the author has decided in advance that Arthur existed in a particular time and place and is then making the sources fit this idea. For example, where the text survives, all surviving early medieval gravestones give the names of the people buried: not one that we know of instead refers to the dead via cryptic and convoluted allusions. The same point stands for other written sources. For a claim to stand that an author is alluding to someone without naming them, a great deal of other, contemporary evidence is necessary about the author, his text, and his subject. If a modern writer has to introduce complex conspiracy theories about why Arthur does not appear in a text, or to account for its silence, you can be sure that the theory is not worth the effort of reading. Again, if the evidence cited is from many centuries after the event, especially after c.1100, then it is worthless. The reasons for this have been given above and at the start of Chapter 4, but let me reiterate the point about consistency. Always check that a modern author is using the evidence consistently, and not simply winnowing out those parts that fit, accepting elements that conform to his or her theory as 'oral tradition' or from 'lost sources' (see above) while ignoring other parts that don't. Many modern writers of pseudo-history have done a great deal of reading of many different sources, sometimes (though admittedly not very often) even in the original languages. This hard work should be saluted but it does not make their theories any more reliable if they do not conform to the rigorous rules of medieval evidence. It is not how much they have read that matters but how well they use what they have read. Contrary to what is often said the difference between academic and amateur writers of history is not that the academics think they know it all; it is that they *know* they *don't* know it all.

King Arthur's heavy cavalry

One of the most frequently stated ideas is that the reason for Arthur's military success was a force of heavily armoured cavalry. It cannot be said too forcefully that there is absolutely no evidence for this contention. None of the three sources that mention Arthur before AD 1000 says that his troops, or even their main battlefield strike-force, were cavalrymen. Mounted warriors were important in early medieval warfare and the Welsh 'heroic' poetry makes many mentions of such fighting men. It is therefore quite possible that fifth- and sixth-century British warlords led bands of horsemen. It must nevertheless be remembered, first, that this statement is no more than a plausible suggestion; second, that therefore it provides no solid basis for further theories about Arthurian warfare; and, third, that this would not distinguish him from, or give him any advantages over, any other early medieval warlord. Reconstructions of Arthur's wars that assume that his men were heavy cavalry start from two other bases, neither of which furnishes reliable support for the notion.

One is that the Knights of the Round Table represent a distant memory of heavy cavalry, an idea sometimes elaborated into the notion that Arthur's men were *cataphracts*. These were very heavily armoured lancers of the classical period who became more important in the late imperial era, encased head to toe in mail, scale, or plate armour, riding armoured horses, and thus looking like later medieval knights. The notion that this superficial similarity derives from a reliable tradition about actual post-imperial warriors is—clearly—nonsense. Were it not so commonly encountered in the Arthurian pseudo-histories, even receiving some support from the eminent earlier twentieth-century archaeologist and historian R. G. Collingwood, it would hardly deserve our attention. *Anyone* writing a romance about a model king in the twelfth to fifteenth centuries, presenting a story to a late medieval royal and aristocratic audience, usually with particular lessons about proper conduct, could not but have the king surrounded by heavily armoured knights. That fact lay at the very heart of the term chivalry, which comes, via 'chevalerie' (horsemen; obviously related to the word 'cavalry'), from the late, low Latin word for horse: *caballus* (whence modern French 'cheval'). Manuscript illustrations of the Arthurian romances have Arthur and his men depicted exactly like later medieval knights, as their audience would have expected. That, to them, was what kings were like. It is absolutely impossible to move beyond this obvious point to *any* notion about the warriors who followed any historical Arthur. Furthermore, the romances (texts and illustrations) present Arthur's enemies as knights too. If they preserve dusky ancient memories of Arthur's men, then, presumably, they also contain dim recollections of his enemies who, it would seem, were cataphracts too, eradicating the explanation for Arthur's dominance. Extending the same point, medieval illustrations, and some written sources too, transpose the heroes of the biblical past into the military realities of their present, making great 'kings' like Julius Caesar and Judas Maccabeus into knights. One would hardly argue that Caesar and Judas Maccabeus led armies of heavily armoured cataphracts on that basis.

The second notion is more academically respectable, deriving from the idea that all Anglo-Saxon warriors fought dismounted. They had no cavalry. This might have made them vulnerable to heavy cavalry charges against which, it is sometimes argued, they had little or no experience. There are many problems with this idea. It is based upon the notion that a simple, cultural and political (even racial) opposition existed between Britons and Saxons and that fifth-century British politics should be envisaged as a straightforward war between these two sides. This is unlikely to have been the case; certainly the idea has no solid foundation. Even while acknowledging the importance of the Anglo-Saxon migration, the difference between Britons and Saxons was more about political identity than deep cultural, let alone biological, divides. For all this, see Chapter 9. Thus if the inhabitants of Roman Britain were familiar with cavalry-fighting then so, one assumes, were those who became Saxons. Finally the idea that the Anglo-Saxons did not fight mounted is very insecure. It is principally grounded in received wisdom, rather than evidence. The *only* pre-Viking reference to whether Anglo-Saxons fought on foot or mounted is in fact to a *horsed* (*equitatus*) Northumbrian army in 670–2. Further, the famous north German bog-deposits show that the inhabitants of the Saxon homelands used horses in warfare. Saxons also served in the late Roman army, which deployed numerous cavalry regiments. Ultimately there is absolutely no prima facie reason why 'Saxon' armed forces in post-imperial Britain should not have fought mounted as often as their enemies. Most importantly, perhaps, it is worth stating that the distinction between mounted and dismounted warriors was not rigid in the early Middle Ages. Warriors fought on foot or on horseback as the occasion demanded. Overall, then, the idea that any historical 'King Arthur' based his successful campaigns upon his unique use of heavy cavalry has no historical basis whatsoever.

Lucius Artorius Castus

Anyone who has seen the 2004 movie *King Arthur* will recognize the name of this candidate for being the historical Arthur, who features heavily in recent pseudo-history. He definitely existed; his sarcophagus (stone coffin), on which were carved details of his career, survives, albeit in fragments. Unfortunately, he definitely existed in the late second and/or early third centuries, long before the Saxon 'invasions' of Britain, and his tombstone is on the Dalmatian coast, far from the British Isles. These facts necessitate slightly different arguments. One is that he was an ancestor of the historical Arthur. Another, pointing in a different direction, is that *this* Artorius lies at the origin of the legends of the great warrior. His exploits were so widely remembered in Britain that he became a legendary warrior, to whom (later on) valiant deeds against the Saxons were attributed. This argument is found, in part, in Higham's *King Arthur: History and Mythmaking*.

Why all this fuss about someone who died in what's now Croatia, two to three hundred years before our 'world of Arthur'? One reason is that Lucius Artorius Castus' sarcophagus describes him as having been a *praefectus* of the legion VI Victrix, stationed in York at this time. Another is that he later led a military expedition of *Britanicimiae*, which seems to have been very successful. Both of these episodes came late in his career, which he ended (probably thanks to his exploits on the expedition just mentioned) as a governor in the area where he was buried. It is often believed that his campaign, with his *Britanicimiae*, was against the Aremoricans of Brittany. Here we stray onto territory familiar from our discussion of another candidate for the historical Arthur, Riothamus (below Chapter 11). It is argued that Lucius Artorius' campaign against the Aremoricans was the basis for later accounts of Arthur's wars across the Channel. No matter that these come nearly a millennium after Lucius Artorius Castus' death. It has also been argued that he commanded Sarmatian cavalry; we will return to this.

As ever, though, with one look at the actual evidence this argument, which at first sight looks suggestive, begins to crumble. The post that Artorius, from an Italian family, held in Britain was probably administrative rather than an active battlefield command. We are not, in any case, told how long he held it for before his expedition. The latter is more problematic than is often supposed. The text describes Lucius as DVCI LEGG [...]M BRITAN{I}CIMIARVM. This can be reconstructed as saying that he led two British legions or that he led *alae* (detachments) *Britanicimiae* (probably a corruption of *Britannicae* or *Britannicianae*). Although these probably drew their name from having been stationed in Britain, the historically attested *alae* and *cohortes Britannicianae* are found in Pannonia (modern Hungary), where they seem to have been transferred in the later first century. None is known in Britain at Lucius Artorius' time. Nevertheless, detachments from the VI Victrix were possibly assigned to Lucius for his campaign, becoming known as *vexillationes Britannicae*. The idea that he took two legions from Britain is unlikely in view of his enemies, as we shall see, and if the legions were called British because of *previous* service in Britain it is difficult to see which ones they could be. The reading as *alae* is probably to be preferred.

Be that as it may, a far more important problem concerns Artorius' opponents. These, as noted, have been identified as Aremoricans. However, the text of the inscription says no more than this: DVCI LEGG [...]M BRITAN{I}CIMIARVM ADVERSVS ARM[... .]S PROCCENTE. The fragment 'ARM...S' has been read as AREMORICANOS but this is quite a leap from what actually survives. Moreover the earliest reading of the inscription, in the 1850s, suggested that the fragment then read ADVERSVS ARME[... .]S, the E subsequently having been weathered away. This would make Aremoricans impossible as Artorius' enemies. Recent commentators have therefore suggested that Lucius Artorius Castus' opponents were *Armenians*, on Rome's eastern frontier. This makes it extremely unlikely that Lucius Artorius Castus has anything whatsoever to do with 'King Arthur'. It is probably also worth saying, in passing, that Arthur's name is never Latinized as Artorius in our surviving early medieval sources, only as Arturus.

King Arthur was a Sarmatian

No he wasn't. I am tempted to leave my comments there, but this idea associating Arthur with the Sarmatians (a semi-nomadic or pastoral group who lived in the Balkans, north of Rome's Danube frontier) has become very popular in modern pseudo-history. The film *King Arthur*, which, like many modern populist books, claimed to reveal the 'true story', subscribed to the idea. If suggesting that Arthur him-self was Roman, these theories argue that Arthurian legend shows strong Sarmatian links. The argument runs something like this: King Arthur's knights represent a dim folk memory of his heavy cavalry; the Sarmatians were renowned for their lance-armed heavy cavalry (sometimes riding partially armoured horses) and were thus similar in appearance and tactics to later knights; some Sarmatians served in the Roman army and some were stationed in Britain. Lucius Artorius Castus (above) is argued to have fought his campaign against 'Aremoricans' with Sarmatian cavalry. Then there is the sword in the stone. The fourth-century Roman writer Ammianus Marcellinus says that the Alans, who lived near the Sarmatians, worshipped a sword stuck in the ground. Some Alans entered the Empire with the Great Invasion and ended up with the Vandals in Africa; others settled around Auxerre and near Valence in Gaul. It is argued that others remained in Brittany and thus became part of the 'Celtic' world. There are other 'resemblances' between various steppes stories and images and elements of Arthurian legend which would be tiresome and unnecessary to relate. On the basis of all this we are asked to believe that the Arthur story is impregnated with elements drawn from Sarmatian presence and influence.

Many elements of this 'argument' have been encountered before. Its bed-rock, the resemblance between ancient lancers and medieval knights, can swiftly be reduced to sand, as described above. In the evidence that we have, Lucius Artorius Castus is nowhere said to have had anything to do with Sarmatians. If he did it is much more likely to have been while stationed in the Balkans than when in Britain. And his campaign was probably not in Brittany/Aremorica at all. Above all, the reference to worshipping a sword stuck in the ground refers to the Alans. Although closely associated with the Sarmatians the Alans were a distinct group; this cult is not specifically attested among the Sarmatians proper. In any case, Ammianus' account of the Alans is not especially reliable. The sum total of evidence for Alan presence in Brittany is the popularity of the name Alan among the Bretons and some place-names which include the element '*alain*'. The name Alan, though, might simply be Breton (meaning something like 'rock') or a local derivation from the Latin name Aelianus, an explanation that also accounts for the place-names. The sword in the stone is first recorded hundreds of years after the Alans' historical existence. If we assume that this represented a folktale that had endured for centuries, then—as noted earlier—we must allow that it might just as easily pre-date the whole 'world of Arthur'. The other 'steppes' influences on the Arthurian story suffer from the same problems: a lack of specific association with Sarmatians, the distance of many centuries between evidence on the steppe and appearance in Arthurian legend, the uncritical assumptions upon which the argument is based. Whatever the historical Arthur was, we can I think be sure that he wasn't Sarmatian.

King Arthur was a 'German'

This—not so much an 'old chestnut' as a new and interesting chestnut—is proposed by Stuart Laycock in his book *Warlords*. Laycock sees Arthur as a 'Germanic' mercenary in the service of a British realm. A figure who suited no one's purposes in constructing the 'bilateral' histories of the early Middle Ages and later (*the* English versus *the* Welsh) could indeed be shifted into legend or forgotten entirely (see Chapter 11). The idea has some attractions, although Laycock accepts too readily the written sources discussed in Chapter 4 and above all the subscription to the view of the period as a simple two-sided struggle between invading English and defending Britons or Welsh. He proposes that 'Arthur' might have been an Anglo-Saxon name, suggesting Eardhere. This looks like a nice idea but, apart from the fact that the name is unknown, a progression from Eardhere (pronounced something like 'Yard-heh-reh') to the Welsh *Arthur* (pronounced something like 'arth-ear') is phonetically unlikely, yet more so when one realizes that it would have to have come from a fifth-/sixth-century form more like Eardachar, with the guttural 'ch' pronounced as in 'Christmas' rather than 'cherish'. Besides, there are perfectly reasonable Celtic etymologies for Arthur, based on the word *arto* (bear), such as 'Arto-rigos' (Bear-King) or, less plausibly, 'Arto-uiros' (Bear-Man). If one wanted a 'Germanic' hero who might be Arthur, one who splashed around, receiving swords from 'ladies' in lakes before dying heroically in the face of the treachery of his household, then the candidate would be Beowulf, whose name— 'Bee-wolf'—means 'bear'. I am not seriously proposing this!

King Arthur was Scottish

There certainly was a historical, Scottish Arthur. He was Artuir, son of King Áedán mac Gabráin of Dalriada. We know nothing about him beyond what Adomnán's *Life of Saint Columba* tells us, written almost a hundred years after Artuir's death. The information could, however, come from an earlier Life written by Adomnán's predecessor in the 630s or 640s, of which Adomnán includes an excerpt. Artuir, says Adomnán, was killed, alongside his brother Eochaid Find, in a battle won by his father against the Miathi. The Miathi are presumably the Maetae recorded in early Roman geographies and thus another of the groups subsumed within the Pictish confederacies reasserting their identity in the post-imperial centuries (see Chapter 11). Artuir's death must have occurred before Áedán's in c.608 because Columba's pre-diction was that he would not succeed his father as king. Thus he was never a king in his own right, though that need not matter, given the HB's description of Arthur. Artuir mac Áedáin *might* be the historical figure behind Arthurian legend but, even if he was, there is nothing else we can say about him. Attempts to do so involve joining the dots from all sorts of snippets, inconsistently cherry-picked from later (second-millennium) sources, whether later Celtic hagiography and folklore or Arthurian romance (French or otherwise), mostly with no relationship to each other, and breaking just about every rule in the book of sound historical methodology. There are even technical problems about whether Artuir is the same name as the Old Welsh *Arthur*, which is what appears in Y *Gododdin, HB,* and the *Welsh Annals.* If one of the late sixth-century Arthurs was the prototype for the legendary warrior, there are no good reasons for choosing which one it was. The only reason to select Artuir, ahead of the others, is that he features in one (single) other written reference. Note too that the earliest securely datable reference to Arthur locates his legend (apart from a number of places that are unknown and unknowable) in the Anglo-Welsh marches. One of Arthur's unidentifiable battles (The Caledonian Forest) is presumably in modern Scotland but another, *Urbs Legionis,* must be in England or Wales. There is, incidentally, no first-millennium source that associates Arthur with Cornwall.

These aren't the druids you're looking for: the pagan King Arthur

That King Arthur was a pagan is commonly stated in novels, pseudo-history, and other New Age Arthurian material. There is no reason to suppose that any historical fifth- or sixth-century Arthur was anything other than a Christian. Two of the three first-millennium sources that mention Arthur explicitly describe him as Christian. The other, Y *Gododdin,* contains precious little by way of religious elements of any sort. Its Christian elements, according to Koch, are later additions. Some of Koch's argument turns on how you understand an ambiguous phrase that might refer to communion, though. Whichever way you read it, as 'communion' or 'a victor's share', the argument easily becomes circular. In any case, Koch rightly states that this has no necessary bearing on the poet's religion or that of his subjects. The western Roman Empire, including Britain, had been heavily Christianized (see Chapter 11) and Gildas did not see paganism, unlike heresy, as a problem with the British rulers of his day. Even Artuir mac Áedáin is mentioned in a Christian context, being part of an army prayed for by St Columba and his monks.

Boozing with Arthur: plotting Arthurian campaigns from pub names

Not very long ago, one Arthurian pseudo-history proposed—and I'm not making this up, I assure you—that the campaigns of Arthur's cavalry (for which see above) could be plotted from the distribution of public houses with the name 'The Black Horsemen'. Presumably this is where Arthur and his troops stopped off for a pint on their way to fight the Saxons, so memorably that, centuries later, when these pubs were named their visit was still remembered. I mention this simply because, out of all the mad theories about King Arthur that I have read, this is probably the craziest and, for that reason, my favourite.

That seems like a convenient place to end this list, as most modern populist pseudo-historical theories about the historical Arthur seem to require you to have had a skin-full of alcohol or other mind-enhancing substance in order to believe them. Thus far, in this book I have set out the evidence, written and archaeological, that exists, how it was used in traditional narratives, and how it is currently employed in academic debate. In Part IV I will propose some new ways of thinking, which, when taken with the preceding chapters, will, I hope, help you into a more, shall we say, sober way of thinking about an era that is fascinating, exciting, and important, whether or not anyone called Arthur happened to have lived during it.

PART IV
New Worlds?

Hey, what did I hear you say?
You know, it doesn't have to be that way.

THE BLOW MONKEYS

8

The Dark Matter
of Arthur

Changing the Framework

Leslie Alcock used to tell a joke at his own expense. One of his favourite typos, he said, came in a bibliography which rendered *Arthur's Britain* as *Author's Britain*. Over the past seven chapters I have attempted to give an accurate account of the evidence available for fifth- and sixth-century Britain and the ways in which specialists study it. I have presented the debates and the positions adopted within them as fairly as possible and set out what seems to be the current consensus (where there is consensus), whether or not I agree. Thus I hope that, although few academics would present the period in these terms today, these chapters constitute a reliable picture of 'Arthur's Britain' as seen in 2012, forty years after Alcock's book appeared. In the next five chapters I move towards 'Author's Britain'. This is a personal essay on how we might rethink post-imperial Britain. Put another way, if you want to know what the evidence is for this period, what problems are involved in its use, what sorts of arguments academic researchers make, and why, therefore, the stories told in modern pseudo-histories about Arthur and his world could not be much further from the 'truth' they purport to represent, you can stop reading here. To reconsider this 'world of Arthur', read on. Be advised, though, that what follows by no means represents accepted academic views; much of it would widely be regarded as controversial.

The present debates about the archaeological evidence, while based upon thorough knowledge of data and sophisticated investigation of sites, suffer from several problems. In this part I draw more attention to these, their effects, and why they should be redressed. I also propose some new ways of thinking about this period which, to a limited extent, will restore something of an 'Arthurian context'. The principal contentions will be as follows:

1. That we must rethink the framework within which we see the period, rejecting the idea that it should be seen in terms of invading Saxons against defending Britons.

2. That the event described by Gildas concerning the arrival of some Saxon federates, which eventually became the standard story of 'the coming of the Saxons', should be placed in the fourth rather than the fifth century.

3. That we must revise our thinking about the mechanics of the Anglo-Saxon migration away from seeing it in simple terms of movement from one (eastern) side of the North Sea to the other, towards viewing the migration in the context of a North Sea 'cultural zone', wherein information and cultural influence passed in both directions around all the regions bordering that sea.

4. That we should consider fifth- and sixth-century British politics in a broader European context, as operating within quite large units.

I will open the door to the historian's 'laboratory' a little wider than has been done thus far and discuss the use of written and archaeological material in slightly more detail. I hope that this will be useful and interesting, especially for readers who are not historians or archaeologists by profession. This might clarify and to some extent demystify the process of historical analysis. It will, however, make for some rather technical sections, which I hope the reader will tolerate.

The tyranny of a narrative

The Arthur of modern pseudo-histories fights at the head of defending Roman Britons (or Romano-Britons, or sub-Roman Britons) against invading barbarian Anglo-Saxons. The era's political history continues to be envisaged in these bipolar terms: 'Britons' on one side; 'Saxons' on the other. Archaeological data are still sifted to detect who (and where) were Britons and who (and where) were Anglo-Saxons. High politics, in the traditional Arthurian view, are a bit like the First and Second World Wars, with a front-line moving steadily from east to west (Figure 8.1). This can be seen very clearly in old (and not so old) illustrations of the coming of the Anglo-Saxons. The Anglo-Saxons storm ashore from their keels (ships)—sometimes they wade towards the land in lines, their ships looking all too clearly like landing craft. (We could also cite the scene of Anglo-Saxon landings from the 2004 film *King Arthur*; tanks and aircraft are just about all that is missing!) Meanwhile, the Britons attempt to repel them from behind rocky barricades. Leaving aside whether or not such an explicitly military reading of Anglo-Saxon settlement is warranted, the absurdity of this scenario is soon realized. Did the post-imperial Britons really line their army up along the shore, just waiting (like some fifth-century version of Field Marshal Rommel) for this Anglo-Saxon D-Day? (Of course it is actually D-Day in reverse, because the 'English' are really 'Germans'.) Would any Anglo-Saxon leader be daft enough to try and get his men ashore at precisely the point where the British army was waiting? It all seems very unlikely.

This example is extreme but not out of place. It is interesting to note how many books on Arthur are penned by retired military men, and just how martial the focus on Arthur is; 'the campaigns of Arthur'

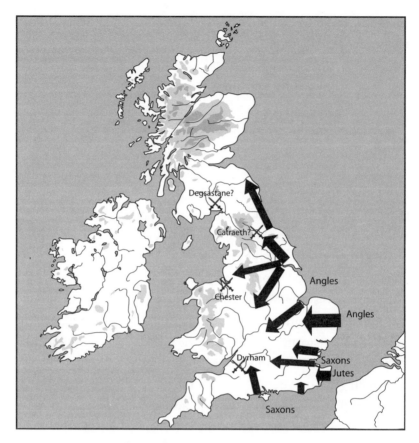

Figure 8.1 The Anglo-Saxon invasion: a traditional image

is not an unknown book title. The spread of Anglo-Saxon material culture was long mapped to locate the 'front-line' of Anglo-Saxon settlement at a particular time. It was thought that forty years of peace after the battle of Mount Badon were visible in a lack of west-wards spread of Anglo-Saxon cemeteries for a generation or so after 500 (this is mistaken for many reasons). In the late 1980s academic archaeologists still thought that areas reserved to the Britons by treaty (reservations?) were detectable from gaps in the spread of putatively Anglo-Saxon cemeteries. In the first decade of the twenty-first century academics continued to claim that British political areas could be identified from such cartographic blanks. Before anything else, we must consider whether there is any reason to think about the fifth century in these binary, ethnic terms.

It is crucial to remember that this view of fifth-century history was created by the early medieval British historians encountered in Chapters 2 and 4: Bede and the authors of the *History of the Britons*, the *Anglo-Saxon Chronicle*, and the *Welsh Annals*. It is also vital to recall that each writer had specific reasons for painting the fifth-century past in these colours. For Bede, attempting to correct what he saw as declining religious and moral standards in his day, it was important that the English had conquered Britain from sinful Britons. The authors of the *HB* and the *Welsh Annals* both wrote at moments when the Welsh were under threat from English expansion. Finally, the idea of an invasion, ousting the Britons and justifying control over territory, was very important in the West Saxon dynasty's ideology in building a unified kingdom of England.

This early medieval picture of post-imperial Britain has nevertheless held sway ever since; at least in implicit and unconscious fashion, it continues to do so. It begins, however, to look decidedly unreliable when analysed critically. Early medieval British political history, when reported in more or less trustworthy records after about 600, rarely (outside an unusual period in the mid- to late tenth century) looks like a neat struggle between Welsh or Britons on one side and English on the other. We more often find the Welsh fighting the Welsh and the English fighting the English. Sometimes allies are summoned from neighbouring kingdoms of a different ethnicity; Anglo-Welsh confederacies fight other temporary alliances of English and Welsh. The seventh century has the best examples. When Mercian Anglo-Saxons under King Penda fought a titanic struggle against the Northumbrian Anglo-Saxons they almost always did so in alliance with the Welsh, earlier perhaps as the junior and later as the senior partner. Penda's Northumbrian enemies (Edwin, Osric, Eanfrith,

Oswald, and Oswy) all spent time as exiles at British, Irish, or Pictish courts. When they regained their thrones, they might well have done so with the aid of their former hosts. Some kings of non-English realms were of Anglo-Saxon birth or products of Anglo-Welsh (or Anglo-Scottish, or Anglo-Pictish) marriages. One recent history discussed politics in terms of northern and southern political arenas rather than as 'Anglo-Saxon' and 'Celtic' zones. British political history between 600 and 900 provides little or no reason to suppose that the period 400–600 saw *the* Britons fighting *the* English according to the 'moving front' model discussed above. Alternatively, if our method was to extrapolate from the period within which we *can* study British political history in some detail to that within which we *cannot*, we would not end up with a picture of this kind of warfare dominating the fifth and sixth centuries. A context for the traditional Arthur figure would not be established.

The obvious riposte to this argument is to draw attention to the important changes that occurred around AD 600, and point out that we cannot simply project seventh- to ninth-century situations back onto the fifth and sixth centuries. This would be absolutely right, but it would not prove that there *was* a simple bipartite struggle between Britons and Saxons in the earlier era; it would just establish that the outlines of history after 600 provide no secure guide to those before that date. We would end up where we started, with no idea what happened in British history between 410 and 597. Yet, the thrust of our analysis is gradually reducing our grounds for believing the traditional picture of post-imperial Britain. That image comes from entirely unreliable written sources, whose picture was determined by the political and ideological agendas of the times when they were written; we cannot even take later history and use it to support the outlines of this traditional image. We can adopt the line taken with the Welsh poetry and argue that the written sources' image of the fifth and sixth centuries is an invention; it didn't pertain when it was created and never had done.

We can, however, follow another tack and argue from analogy with the far better documented contemporary European mainland. This might provide clues about what the outlines of fifth- and sixth-century British political history could have been like. Indeed a lack of awareness of fifth-century mainland Europe bedevils most writing about immediately post-imperial Britain. It is commonly believed that this period saw the Roman Empire fighting off hordes of invading barbarians. In other words, the situation across the Channel was much the same as that traditionally envisaged for 'Arthur's Britain': Romans versus barbarians; Britons versus Saxons. It is, however, slowly and steadily (in spite of increasingly shrill rearguard actions by adherents of the traditional view) becoming clear that this was generally *not* what the fifth century was like in western Europe. The end of Roman Britain, discussed at the start of Chapter 2, hints at the reality of the situation. Even during severe barbarian attacks, the first priority of imperial commanders was, and remained, dealing with *Roman* rivals. In the first decade of the fifth century, in spite of large numbers of Vandals, Alans, and Sueves crossing into Gaul and then Spain, or the rebellious Gothic army in Italy, the imperial leaders' principal activities hardly concerned barbarians. It is only modern surmise that Constantine 'III' penned the invaders into northern Gaul in 407/8. Contemporary accounts can suggest that he took little or no notice of the barbarians. He certainly made no move against them in 409–11. Like his opponents, he was more concerned with securing control of the Empire. Barbarians could always be mopped up afterwards. In Italy in 409, the Roman senate itself joined Alaric's Goths in raising a usurper, Priscus Attalus. Such non-Roman allies occur repeatedly during the numerous usurpations and rebellions of Honorius' reign.

The prioritization of Roman threats had long been a pattern in Roman politics. Barbarians were enlisted as allies and during civil war it was not unknown for Roman leaders to pay them to attack, and thus distract, their imperial rivals. The army recruited large numbers of troops from beyond the frontiers; it always had done. Furthermore, the army itself had adopted consciously barbarian identities during the fourth century. There was thus nothing very strange about either the involvement of barbarian allies in Roman civil wars or imperial commanders deciding to leave barbarian raiders as something to sort out after the more important issue of their Roman opponents had been resolved.

This pattern remained for the rest of the western Empire's history. Regional aristocratic factions made common cause with armies stationed in their areas—forces increasingly made up of barbarians as the taxation and recruiting base shrank. None sought separation; like their predecessors they wanted to control the imperial court and thus the whole Empire. The actions of the Goths of Toulouse, for example, are entirely in line with those of the Aquitanian nobility right through to the late fifth century and even beyond—given that Gallo-Roman 'senators' fought for the Goths against the invading Franks in 507. The higher echelons of the Roman aristocracy in the Rhône valley were, from the very start, in cahoots with the Burgundians stationed there from the 440s. And so on. We must also remember that these 'barbarians' were, increasingly, not invaders from outside, but people who had largely grown up (and usually been born) within the imperial territories and who formed armies stationed by the Empire's government in the areas in question. The Vandals were the key exception, seizing North Africa in the 430s. Even here most of the 'Vandals' who took Carthage in 430—even Geiseric, one of the fifth century's arch-barbarians—were born and grew up in Gaul or Spain. Furthermore, after 442 their occupation of Africa was recognized by treaty and the Vandal leader was linked to the imperial house by marriage. In spite of their bad press, the Vandals soon attracted Roman Africans to their cause and formed another faction in imperial politics They became an especially dangerous faction after the assassination of Valentinian

III (455), whose daughter was married to Geiseric's son. This event pushed the Vandals' faction out into the cold. The problem was that none of these factions ever managed to defeat all the others and achieve its objective: control of the whole western Empire.

Further, when Valentinian III was assassinated, the legitimate male line of the imperial dynasty came to an end. Belonging to the imperial royal house had been a trump card that all accepted, especially in the second quarter of the fifth century. With the demise of the Valentinianic-Theodosian dynasty, which had governed the Empire since 364, a further problem came to the fore. No faction (with the possible exception of the Vandals') could claim a legitimate right to rule that its rivals would accept, short of being forced to. By the 470s it became apparent that even controlling the heart of the Empire, Italy itself, did not bring the material or ideological resources necessary for effective offensives against rivals for power. In this stand-off, regional Romano-barbarian factions crystallized into the post-imperial kingdoms: the Franks in northern Gaul, the Goths in south-ern Gaul and northern Spain, the Burgundians in south-eastern Gaul, and the Vandals in Africa. Italy fell under the control of its own regional army, whose commander, Odoacer, declared himself king. Much of Spain saw no clear winners in the struggle for local power by 500. Instead there was a variety of contending powers: a Suevic king-dom in the north-west, the Goths of Toulouse, extending their authority into the peninsula by the 490s, and various shadowy local rulers, principally of Roman origin (bishops, local senates, and so on), but sometimes in association with 'barbarian' soldiers. Again, one must remember that most of these 'barbarians' were actually born and raised inside the Empire and were thus in many ways as Roman as anyone else.

This has taken us far from the shores of post-imperial Britain but the digression is vital. It shows that the norm for fifth-century politics was *not* warfare between defending Romans or 'Romano-provincials'

(Romano-Britons, Romano-Gauls, Hispano-Romans, etc.) and invading barbarians but struggles between factions, usually of Romans allied with barbarians. If the traditional 'moving front' picture of post-imperial Britain is right, with Romano-Britons on one side and barbarian Anglo-Saxons on the other, Britain would be the only part of the fifth-century Roman world to see this sort of conflict. But such a claim to uniqueness would have no basis. Its foundations lie in history created to suit later political agendas. The picture of 'Britons versus Saxons' did not even pertain when those sources were written. This insight allows us to reassess the most important aspects of post-imperial Britain.

Vitally, it permits us to sidestep the issue of Romano-Barbarian 'collaboration'. If one is held prisoner by the traditional narrative one might wonder why the 'natives' would 'cosy up' to the invaders, or decry those who did as traitors or 'Quislings'.[1] If one sees the regional factional alliances of 'barbarian' armed forces and 'Roman' aristocrats as working within the frameworks of imperial politics, to attempt to attain control of and recreate the Empire on the fourth-century model, and especially when one sees that the driving forces in such alliances were as often as not the Romans rather than the barbarians, then such ways of seeing the provincials' activities, so obviously coloured by experiences of the Second World War, become quite irrelevant.

Gildas and 'civil war'

Escaping the old framework requires us to look again, in some detail, at two of the traditional narrative's principal supports. The change of perspective enabled by the preceding discussion allows a potentially

---

[1] Since 1940, this name has frequently been given to members of collaborationist national governments in the service of occupying powers, drawing its name from Dr Vidkun Quisling, leader of the pro-Nazi government of occupied Norway between 1940 and 1945.

significant re-reading of Gildas' narrative. This concerns the sides involved in the war that culminated in the siege of Mount Badon. Since the eighth century it has been assumed that this conflict was between 'Britons' and 'Saxons' but Gildas does not say so. Studying the convoluted 'Badon sentence' (discussed in Chapters 2 and 4) in its context reveals the following sequence:

1. Rallying of the Britons under Ambrosius, and their defeat of the Saxons (ch. 25.2–3);
2. The war that led to Badon lasted forty-three years and a month (ch. 26.1);
3. Gildas famously says that the cities are depopulated and the land laid waste, 'external wars having ceased, but not civil ones' (ch. 26.2).

You can read this in two ways. Traditionally, the 'Badon war' was a continuation of Ambrosius' Saxon war and the rest of chapter 26 is a commentary on what happened *after* Badon: wars between Britons broke out. Alternatively, however, the division between chapters 25 and 26 might be more significant. In *this* reading the Saxon war *stopped* with Ambrosius' victory, but this was followed by a forty-four-year war between, as Gildas puts it, 'citizens' (*cives*) and 'enemies' (*hostes*; also called rascals: *furciferes*)—barbarians or Saxons are not actually mentioned. The second verse of chapter 26 thus comments on the first: external wars had stopped (with Ambrosius' victory) but civil wars hadn't (that is forty-four years of strife up to Mount Badon), laying waste the country. In Roman political vocabulary an opposition between citizens and enemies need not mean one between *Roman* citizens and *barbarian* enemies; it could mean one between loyal citizens and rebels. There's no decisive way of choosing between these readings; both are possible if one stops reading *On the Ruin...* in the light of interpretations of it made from the eighth century onwards. The latter 'civil war' interpretation should be retained as a possibility. It would be entirely in line with the general course of fifth-century political history.

Arthur's battles revisited

Freeing our thinking from the constraints of the 'Britons versus Saxons' framework allows us to see Gildas' story more in terms of what it actually says, casting doubt on one support for seeing the defining feature of fifth-century British history as a conflict between defending Roman Britons and invading Anglo-Saxons. The other major support—although we have already seen that it is a pretty weak one—is the *Historia Brittonum*'s discussion of the 'Twelve Battles of Arthur', evidently a long war between the Saxons and the Britons, united under the great warrior. Chapter 4 discussed the current state of play concerning this famous chapter (56) of the *HB*, leaving its status somewhat in limbo. Is it a genuine fragment of a lost poem, reflecting Arthur's actual battles, or is it part of a later poem, grouping famous battles around a mythical or semi-mythical figure? Or is it not even that: simply an early ninth-century Welsh composition by the *HB*'s author? I believe that this last possibility is correct: the *HB*'s list *does not* represent any sort of lost Welsh poem. If you have read the 'battle list' before, the version in Chapter 2 might have seemed unfamiliar. I included the first and last sentences, about the Saxons, which are almost always left out, making the 'lost poem' interpretation more attractive. There is no textual reason to omit these sentences, which immediately renders the 'lost poem' reading less plausible. If you read them closely you will note that they are quite similar. In both we hear of the Saxons' growth in numbers in England, with rulers coming from elsewhere. The first tells us about the foundation of the southernmost Saxon kingdom (Kent) and in the last we hear of the creation of the northernmost, Bernicia (Northumbria's northern half). This south/north parallelism in the *HB* has already been mentioned: Vortimer's siege of the Saxons on Thanet in Kent (the far south) and Urien's siege of the Bernicians on Lindisfarne (the far north) are very similar. The last sentence of chapter 56 'mirrors' the first.

Early medieval writers frequently used a 'mirroring' stylistic device, known as 'chiasmus' or 'chiastic patterning'. The name comes from the Greek letter Chi (X) which can be seen as two halves meeting at a crux (or cross). Passages were structured to match each other on either side of the crux containing the—literally—*crucial* message. This clue allows a re-examination of the structure of the passages between the 'bracketing' statements about Saxons. It might simply be that the 'battle list' is itself the crucial passage, enclosed within these mirroring opening and closing comments. That would allow us to retain the idea that the list itself is translated from a poem, more or less intact. However one views its historicity, it would still be a discrete, separate element.

A close reading destroys this possibility, however. The whole passage is chiastic. It begins with the description of the founding of Kent (32 words in the Latin text) before introducing Arthur and describing him as *dux bellorum* (16 words). A four-sentence, 45-word section detailing the first seven battles of Arthur follows, before we reach a long sentence (47 words) on the eighth battle (of *Castellum Guinnion*). This long sentence is the crux of the passage. After that we have four more sentences (44 words) on the ninth to twelfth battles, ending with the word Arthur. Following that is a brief summing up comment (13 words) about Arthur, describing him as *in omnibus bellis victor* ('victor in all battles'). Finally we have the concluding comment about the foundation of the most northerly of the English realms: Bernicia.

The passage can be set out, slightly differently, as in Figure 8.2, using the usual notation, where 'A¹' indicates the 'mirror' of 'A'. Apart from a slight imbalance between sections A and A¹, the elements match in length as well as subject matter. This is unlikely to be

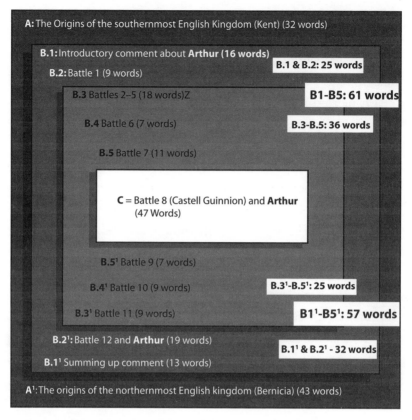

Figure 8.2 The structure of *HB* chapter 56

coincidence. The three sections about the battles are of almost exactly the same length. This permits vital conclusions. There is no structural border between the opening and closing passages about Saxons and the section about Arthur's battles. They are all seamlessly part of the same composition. Given the careful balancing of the elements—in Latin—this *must* mean that the *whole* chapter was composed by the *HB*'s author. As this passage is the 'hinge' in moving from the *HB*'s history of southern wars against the Saxons to the account of such wars in the north, its layout makes further sense, embedding it further within the *HB*'s structure and underlining that the whole is a single composition.

There are curious numerological elements too. The whole passage is 240 words long (twenty times twelve, twelve being the number of battles); the figure of 960 for the men laid low in a single charge is four times the 240 words of the passage (or eighty times twelve). And so on.

The middle eleven sentences *cannot*, therefore, be a simple translation of a lost Welsh poem. The analysis shows that, wherever he got them from, the author could only find *nine* battles: Glein, Dubglas, Bassas, *Cat Coit Celidon*, Guinnion, 'castle of the legion', Tribruit, Agned [or Bregoin], and Badon. Dubglas is made into four battles and given a location in 'Linnuis', and the Caledonian Forest has its name in Welsh as well as Latin to add sixteen words and balance the first section about battles (B.2–B.5) with the last (B.5^1–B.2^1). The extra battles at Dubglas also bring the count up to a more numerologically significant twelve. Without that lengthening we would have, overall, four battles, then *Castell Guinnion*, and then four more battles.

A key revelation is that the important battle for the *HB*'s composer was not Badon but *Castell Guinnion*, to which the author devotes as many words as to the whole preceding group of seven (or four) battles or the succeeding group of three. If we knew what, when, or where *Castell Guinnion* was we might understand the whole passage. Sadly we don't. Even if we have discovered the key we still can't find the door! The title the author of the *HB* gives Arthur, *dux bellorum* (leader of the battles), is similar to Constantius of Lyon's description of St Germanus before the Alleluia Victory, *dux proelii* (leader of the battle). This must be seen in the light of the Christian emphasis laid upon Arthur's campaigns.

The *HB* was composed in a period of English aggression against the Welsh. According to the *Anglo-Saxon Chronicle*, in 830 (the year after the *HB*'s composition), King Ecgberht of Wessex (Alfred the Great's grandfather) 'led an army among the Welsh and reduced them all to humble submission to him'. The *Welsh Annals* make no mention of Ecgberht's campaign. It might well be that by 'the Welsh' the

Chronicle meant Cornwall ('West Wales') rather than 'North Wales'. Even so, the rumblings of all this might have been heard in 828–9 when, again according to the *Chronicle*, Ecgberht conquered Mercia and received the submission of the Northumbrians.

The *Chronicle*'s account of Ecgberht's supremacy is demonstrably questionable. If he ever ruled Mercia directly, it was not for long, and indeed the Mercians seem to have regained their supremacy by the later 830s. Nonetheless, in 828–9 a Welsh writer might have found it politically advantageous to compose a history in which the Britons united under a great, divinely favoured general who smote the Saxons at all points of the compass. In this context, perhaps, its author used the legendary figure of 'Arthur the Soldier', about whom he clearly knew, as the 'wonders of Britain' section makes clear, as the peg on which to hang these battles. He is a rousing hero, someone to emulate, employed (in this precise context perhaps even invented) to encourage the ruler of Gwynedd to take up arms and lead the kings of the Welsh against the English. Arthur's non-regal status would not be coincidental. Merfyn 'the Freckled' took the throne at the end of a period of internecine strife, probably violently, and his claim to the throne was dubious. He was the first king not to claim descent from the direct, male royal line of Gwynedd. The *HB* thus seems to be stressing that you don't need to be of royal stock to lead the Britons against the hated English. In this light, the 'battles of Arthur' *might* be mock-antiquarian names for important places in early ninth-century politics, rather than corrupted but genuine names of actual fifth- or sixth-century battles. It is incontestable that if there is an historical core (or cores) to the *HB*'s list we can neither identify nor know what the author has done to it, not least in translating it (or them) into Latin.

That said, let me underline that my analysis doesn't show that our author's list of eight battles did not come from a single source; it does *not* prove that there never were any battles with the names given in the

1. The Landing of the Jutes at Ebbsfleet. A traditional image of the coming of the Anglo-Saxons.

2. A modern image of the historical Arthur. Angus McBride's evocative depiction of post-imperial British warriors.

3. Peter Dennis' reconstruction of the British hill-fort at Dinas Emrys in Wales.

4. The 'capital' of Dalriada. The Scottish stronghold of Dunadd.

5. The Pictish fort at Dundurn at the head of Strathearn.

6. A more modern image of the coming of the Saxons. Angus McBride's picture of 'Sutton Hoo Man' (centre) and other early English warriors.

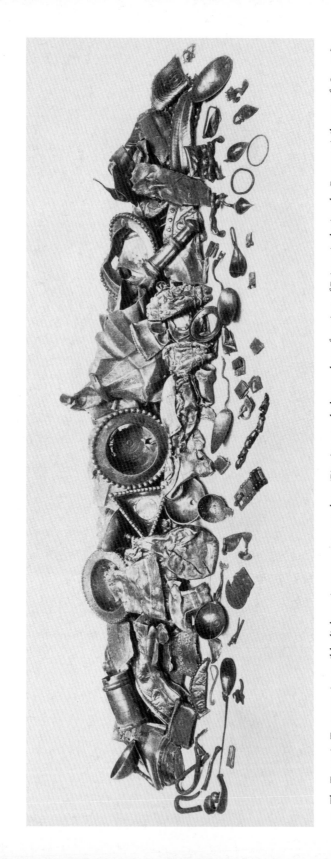

7. The Traprain Treasure. A possible diplomatic payment to southern 'Picts' to watch the northern frontiers of Britannia during the Roman civil wars of 383–413?

8. By South Cadbury was that Camelot? The Iron-Age hill-fort of South Cadbury, partly excavated by Leslie Alcock.

9. A classic object in Salin's Style II from around the end of the 'World of Arthur'. The reliquary buckle from Sutton Hoo Mound 1.

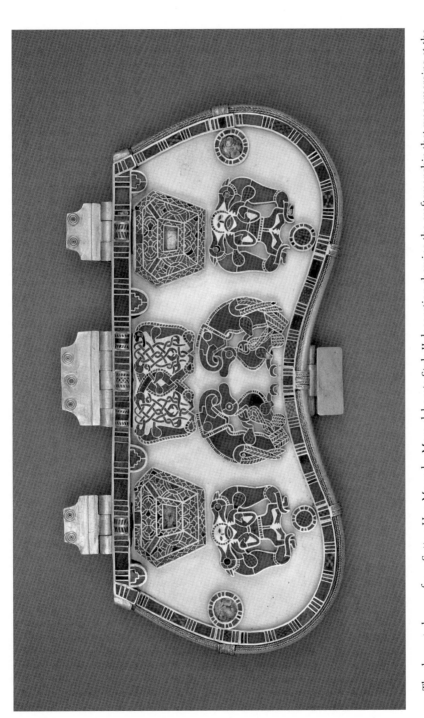

10. The decorated purse from Sutton Hoo Mound 1. More elaborate Style II decoration showing the craftsmanship that was emerging at the end of our period.

11. Tintagel. A fortified promontory fort which was linked into an exchange network that reached as far as the eastern Mediterranean. Tintagel later acquired many Arthurian associations.

12. A defence against the Saxons? Or a fortified depot safeguarding Roman Britain's crucial links with the rest of the Empire? The mighty walls of the 'Saxon Shore' fort at Richborough (Kent).

13. Glastonbury Tor. Philip Rahtz excavated here 'at the wrong time'.

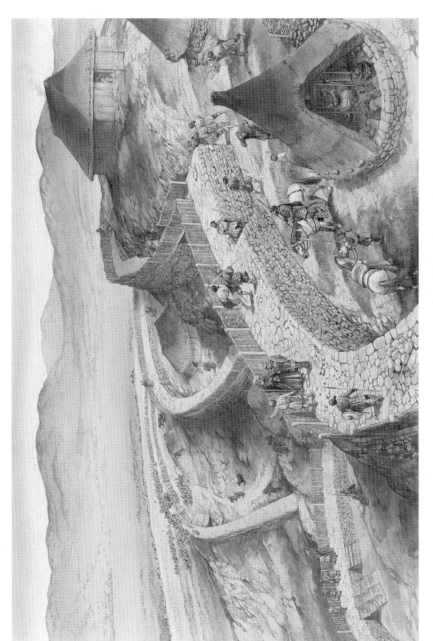

14. Peter Dennis' reconstruction of Dundurn under attack.

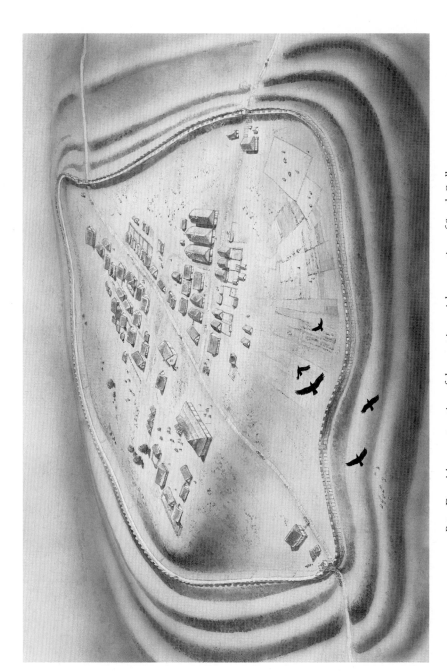

15. Peter Dennis' reconstruction of the post-imperial occupation of South Cadbury.

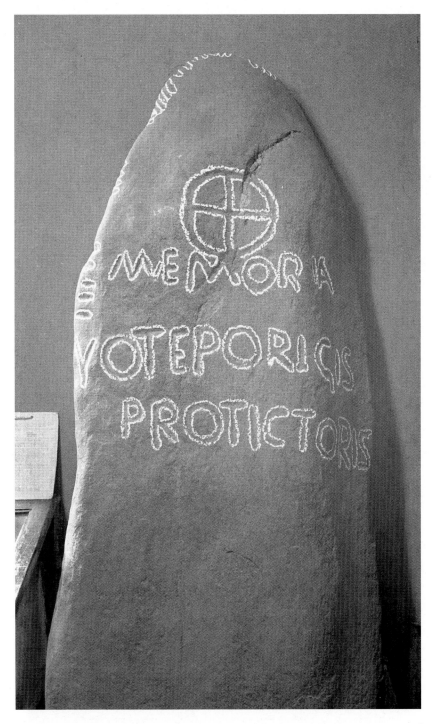

16. The Castell Dwyran Stone. Possibly a memorial for the King Vortiporius 'Tyrant of the Demetae', mentioned by Gildas.

17. The Pillar of Eliseg. A last trace of the traditions of 'Good King Vortigern'?

HB. It does *not* demonstrate that no such battles were fought by someone called Arthur. It doesn't definitively explain why our author, even if cobbling the list together from various sources ascribing the battles to other warlords, decided to attribute them all to someone called Arthur or why this figure was so important to his message. There is no doubt that Arthur *is* of crucial significance within the chapter.

I can offer one life-line to pro-Arthurian optimists. My analysis suggests that in writing this passage the *HB* author essentially knew of nine battles, which he made up into twelve, by creating three extra battles at *Dubglas*. It lies beyond reasonable doubt that the author knew about Badon from Gildas and/or Bede and knew from them that it ought to come at or about the end of the war. He might thus have added that battle to the list. Possibly, then, our author knew of *eight* battles of Arthur, perhaps indeed from a lost list or poem about a historical Arthur. He could, however, equally well have taken them from several, diverse Welsh heroic sources with no Arthurian connection at all.

What the analysis *does* do is demolish the idea that we have here an intact, genuine snippet of a 'bardic' source. It is an early ninth-century composition and therefore—in the form that we have it—all its details and its message *must* belong to *c*.828. No argument can be securely built on *any* element of *HB* chapter 56 on the grounds that it reflects earlier tradition. We cannot get beyond our ninth-century Welsh writer to his sources, whatever they were or indeed *if* ever they were. Finally, *if* the author of the *HB* was the first to take the battle of Badon from Gildas and/or Bede and ascribe it to Arthur, then he could also have been the first to place Arthur in the post-imperial period.

Archaeology and the end of Roman Britain

A view of the fifth century in broader perspective thus renders the traditional framework unlikely; of the principal sources for the fifth century as a time of war between 'Britons' and 'Saxons', one can be read as being about internecine strife and the other demonstrated to be a ninth-century composition for political purposes. Before we dive further in the murky waters of fifth- and sixth-century British politics, there are other issues that must be re-evaluated. The first is the fate of Roman society, culture, and economics in Britain.

Chapter 5 presented the debate over the archaeology of the end of Roman Britain. Widespread evidence suggests collapse and dereliction but arguments have been put forward against this view, claiming that there was much greater continuity. In my view the evidence for cataclysmic socio-economic collapse cannot be circumvented. None of the arguments against a serious rupture is very compelling. We can take first the analogy with black earth found at Birka, used to claim that similar levels on Roman towns also reflect dense occupation. The main problem here is that the Birka black earth was filled with finds and evidence of manufacture and craftsmanship; the black earth above Roman towns typically contains only residual fragments of the last Roman pottery-types. Palaeobotanical analysis of these soils, in Britain and abroad, frequently suggests that it has the profile of scrub or waste-ground. Similarly, the 'layers' lying above the latest Roman phases at Wroxeter were sterile in terms of diagnostic artefacts. Urbanism is not a simple matter of lots of people living together in a small area; it is a pattern of relationships with other settlements. Town-dwellers must be fed and must therefore provide something in return for that food, either money or specialist manufactures or services. If it is money, where do they obtain this from? There is no trace of any production on the sites of old Roman towns. Nor is there evidence of trade, bringing in things that town-dwellers could exchange for subsistence supplies. The distribution of Mediterranean pottery arriving in western Britain is not market-based and there is, finally, no sign of coinage still being used as such. It is entirely incredible that a town could exist for 200 years and remain artefactually completely invisible. Other buildings, such as the handful of *Grubenhäuser* (sunken-featured buildings) found at Canterbury, are no different from those found on rural sites. They simply represent people living on the sites of former towns, rather than continuing urban life. There are increasing signs of continuing use of the *fora* in western British towns (Chester, Exeter), but while these might reveal the site's continuing high status, they do not convincingly demonstrate urbanism.

Otherwise the 'continuity' argument focuses on theoretical explanations for the absence of evidence. People *could* have used old coins; they *might* have continued to use old pottery (sometimes they demonstrably did). These attempts to account for silence are convoluted and unconvincing. When coinage dried up earlier in Romano-British history, the Britons minted their own, sometimes by clipping the edges off the most recent official coins and minting new, imitation ones from the metal so obtained. They did not do that in the fifth century. The sudden demise of vigorous pottery industries which, at best, now produced only a limited range of simple, undecorated types can only be explained by severe economic decline. The 'fashion' explanation for the abandonment of villas carries little conviction and the 'rejection of Rome' argument even less. For centuries previously, Roman aristocratic life had turned on the villa; for centuries afterwards western European elites tried to be as Roman as possible. If abandonment means the political 'rejection' of Rome it is odd that it was so universal. Where are the villas of those who wished to continue claiming a Roman identity? If this argument is to be believed, we have a rare example of complete political consensus. Even the more plausible variations on this argument fail to persuade. Where they could afford it (for example in Aquitaine), post-imperial elites (civic *and* military) maintained their retinues *and* their villas. However one views the problem, one cannot escape the point that the villa abandonment was produced by severe economic constraints in a period of dramatic collapse.

It is frequently suggested that Britain was not very Romanized or harboured anti-Roman feelings. This has recently been suggested on the basis of analogy with western European empires. Yet these empires lasted for much shorter periods than did the Roman Empire and were often acquired and governed very differently, with dissimilar attitudes about 'conquered' or colonized peoples. After 350 years, the survival of pre-Roman identities and cultures is unlikely, as is a continuing sense of 'colonized' and 'conquerors', given that the ruling elite and 'occupying military' of late Roman Britain must have been overwhelmingly of British extraction. The 'post-colonial' view of the post-imperial era suffers from seeing the Empire as 'withdrawing' from Britain, in a similar way to the British and French retreat from empire after the Second World War. This is quite mistaken. The changes in late Romano-British archaeology, therefore, have nothing at all to do with any lessening of Britain's Roman-ness. They seem rather to show that the British provinces were far more closely bound into the imperial edifice than had earlier been the case.

A variation on this theme suggests that post-imperial Britain was a 'failed state'. There are certainly elements within the data that suggest that the Romano-British city-districts retained their own identities. The data allow us to postulate that these *civitates* were important building blocks within post-imperial kingdoms. In that context it is likely that the inhabitants of these originally tribal administrative units might have fought each other during the centuries that concern us. None of that, however, implies a failure to incorporate the Britons into the Roman Empire, or age-old tribal hostilities simmering away until the strong hand of Roman rule was removed. As ever, the argument suffers from an ignorance of the broader imperial context. Identities based around *civitates* remained important wherever these formed the basis of imperial administration (like Gaul). Civic pride and competition between cities was a well-known dynamic by which imperial government had made itself effective. In the late and post-imperial period competition between *civitates* found new forms, such as local saints' cults and even, occasionally, different ways of measuring time. They were not always peaceful either. *Civitates* were the principal administrative units of the Merovingian Frankish kingdoms and formed the basis, as far as we can tell, for the raising of armies. In southern Gaul there are many references to the men of particular *civitates* under arms, often fighting each other. Moreover, during crises fighting between the *civitates* sometimes broke out without official, royal permission. None of this means that the peoples of Gaul had never been integrated into the Roman Empire or that the rivalry between, say, the men of Tours and those of Bourges perpetuated an age-old hostility between the Turoni and the Bituriges. The Gallic evidence that could be used to support a 'failed state' hypothesis is probably stronger than that from Roman Britain. Yet such a conclusion from it would clearly be mistaken. As the Roman government fractured in the fifth century, there was obviously a great deal at stake; it was competed for with considerable violence. To this extent, the failing state model is descriptively adequate. However, the fighting and competition were not based upon ancient enmities or hostility to Rome. Nor were they founded in separatist desires. They revolved around attempts to control the Empire on the fourth-century model.

What, then, produced Roman Britain's rapid demise? It is difficult to avoid the chronological link between this collapse and the Roman government's withdrawal from Trier to Italy from 381. The removal of the source of patronage from the north-western provinces was probably one reason for Magnus Maximus' usurpation in 383. Maximus reigned from Trier for about five years and was remembered in western sources as a good emperor, in spite of being a usurper. His memory was especially significant in Britain. After his defeat (388), the imperial court did not return to the north of Gaul. For four years it was based on the Rhône at Vienne, south of Lyon, but thereafter it moved definitively to Italy, first to Milan and then (in 402) to Ravenna.

This was, it seems, crucial to Romano-British social order. Far from being, as is often said, a peripheral region hardly touched by the Empire, fourth-century *Britannia* was inextricably bound into the imperial system. Chapter 4 described its prosperity and stability but also its aristocrats' comparatively limited wealth (except possibly along the border between the highland and lowland zones). Wealth, we saw, came from profits from providing grain (and perhaps other supplies) for the imperial Rhine army, and the state and its patronage ensured the British elite's position.

Nevertheless, the retreat of central authority to Italy need not, in itself, have had dramatic effects. However, the collapse of the young Emperor Honorius' court into internal faction-fighting and Honorius' inability when he came of age led to those holding power concentrating on ensuring that they continued to do so. The factions in Ravenna bickered with the eastern court in Constantinople. Further distractions were caused by an attack on Italy by Alaric's rebellious Gothic army in 401–2 and another Gothic invasion of Italy, from beyond the Danube, in 405. All this meant that regular government was not restored to the north-west before the 'Great Invasion' and the usurpation of Constantine 'III'. This effectively ended the old taxation system, which had not only brought coinage into Britain but had also provided the main role of the imperial bureaucracy, which maintained the social position of the British aristocracy. As taxation involved levying and transporting foodstuffs, this probably also hit the wealth of the British elite. The Roman system worked on the regular distribution and redistribution of offices, oiling the systems of patronage and precedence. With the imperial court seemingly uninterested in, or incapable of, having any effective presence in the island, the build-up of social and political tensions over a decade can readily be imagined. In this situation it is not surprising that a usurper emperor was raised, or that Gildas thought appeals for help had been sent to Rome.

If the 'Great Invasion' preceded the 406 usurpations, we can see the latter as a response to this attack. If, however, it came later, we must seek another explanation for the British army's actions. Romano-British archaeology suggests a profound socio-economic crisis from the end of the fourth century, which I have linked to a breakdown of the direct governmental authority that had become essential to social stability in Britain. Constantine 'III' did not try to make Britain independent or separate but tried to restore the fourth-century style of government in the west, ruling from Gaul. The 'Great Invasion' would thus be a last straw if it came before the usurpations, and a spur to Constantine's actions if it came later.

Constantine's attempt failed and no government was restored. In this context we must reconsider 'Honorius' Letter' and the account of the British provincials' own actions in 409–10. These have been consistently misunderstood in recent writing on the end of Roman Britain. We do not know for sure that Honorius' letter (or rescript) was sent to Britain rather than Bruttium but, if it *was*, the common interpretation of events still does not follow. We do not have the letter's actual text—only Zosimus' account of its dispatch, written in Egypt almost a century later. What the Emperor wrote might have concerned local law and order rather than large-scale strategic issues. On a couple of occasions in his troubled reign, Honorius had cause to issue rescripts, surviving in the *Theodosian Code*, compiled under his nephew Theodosius II, which temporarily waived the usual ban on citizens bearing arms so that local authorities could defend themselves against bandits or redress problems of local order. It is possible that the document Zosimus saw (or heard or read about) was like this—understandable enough in the circumstances of 410. Nonetheless, nothing in Zosimus' account gives the impression that this was a permanent solution. It is unimaginable that a Roman emperor would write to the cities of a diocese granting them independence. Nor did the Britons want that. A severe barbarian raid apparently took place in 409, mentioned by Zosimus and, possibly, the *Gallic Chronicle of 452*. After Constantine's usurpation Britain's garrison must have been tiny, leaving the island more or less defence-less—another index of how seriously the Romans really took 'the barbarian threat'. This and other defeats for Constantine 'III' and his forces spurred the Britons to expel his officials, as his empire unrav-elled (as Zosimus tells us). Now, the Britons asked the Emperor for the restoration of 'legitimist' Theodosian officials (and troops). They surely wanted the resumption of traditional management and regula-tion of government, offices, promotions, and so on. In 410 Honorius was in no position to comply, so he wrote back telling the Britons, effectively, to 'hold the fort until the relief gets through'. The ghost-document of 'Honorius' Letter' is therefore no basis to assume Roman abandonment or withdrawal, let alone some sort of Unilateral Declaration of Independence by the British *civitates* in 410. The point of this exchange of letters (assuming it took place at all) is quite the opposite: it is about the diocese of *Britanniae* ('the Britains') declaring itself part of the legitimate Roman Empire once more.

'To the legions leaving Britain for the last time to shore up a crum-bling continental empire ...' This quote, from a recent work by a very fine scholar, shows just how deeply ingrained the traditional narra-tive is. How often is the legions' movement described as a 'with-drawal', rationalized as being to defend Rome, and coupled with the date 410? Yet every element of the image is completely wrong. We know of no troop-movements from Britain to the mainland in 410. The last documented movement (in 407) took place not to 'shore up a crumbling Empire' but to win control of one in a civil war. Finally, these troops were not 'withdrawing' to defend Rome against barbar-ians but 'advancing' against other Romans.

In lowland British society this situation would clearly render the aristocracy's position more precarious. Without the Empire support-ing its status and privileges, or providing order within the class, competition for local authority heated up. In the 390s the Britons had already turned to other means of establishing political ascendance. Bishop Victricius of Rouen visited the island to resolve a dispute over correct religious belief. The accusation of heresy was, we have seen, a means of denigrating political opponents that raised its head more than once later in the fifth century, as the breakdown of authority gathered pace. The aristocracy was compelled to withdraw to its local communities to maintain support and position against rivals. Unsurprisingly towns, no longer necessary nodes of imperial governance and politics, withered. As support had to be bought in gifts and as military retinues became necessary, the surplus remaining in the local elite's hands dwindled. What was left was insufficient to maintain elaborate dwellings, let alone support craft specialists, tradesmen, or organized industries. The result was the archaeologically visible meltdown. In the highland areas, though, a quite different set of circumstances pertained, to which we shall return.

East to west? (1)

One final element of the 'tyrannical' traditional narrative remains to be briefly considered. It looks like its most reasonable component, too: the assumption that Saxon settlement spread gradually from east to west. However, if one looks at the creation of barbarian kingdoms elsewhere, we might wonder whether this assumption is as natural as it at first seems. Rather than spreading their territory slowly to the south-west, the Goths, from north of the Danube, found themselves in Aquitaine by 418, with no Gothic territories between there and their homelands. The Vandals who crossed the Rhine in 405/6 were in Spain by 409 and eventually created a kingdom in Africa in the 430s. These, it could reasonably be objected, were rather different migrations from that of the Anglo-Saxons, so let us look at the Saxons' Frankish neighbours. The Frankish

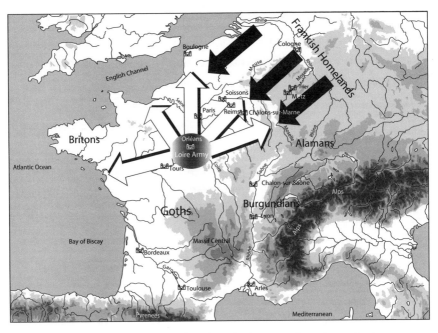

Figure 8.3 The Frankish political takeover of northern Gaul

conquest of northern Gaul has long been seen in similar terms to those of the Anglo-Saxon expansion into Britain, as a 'moving front', in this case progressing steadily from north-east to south-west. This was certainly part of the equation. However, contemporary accounts show that Frankish troops were active on the Loire and around Paris by the 450s. These were led by the family that ended up creating and ruling the Frankish kingdom in Gaul: the Merovingians. A crucial reason for their success was doubtless their command of this Frankish force in Roman service and their control of the more prosperous, southern regions of the Paris Basin. Northern Gaul was therefore quite likely absorbed by the Franks from two directions (Figure 8.3). A military source with strong Roman connections spread control northwards from the Loire while other Franks, often relatives of those on the Loire, were drawn southwards and west-wards across the Rhine into the political twilight zone of northern Gaul. This is a model we should remember when reconsidering the other defining element of the usual framework for post-imperial lowland Britain: the coming of the Anglo-Saxons.

9

Rethinking the Anglo-Saxon Migration and Settlement (1)

When Did the Anglo-Saxons Come to Britain?

ಶ⧓ಬ

This chapter can open with a simple statement: there was an Anglo-Saxon migration. Saying so might hardly seem worth the effort but, as we have seen, some have argued that there wasn't, or that hardly any Anglo-Saxons came to Britain. Unfortunately the debate over the Anglo-Saxon migration has all too often been characterized by extreme silliness and sloppy thinking on *both* sides.

Migrations do not always (or indeed often) show up especially well archaeologically. Objects cannot move without people to transport them, but they can do so in many ways without people permanently changing residence. People can alter dress fashions to ape those of another region. Burial customs and artistic or architectural styles can spread into other areas without permanent population movement. On the other hand, large numbers of people can migrate but adopt the material culture and customs of their new home, rendering their migration archaeologically invisible. For example, in the first four centuries AD many thousands of people moved from *barbaricum* to serve and settle in the Roman Empire but left almost no archaeological trace. That which they did leave is entirely Roman in form: their names on otherwise typical Roman tombstones. So, some archaeological evidence claimed to prove migration is nothing of the sort, but there is no reason why migrations should leave any archaeological trace anyway.

Yet, the movement of people from the coastal regions of Germany and Denmark is just about the *only* fifth- and sixth-century western European migration which is—indisputably—attested archaeologically. That, however, leaves a series of trickier and considerably more important questions. When did the migration take place? Are all the cultural changes that occurred in the fifth-century British lowlands proof of migration? Does migration itself *explain* the changes? What explains the migration? Above all, given what was said about fifth-century politics in Chapter 8, is the continuing archaeological search for 'Britons' and 'Saxons' not in fact missing the point completely?

When did the Saxons come to Britain?

The first question to reconsider is the date of the migration. Archaeological traces of Anglo-Saxon presence in lowland Britain begin to appear around 430 and most commentators have extrapolated from this that the Anglo-Saxons' arrival in Britain took place at that time. This conclusion looks logical enough but it doesn't necessarily follow. An important insight during the last thirty years has been that the archaeological record isn't produced just by chance. In its own way it is just as much an expression of ideas as the written sources, even if those ideas might be expressed subconsciously through use as well as through design, manufacture, or construction and even if they cannot often be recovered as clearly from this evidence. When people build a house, its layout tells us much about ideas of privacy or communal living. Modern building regulations inform us about our society's views on privacy, public health, hygiene, and many other things. Even random-looking rubbish disposal conforms to social norms or ideas. Costume is deliberately chosen to make a statement, whether of simple conformity or as an outlandish expression of individuality. The archaeological record doesn't passively *reflect* what people do; people actively *create* it through innumerable daily choices.

The appearance of 'Anglo-Saxon' archaeology thus reveals the date at which people chose to *demonstrate* their Anglo-Saxon identity through their material culture. This, obviously, need not correspond to the date at which people with that identity arrived in an area. Famously, the first generation of West Indian immigrants into post-War Britain would have left little archaeological trace. Clear manifestations of an African-Caribbean identity appeared only with their children and grandchildren. Intolerance and racism led to the parents' desire to fit in by adopting white British culture being replaced by their children's proclamation of and pride in their own identity.

This analogy is useful. For the barbarians, the Roman Empire was a culturally dominant and militarily *dominating* force, seen as the source of wealth, power, and socio-political prestige. It is unsurprising that the thousands of barbarians who migrated into the Empire between the first century before Christ and the end of the fourth century AD left no distinctive remains. The Romans saw northern barbarians as practically sub-human, almost as animals. This might usually have been truer of ideas than everyday behaviour but it could all too frequently be turned into very brutal practice. As a periodic show of Rome's military domination, the army could be unleashed on settlements over the border with orders to kill every living thing. It was only appropriate that 'sub-human' barbarian prisoners should be thrown to wild beasts in public spectacle. Outside the army, where barbarian ferocity had a certain cachet, this was not a world where one proclaimed barbarian identity. In any case, barbarian immigrants wanted to *become* Roman; they eagerly adopted the traits that would make them so. Through most of the fourth century, barbarian army officers usually adopted a Roman name.

As we have seen, 'federate' metalwork and 'Romano-Saxon' pottery are no longer thought to reveal fourth-century Saxon presence in Britain. However, for reasons just outlined, one should not expect archaeological evidence of Saxon settlers in a fully functioning fourth-century Empire. While our archaeologically visible settlers from north-west Germany *could* have first arrived around 430, they could also have been there for some time before that date. Two questions arise: what made the Saxon settlers manifest their non-Roman identity in the fifth century, and—if these people *had* been settled in Britain before *c.*430—why was the non-Roman material they used current for *c.*430 and not older—heirlooms? For answers we must look to the causes and nature of migration, but first we must return to close examination of the sparse written record. This might suggest that the initial, official Saxon settlement took place rather earlier than usually believed.

Gildas' proud tyrant

Gildas' narrative provides important support for this possibility. His historical section comprises four parts: a 'Roman Section' (chapters 5–6), about the conquest of Britain; a 'Christian Section' on the evangelization of the island (chapters 8–12); the 'Northern Section' (chapters 13–21), relating Scottish and Pictish attacks after the end of Roman rule; and an 'Eastern Section' recounting Saxon attacks (chapters 22–6). Most people skip straight to the last two sections, preventing them from seeing clearly how Gildas writes. An outline of the 'Northern' and 'Eastern' sections was given in Chapter 2. This account is usually read much as was done there, as a single sequence of events. The 'Eastern Section' simply follows directly from the 'Northern Section'. First there was a series of northern wars against the Picts and *then* a sequence of events involving the Saxons in the east.

It is now very difficult for historians to read Gildas purely in terms of what he says, without being influenced by all the glosses and interpretations later piled upon his very basic account. Looking at the historical section in its entirety shows what Gildas' point was. The introductory section describes Britain's 'green and pleasant land' before showing how the Britons are faithless and rebellious but never have the courage of their convictions. The Roman Empire easily conquers them and, though the Britons rebel under Boudicca when the Romans are distracted, they flee when the legions return. Gildas then passes on to his Christian Section. Christianity in Britain was at first pretty lukewarm but then the tyrant Diocletian launched a terrible persecution. Many Christians were slaughtered and others apostatized. However, some martyrs provided a fine example of courage. Gildas names St Alban at Verulamium (St Albans) and Sts Julius and Aaron, possibly at York. Others hid in woods and caves until the persecution passed. After it did, the Britons entered a period of piety, rebuilding churches, celebrating feast-days, and generally being pure in heart. Alas, this gave way to sin in the form of Arianism, an eastern heresy concerning whether Christ and God the Father were of the same or merely of similar substance.[1]

You might have spotted the clear parallels between this 'Christian Section' and Gildas' 'Northern' and 'Eastern' sections, as described in

---

[1] Here is something to ponder. Arianism is the only heresy that Gildas mentions by name in the *De Excidio*—Pelagianism, supposedly the British heresy par excellence, receives no mention and nor do any of the myriad other heresies that beset the late antique Church. In Gildas' day (whenever during the later fifth and sixth centuries that was), Arianism was a heresy most associated with the Goths, and in Chapter 4 I mentioned that Gildas' name has a Gothic resonance. Might this be more than coincidence?

Chapter 2. The lukewarm reception of Christianity mirrors the feeble early attempts at defence; the persecution parallels barbarian ravaging and the results are similar; the apostates match those who surrendered to Picts or Saxons. The rallying heroes are the martyrs and Ambrosius Aurelianus. Locations are given for the sites of martyrs' triumph over death and for the great victory at Badon Hill. Note how Britons hide in caves, forests, and other wild landscapes, whether from ravaging barbarians or merciless persecutors. The persecution's blowing over mirrors the barbarians 'going away' or retreating. An era of sin and decline always follows a victorious one. Gildas' point, as part of his sermon, is that the Britons cannot properly manage themselves without being chastised and tested by God. Heroes arise to show them the way, but the perfidious Britons never see the lesson for long, before sliding back into their old ways. They are treacherous and faithless, to their Roman rulers and to God. This is the crucial background to Gildas' main argument. The Britons must be led; they must have guidance and good examples. Yet, the leaders of the Church, of all people, are not fulfilling this role.

Gildas stacks up three loosely historical 'case studies' to hammer home his lesson. In this light, we can look again at how closely the stories told in the 'Northern' and 'Eastern' sections parallel each other, as was probably clear from the summary in Chapter 2 (Figure 9.1). Half-hearted defence is accompanied by appeals for help from outsiders. When these fail there is barbarian onslaught. The Britons rally and their enemies are driven off but this only ushers in a period of vice. Gildas' tale is *extremely* stylized. Furthermore, the 'Northern' and 'Eastern' sections are separated by the word *interea*: 'meanwhile'. This is sometimes used more poetically to mark a break in the narrative but either way some unspecified overlap is implied between the section about the Saxons and that dealing with the Picts and Scots. Talking of the sexual excess that followed the victory over the Picts, Gildas ends his 'Northern Section' with the phrase *et sicut nunc est*:

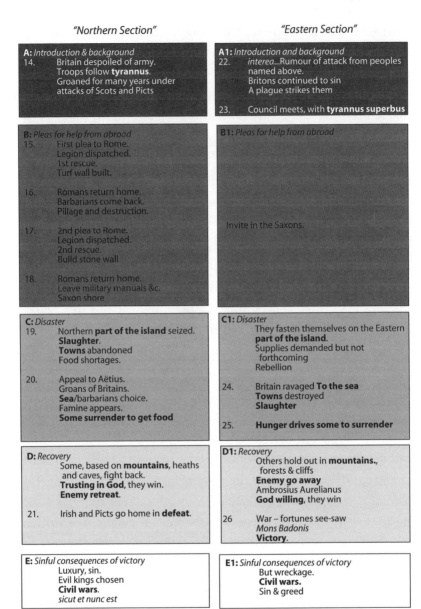

"Northern Section"   *"Eastern Section"*

A: *Introduction & background*
14.   Britain despoiled of army.
         Troops follow **tyrannus**.
         Groaned for many years under
         attacks of Scots and Picts

A1: *Introduction and background*
22.   *interea*...Rumour of attack from peoples
         named above.
         Britons continued to sin
         A plague strikes them

23.   Council meets, with **tyrannus superbus**

B: *Pleas for help from abroad*
15.   First plea to Rome.
         Legion dispatched.
         1st rescue.
         Turf wall built.

16.   Romans return home.
         Barbarians come back.
         Pillage and destruction.

17.   2nd plea to Rome.
         Legion dispatched.
         2nd rescue.
         Build stone wall

18.   Romans return home.
         Leave military manuals &c.
         Saxon shore

B1: *Pleas for help from abroad*

         Invite in the Saxons.

C: *Disaster*
19.   Northern **part of the island** seized.
         Slaughter.
         Towns abandoned
         Food shortages.

20.   Appeal to Aëtius.
         Groans of Britains.
         Sea/barbarians choice.
         Famine appears.
         Some surrender to get food

C1: *Disaster*
         They fasten themselves on the Eastern
         part of the island.
         Supplies demanded but not
         forthcoming
         Rebellion

24.   Britain ravaged **To the sea**
         Towns destroyed
         Slaughter

25.   **Hunger drives some to surrender**

D: *Recovery*
         Some, based on **mountains**, heaths
         and caves, fight back.
         Trusting in God, they win.
         Enemy retreat.

21.   Irish and Picts go home in **defeat.**

D1: *Recovery*
         Others hold out in **mountains.,**
         forests & cliffs
         Enemy go away
         Ambrosius Aurelianus
         God willing, they win

26   War – fortunes see-saw
         Mons Badonis
         Victory.

E: *Sinful consequences of victory*
         Luxury, sin.
         Evil kings chosen
         Civil wars.
         sicut et nunc est

E1: *Sinful consequences of victory*
         But wreckage.
         Civil wars.
         Sin & greed

Figure 9.1 The structure of Gildas' historical sections

and thus it is now. Rather than narrating a single sequence of events, Gildas tells his moralizing, stylized story twice, once in regard to northern foes and once (in a separate 'case study') with relationship to enemies in the east. This breaks the chronological linkage between the letter to Aëtius (in the 'Northern Section') and the reference to Ambrosius' grandsons holding power in the present (in the 'Eastern Section'). This permits us to telescope the chronology of *On the Ruin* ..., possibly moving Gildas' composition up to half a century earlier than the usual date of *c.*540. The clear parallelism implies that the unnamed tyrant mentioned at the start of the 'Eastern Section' is very likely the one, similarly not named but alluded to as the 'bloody tyrant', at the start of the 'Northern Section': the usurper Magnus Maximus. As it happens, Vortigern's name ('highest ruler') could be read as a translation of the Latin *magnus* or (better) *maximus tyrannus*, which can mean Magnus or Maximus the Tyrant but also great, or greatest, tyrant. As well as being a personal name, *magnus maximus* means 'great the greatest': a suitable name for a proud tyrant. The Spanish Christian writer Orosius punned on this fact within a generation of Maximus' death. That could be coincidence but the traditional argument, seeing 'the proud tyrant' as Gildas' pun on the name 'Vortigern', puts the cart before the horse. Although Gildas can be very allusive, he usually names his tyrants; all five reigning tyrants that he complained against are named, as is the *tyrannus* Diocletian at the start of the 'Christian Section' and the tyrant Magnus Maximus at its end. What's more, the 'pun' argument selects only one of Gildas' descriptions: 'proud tyrant' (*tyrannus superbus*). There are two other allusions. Magnus Maximus is alluded to as the 'bloody tyrant' at the start of the 'Northern Section' and 'the proud tyrant' appears as 'the unlucky tyrant' slightly later in the 'Eastern Section'. *Tyrannus infaustus* (unlucky tyrant) could just as easily be a pun on the names Faustus or Felix ('lucky'). *Tyrannus superbus* is selected as a pun solely because it might fit the name Vortigern, which first appears 200 years after Gildas' day. It is at least as likely that that the character Vortigern is an outgrowth from a misunderstanding of Gildas' obscure Latin narrative.

This suggestion gains plausibility if one examines Magnus Maximus' reputation in the late antique West. Maximus was generally well regarded, probably for two reasons. He had his capital at Trier, maintaining the late third- and fourth-century tradition of giving the Gallic aristocracy easy access to the imperial court. This was also, as described, important for the British elite and for the island's prosperity and it ensured economic and social stability for the north of Gaul. The other reason for Maximus' good reputation was his impeccable Catholic credentials, especially since he reigned at the same time as the Arian dowager empress Justina, who caused serious problems for St Ambrose, Bishop of Valentinian II's capital city, Milan.

Maximus' fellow Spaniard Orosius, whose *Seven Books of History* Gildas may well have read, says he was a fine emperor apart from the fact that he had seized the throne illegitimately. Rufinus of Aquileia, whose Latin translation and two-book continuation of Eusebius' *Ecclesiastical History* was certainly used by Gildas, has nothing very damnatory to say other than calling Maximus (technically correctly) a *tyrannus*. Rufinus' ire is reserved for Empress Justina. However, Gildas probably got the idea from Rufinus that Emperor Gratian, whom Maximus had murdered, led a 'most religious' life. The Aquitanian Sulpicius Severus is complimentary about Maximus in his *Dialogues* and, though less effusive in his influential *Life of Saint Martin*, still describes him in positive terms. In the mid-fifth century, Sidonius Apollinaris, delivering a praise-poem (panegyric) to Majorian, the first emperor to set foot in Gaul since the 390s, implied that, as far as Gauls were concerned, Maximus was the last decent emperor before Majorian. Set against the positive role that Maximus, as Macsen Gwledig, played as a legitimizing founder of British kingdoms, Gildas' animosity towards Maximus becomes yet more unusual.

To get a description of Maximus that is as hostile as Gildas' you have—unsurprisingly—to go to Italy and sources close to the legitimist court of Theodosius I: Pacatus' panegyric delivered to Theodosius on the occasion of Maximus' suppression; Ambrose's account to Valentinian II of his confrontational visit to Maximus' court; Ambrose's funerary oration for Theodosius; and Paulinus' Life of Ambrose. Whether Gildas had access to any of these is unknown.

Gildas' unrelenting hostility towards Maximus is surprising, especially given Maximus' Christian orthodoxy. Maximus put it about that his invasion of Italy in 387 was a response to the Milanese court's Arianism: Arianism, a 'poison' 'vomited' on Britain by a 'foreign snake', is the only heresy named by Gildas. Even if deriving his opinion from a Theodosian source, Gildas' choice of this view over others that were certainly (like Rufinus') or possibly (like Orosius' or Sulpicius') available to him requires explanation. In western European historiography north and west of the Alps, Gildas' antipathy towards Maximus stands out like a sore thumb. It is difficult to avoid concluding that it stems from something very specific to Gildas; perhaps something specifically British. I suggest that that 'something' was that it was—or that Gildas thought it was, which is a crucial distinction—this 'proud tyrant' who had called in the hated Saxons.

Two other curiosities might support this argument, though neither is very weighty. Maximus' council or consilium features very strongly in the accounts of his reign. The main 'black mark' against him in most western eyes was his sentencing the heretic Priscillian to death (Priscillian thus acquiring the dubious distinction of being the first person executed for heresy). Much of the blame tended nevertheless to be shifted onto the shoulders of the sycophantic bishops in his council. Perhaps this somehow relates to the mention of the Proud Tyrant's council being responsible for summoning the Saxons? The other comes in a letter (number 40) from Ambrose of Milan to Theodosius I, urging him to thank God for his victory over Maximus.

During his final war against Theodosius, Ambrose claims, Maximus suffered defeats by Franks and Saxons. This is the only association of Maximus with Saxons but there seems no reason to dispute it. One is tempted to wonder whether this was the 'Saxon revolt' ...

This argument, if accepted, moves the Saxon settlement described by Gildas from the usually supposed date in the second quarter of the fifth century back to the 380s. Such a centrally administered settlement, as is implied by Gildas' accurate use of technical terms like *foedus* and *annonae*, seems to imply a centrally administered settlement. This would make more sense in the context of the functioning late fourth-century Empire than in the economic crisis of the second quarter of the fifth century.

Nennius' numbers

To pursue this argument we must examine the *Historia Brittonum*. This has various things to say about Maximus and Vortigern and gives us two dates for the Saxons' arrival (*adventus Saxonum*), one in 428 and the other during Gratian's reign, in 374. The latter comes close to the date in Maximus' reign that I am suggesting. In Chapter 4, we saw how Bede calculated that the *adventus* occurred between 450 and 455. How did the *HB*'s author ('Nennius') come up with his dates? Any answer requires us to consider the *HB*'s sources and their reliability. It has commonly been suggested that the *HB*'s author knew of a now lost set of British annals or other historical material closer to the fifth and sixth centuries. If the *HB* derived its fifth-century date for the *adventus* from a trustworthy source, this would argue against the fourth-century date just proposed from Gildas—assuming of course that the two writers were discussing the same event.

The *HB*'s writer had access to the works of Gildas and Bede, whose reliability has already been discussed. We examined his passage about Arthur's battles and its sources in the last chapter and concluded that it was his own work. He (assuming it was a he) also used English and

Welsh royal genealogies. For the period after the late sixth century, the HB may have drawn upon poetic sources, given that it mentions some bards by name, and other Welsh historical texts. These may have been of reasonable reliability. This is a period from which adequate records do survive. Often the HB's account does not tally with others, like Bede's. Given Bede's own agendas, this does not make the HB's version untrustworthy; it simply renders it difficult to decide which account to follow. The HB's author certainly worked his sources into his overall scheme, employing parallel phrases to make the story of the north mirror that of the south (see Chapter 8). Nevertheless these later sources do not bear upon the precise question that concerns us here.

The author also used a life of St Patrick, based upon the saint's own *Confession* but infused with the legends that had accrued about the Apostle of Ireland by the ninth century. He drew upon strange miraculous material about St Germanus of Auxerre. This is quite unlike anything in Constantius of Lyon's Life of the saint, and the HB itself makes it clear various versions of this story circulated in ninth-century Wales. The saint in question might be a different Germanus, a Welsh St Garmon, but this seems unlikely. About forty years after the HB's composition a British Bishop Marcus told Heiric of Auxerre, a devoted publicist of Germanus' cult, about the saint's British miracles, which he either drew from the HB itself or from the same sources. It is just possible that it was Marcus himself—described as old in the 870s—who wrote the HB. To this list we can add other sources which have not been preserved: the story of Ambrosius/Emrys and Vortigern, the materials employed for the account of Vortigern, Hengist, and Vortimer in Kent, the list of 'wonders of Britain', and a curious history of the nine (or seven, according to the 'elders of the Britons') Roman emperors who ruled in Britain. This last is more than oral tradition as it employed classical histories.

The main conclusion to draw is that, aside from Gildas and Bede, these sources are almost entirely legendary. Wherever we can check them against earlier, more trustworthy materials they are revealed as unreliable. This raises a huge obstacle for anyone arguing that the *HB*'s account of the fifth century and the Saxons' arrival was based on lost histories. Even were this the case, there would be no reason to suppose that such sources were any more trustworthy than those of Emrys, Vortigern, and Germanus. We would have no grounds for thinking that, beyond the invocation of historically existing characters, they presented an accurate portrayal of fifth-century events. We must return to the point made at the start of Chapter 4. Medieval histories were written for quite different purposes from modern ones. It is interesting that the composer of the *HB* tended to leave his sources discrete and allow them to say their piece, as in his various accounts of Magnus Maximus and different versions of Vortigern's death, but this does not increase their inherent reliability.

The preceding catalogue nevertheless omits one important group of sources: those drawn upon for the *HB*'s measurement of time. This is principally found in *HB* chapter 66 but other comments are scattered throughout the work (Figure 9.2). Here we can identify other sources, contemporary with the fifth century, which still survive. These passages include dates referring to Vortigern and other British fifth-century events. If, for now, we leave aside the rest of its narrative, are the dates given by the *HB* for the *adventus saxonum* reliable? Do they represent fifth-century record 'fossilized' in this ninth-century history or are they, like Bede's dates, a later scholar's more or less educated guesses? Answering this question requires not merely mental arithmetic but awareness of two or three chronological systems and two different ways of counting, as well as every effort not to slide from one to another (something the *HB*-author himself did not manage)! Entering the world of 'Nennius' numbers' requires a deep breath and a strong coffee, if

Measurement	Number of Years	*HB* reference
From the Creation to the consulship of Constantine and Rufus	5,658	Ch. 66
From the execution of Maximus to the coming of the Saxons	40	31
From the consulate of the twins Fufius and Rubellius to the consulate of Stilicho	373	66
From the Incarnation to the coming of Patrick to Ireland	405	16
From the Incarnation to the coming of Patrick to Ireland (as 23 cycles of 19 years)	438	16
From the coming of Patrick to Ireland to the present year (as 22 cycles of 19 years)	418 + 2 in the Ogdoad	16
From the consulate of Stilicho to that of Valentinian III and the reign of Vortigern	28	66
From Cunedda, who drove the Irish out of Britain, to king Maelgwn of Gwynedd	146	62
From the regin of Vortigern to the strife between Ambrosius and Vitalinus, or the battle of Guoloph	12	66
From the Coming of the Saxons to the consulate of Valerian and Decius	69	66
From the Coming of the Saxons to the 4th year of king Merfyn of Gwynedd	429	16
From the death of St Patrick to the death of St Bridget	60	16
From the birth of St Columba to the death of St Bridget	4	16
From the Passion to the current year	796	4
From the Incarnation to the current year	831	4

Figure 9.2 The *HB*'s chronological measurements

not something stronger. To spare you some of that pain I have restricted myself to the key points.

One important observation is the remarkable degree of error and inconsistency in the *HB*'s chronological calculations. The author calculated the present year variously as AP (the 'Year of the Passion': see below) 796, AD 825, AD 831, and AD 857. The fourth year of King

Merfyn Frych ('the Freckled'), mentioned in *HB* 16, was AD 828–9, equating with none of his calculations. This nevertheless seems to have been, for him, the current year. For reasons that we will see in a moment, AD 831 ought to equate with AP 804, not AP 796 as the *HB* states, and, conversely, AP 796 should be AD 823 rather than AD 831.... Our author clearly did not cross-check his sources, but took each on its own terms and let it stand.

This confusion is not surprising. The author was familiar with at least two chronological systems. He knew the common *anno passionis* (AP: the Year of the Passion) system and the more 'new-fangled' *anno domini* calculation (counted from the Incarnation). Christ's passion was believed to have occurred in the consulate[2] of the twins Fufius and Rubellius (AD 29) so there ought to have been, by antique reckoning, twenty-nine years between AP and AD dates; we would see the difference as twenty-eight.[3] However, according to the calculations generally accepted in late antiquity, the difference between the AP year and the AD year was, as we would reckon it, twenty-seven (or to contemporaries twenty-eight). Thus AP 401 is the year we think of as AD 428. Note, though, that at HB 4 our author thinks there were, by his counting, thirty-six years between AP and AD dates...As if this were not enough, two ways of establishing the date of Christ's passion circulated in late antiquity. One placed the crucifixion in Tiberius'

---

[2] The Romans designated years according to the two men who held the first pair of consulships in that year.

[3] The Romans and their heirs counted the numerical difference between days and years differently from modern westerners. They counted the first and the last numbers *inclusively*, rather than simply deducting the start date from the end date. The day after the *Kalends* of March (2 March) was counted as the sixth day before the *Nones* of March (7 March) rather than the fifth as one might expect. Thus the *HB* counts the difference between the consulate of Valentinian and Theodosius (425) and that of Felix and Taurus (428) as four years rather than three (*HB* 66). It is also why it calculates twenty-three nineteen-year cycles as 438 rather than 437 years (*HB* 16). When studying Nennius' calculations it is important to remember this and not to slip back and forth between modern arithmetic and antique 'inclusive' counting to suit one's argument.

fifteenth year, the other in his eighteenth. This produced dates that were (by antique counting) four years apart. It is not uncommon in fifth-century history to find an event, dated to one year in one source, placed four years later in another.

However, the author's use of consulates is fairly correct and consistent. From this we can deduce that the *HB* used a *consularium* (a list of years identified by their consuls) or a chronicle or Easter Table based upon one. Numerous such sources existed in late antiquity. We can further conclude that his list counted its years by the AP system. In *HB* 31 the author dates the *adventus saxonum* to AP 347. He also states that the consulate of Felix and Taurus was in the 400th year since Christ's incarnation. This is wrong but it *was*, as usually counted, the 401st year since Christ's *passion*. This is important because it shows that the author could slip from one chronographical system to the other without realizing.

Our author's odd statement that from the time of Magnus Maximus the Romans' rulers were called consuls suggests his *consularium*/chronicle source began with Maximus. His calculation of the number of years from Creation to the consulate of Constantine and Rufus suggests that it ended in 457. If this were a continuation of Jerome's *Chronicle* it would have started, or had a break in the text, after 378, making Magnus Maximus' usurpation one of the earliest events recorded; certainly the first to mention Britain. Prosper's mid-fifth-century *Chronicle*, written in Aquitaine and dated according to the AP system, fits the bill, and chapter 29 of the *HB* is indeed a jumbled sequence of quotes from Prosper. Bede also used this source. However, Prosper's *Chronicle* ended with Valentinian III's death (455). Nevertheless, some manuscripts of Prosper continue the story to 457. Perhaps the *HB*-author used a version like this.

Earlier analyses have thus suggested that the author also used Victorius of Aquitaine's fifth-century *Cursus Paschalis* (loosely, *Easter Sequence*), which counted in AP dates and stopped in 457. Victorius started with the consulate of Fufius and Rubellius in which the first 'Easter' occurred, so the difference between that and Stilicho's first consulate (*HB* 66) could be worked out from his writings. Both sources (Prosper and Victorius) could well have had comments introduced into them during the 350 or so years between their composition and that of the *HB*, and we can repeat the possibility that the author's copy of Prosper itself continued down to 457 to harmonize with Victorius. A different Easter Table was apparently also used, set out (unlike Victorius') according to a nineteen-year Easter Cycle. This source seems to have counted in AD dates and it was from here that the *HB*-author derived his chronology for Irish events (see Figure 9.2).

There were, by antique counting, twenty-eight years between AP and AD dates and the author twice seems to make an error of twenty-eight-years. He says that the *adventus* took place in AD 400 but his mention of the consulate of Felix and Taurus (*HB* 66) and of a forty-year period of fear after Maximus' death (388: *HB* 31) suggests he meant 428. The other indication of confusion comes when the author says (*HB* 16) that the *adventus* occurred 429 years before King Merfyn's fourth year. This would work out at AD 400/1 (Figure 9.3). Our author or his sources seem to have stressed a '400th year', either since Christ's

Event	AD date
Consulate of Fufius and Rubellius, 'the twins'	29
429 years before the 4th year of Merfyn of Gwynedd	400
Consulate of Gratian and Equitius	374
AP 347	374
(First) Consulate of Stilicho	400
(First) Consulate of Theodosius (II) and Valentinian (III)	425
Consulate of Felix and Taurus	428
Consulate of Constantine and Rufus	457
4th year of king Merfyn of Gwynedd	828–29

Figure 9.3 Chronological fixed points in the *HB*

birth or since his passion. Stilicho's first consulate (400) was used as a fixed point. Sometimes, the author evidently forgot to convert from AP to AD or forgot which system or method he was using. At least once he deducted twenty-eight from, instead of adding twenty-eight to, the AP date to arrive at the year AD. Arguments based upon internal consistency and numerical logic within the *HB* start on shaky ground.

If the *HB*-author had these sources available, where does that leave his comments about the *adventus saxonum* and the other British events (Figure 9.4)? Possibly he found the entries relating to Vortigern, the Saxons, and the strife between Ambrosius and Vitalinus in his sources. I think, though, that the problem is solved quite simply. St Germanus mattered to the *HB*-author and to early medieval Welsh politics generally. The *HB* hushes up the Britons' heresy and presents Germanus' visit as a moral 'crusade'. On the 'Pillar of Eliseg', a stone column erected in neighbouring Powys a generation or so after the *HB*'s composition, the kings of Powys claim Vortigern (there a son-in-law of Magnus Maximus) as their founder and say that his son Brittu was blessed by St Germanus. Germanus had (literally) become a political touchstone.

Now, in Prosper's *Chronicle*, the *HB*'s author would read that Germanus came to Britain in the consulate of Florentius and

Chronological Index	HB reference
The *imperium* of Vortigern was in the consulate of Theodosius and Valentinian	66
The *adventus saxonum* was in the consulate of Gratian and Equitius	31
The coming of the Saxons took place in AP 347	31
The *advents saxonum* was in the consulate of Felix and Taurus	66
The coming of the Saxons took place in the 4th year of Vortigern's rule	66
The *advents saxonum* was in the 400th year since the incarnation of the Lord	66

Figure 9.4 The *HB*'s chronology for fifth-century Britain

Dionysius (AD 429) in response to appeals from the island. He knew that when Germanus arrived in Britain Vortigern and the Saxons were already up to no good, and that when he was in Britain Germanus participated in a campaign against Saxons. It is therefore not difficult to see why he simply placed the arrival of the Saxons a year before Germanus' arrival. Even if this entry was already interpolated in the author's sources, it probably got there via the same calculations. There are other reasons why his sources might have stressed AP 400/1 as a fateful year, and this might have convinced the author that this was when the Saxons arrived in Britain.

By the HB-author's calculations, the year of composition (AD 828–9) was the 401st year since the Saxons' arrival (AD 428) which itself took place in the 401st year since Christ's passion. This would be a good year to argue for militant opposition to the English, perhaps claiming that this would be the year of their expulsion. 400 years before their arrival; 400 years before their being driven out: a neat symmetry. This might suggest that the author of the HB already had reason to think that the *adventus* occurred in 428, although he could just as easily have placed it there for rhetorical purposes or because he had already estimated that that was about the right date. This would be a very attractive idea, were it not for one thing. On the only occasion that he counted the years from the *adventus* to the present day, the author confused his chronological systems. He deducted the AP date from the current AD date to calculate that 429 years had elapsed since the Saxons' arrival. This suggests that the 401st year since the *adventus* cannot have been uppermost in his mind at that point at least. This highlights the inherent difficulties in any argument asserting what the HB author 'would have' known or what inconsistencies he 'would have' appreciated.

All that, however, leaves unexplained the HB's other date for the *adventus saxonum*, in Gratian's reign, and why he thought it took place in Vortigern's fourth regnal year. The 'Gratianic' date is a simple error.

We've seen how the author could slip from one dating system to the other and convert dates from AP to AD the wrong way. We've also noted that at one point he mistakenly calculated that 429 years had passed between the *adventus* and the current year. Such a calculation would place the *adventus* in the year which we think of as AD 400 but, clearly, the *HB* author thought this had taken him back to AD 428— the year he otherwise always uses for the Saxon arrival. He seems then to have decided to convert this to an AP date and counted back another twenty-seven years (twenty-eight as he saw it). This brought him back to AD 373. Although the date he gives is 374, AP 346 in his source, listing the consuls correctly as Gratian and Equitius, this is probably within an acceptable margin of error. After all, King Merfyn's fourth year spanned AD 828–9, and the author's own calculations of the 'present year' were inconsistent. The *HB*'s late fourth-century date for the *adventus saxonum* is therefore an arithmetical mistake.

The statement that the Saxons arrived in Vortigern's fourth year is, I propose, included to resonate with the present day. The author wrote in the fourth year of King Merfyn of Gwynedd. According to the Welsh Annals, the Saxons burnt the Gwynedd stronghold of Degannwy in 822 and took under their control the kingdom of Powys, which claimed to be founded by Vortigern. In Chapter 8 we saw the *Anglo-Saxon Chronicle*'s unverifiable claim that in 830, the year after the *HB*'s composition, all the Welsh kings submitted to Ecgberht of Wessex. This seems like a very appropriate context for a North Welsh writer to present his king with a history showing what came of deals with the English. No surrender! I argued earlier that this explains his composition of an elaborate passage about Arthur, smiting the Saxons left, right, and centre. The *HB* was a highly political response to a very specific set of circumstances.

We can, therefore, safely explain both of the *HB*'s dates for the *adventus* as calculations dating to 828–9, made from the different sources available to its author, and by basic human error. No significance can be attached to the HB's recording of two very different dates; its author envisaged a single event. The date of 374 is not significant.

Other traces of the 'lost annals'?

This nevertheless leaves two other statements:

1. 'From the reign of Vortigern to the discord between Ambrosius and Vitalinus are twelve years, which is *Guoloppum*, that is *Catguoloph* [the battle of Guoloph].' (HB 66)
2. 'From the year when the English came to Britain and were received by Vortigern to Decius and Valerian are 69 years.' (HB 66)

Do *these* indicate lost fifth- or sixth-century British annals? They are conundrums to be sure. The strife of Ambrosius and Vitalinus, the battle of 'Guoloph', and its distance of twelve years from Vortigern's reign (thus *c.*436 by the author's reckoning) are difficult to account for except by assuming that the author found them in his sources. One can suggest that the author (or his source) confused other events and people mentioned under those years in Prosper's *Chronicle*, such as the fighting between Aëtius and Litorius and the Goths, and corrupted the names. It is difficult, however, to make such propositions carry conviction. Given that Ambrosius is mentioned by Gildas, the safest and simplest solution might be that a British event had indeed been entered into the author's chronicle source under 435 or thereabouts. What the strife was about, who Vitalinus was, where Guoloph was (Wallop in Hampshire is usually proposed), and who won, we can no longer know. There is, however, another faint possibility, to which I will return.

That leaves the sixty-nine years from Vortigern's *imperium* to the consulate of Valerian and Decius. There is no simple solution here. Working forward sixty-nine years from 428 brings us, by antique reckoning, to 496. No Decius or Valerian held the consulate in that year; no one did. One can scurry about in the annals looking for people with similar names. Various members of the Decii, a great senatorial dynasty, held the consulate in the late fifth century: Flavius Caecina Decius Maximus Basilius in 480, Decius Marius Venantius Basilius in 484, Caecina Mavortius Basilius Decius in 486, and Decius Iunior in 529 (not to mention their relatives Basilius Venantius Iunior in 508, Vettius Agorius Basilius Mavortius in 527, and Paulinus Iunior in 534). None of these comes close to the right year, though, and none had a colleague called Valerian or anything similar. Even those called Decius are usually called by one of their other names in the consular annals (e.g. Basilius in 480; Venantius in 484). If one looks for consular names that might have been corrupted into Decius and Valerian, the closest one can get are the Volusianus and Dexicrates who held office in 503. However, Dexicrates does not appear in western sources so the *HB*-author did not know about him. None of this looks very convincing. Nor can one solve the riddle by going *back* instead of forward from 428.

Even less plausible alternatives have been proposed, such as later editing out of what the *HB*-author *really* mentioned. One suggestion for the latter has been the battle of Mount Badon, the date of which comes out at 496 *if* you assume Gildas was writing in 540 exactly and *if* you assume that he meant that the battle occurred forty-four years *before* his writing; neither assumption is secure.

The most scholarly solution advanced to date was presented by David Dumville in 1974. This assumed that the manuscript was corrupt and that the scribe made an error in jumping from one bit of text to another. Dumville suggested that *Decius* was an error for *Aecius*, a variant spelling of Aëtius. He then proposed this ingenious reconstruction, which I have translated (the bit of text the scribe skipped over is italicized): 'From the year when the English came to Britain and were received by Vortigern to [A]ecius and Valer[*ius four years and from Aecius to Valer]ian* are lx[*xx*]ix.' Aëtius held the consulate with Valerius in 432 and another Valerius, sometimes Valerianus, held it in 521, eighty-nine years after Aëtius and Valerius. A corruption of lxxxix (89) to lxix (69) is easily enough envisaged. It is a very clever solution. Why, though, did the 432 consulate of Aëtius and Valerius matter to the *HB*-author or his source? Actually there are, by the author's calculations, five years between 428 and 432, but that is easily incorporated in Dumville's reconstruction. A bigger problem is that there are ninety (xc) years between 432 and 521 by the *HB*'s method of counting. One can assume that the author counted incorrectly (as he demonstrably did elsewhere) but then the explanation starts to look a bit *too* clever.

I offer this conjecture, which may be no more satisfactory than the others. There was no consul in 496, but a source called the *Paschale Campanum* (an Easter Table from Campania, Italy) recorded that in this year many people feared that Antichrist would appear. This was because they calculated that it was 6,000 years since Creation. Decius and Valerian were two great third-century persecuting emperors. The *HB*'s chronicle source, which I suggested might have been a version of Prosper continued to 457, might (in its entry for 428) have *prophesied*, or more likely reported a prophecy, that in 496 would come (or return) Decius and Valerian as Antichrist. This calculation of Antichrist's date, and this fear, were not uncommon in the later fifth century. In the ninth century, the *HB* simply misread this reference to a prophecy as the record of a consulate. AD 428 was reckoned as AP 401, the first year of the fifth century since the crucifixion and the year 400/1 seems to have been stressed in the *HB*-author's sources. It could well have been a year when discussions of the coming of Antichrist were common. This attention might have been a further reason why the author placed the Saxons' coming in that crucial year.

A problem is suggested by the *HB*-author's computation of the years of the world, which comes nowhere near 6,000. However, most of the *HB*'s numbers for the years since Creation are taken from Victorius and Prosper. They were, then, current even in the fifth century when this belief in Antichrist's imminent appearance was common. If the source simply reported the prophecy rather than subscribing to it, the discrepancy between the present year's date, worked out since Creation, and its proximity to a 'Year 6000' apocalypse in 496 would not matter. A more serious problem is that this prophecy is not entered under 428 in any surviving manuscript of Prosper or Victorius. It would have to have been entered into the manuscript, whether under 428 or 457, or under 496 in a manuscript of Victorius, very early on, between 457 and 496. This is not a fatal objection; plenty of other people were adding entries to both sources across the fifth-century West. This solution might now seem, like Dumville's, over-elaborate. Nevertheless it has important advantages over all those suggested to date. It requires no change at all to the text, whether in the vocabulary, orthography, or syntax, or in the names or numbers mentioned, and presumes no later censorship or missing phrases. The *HB*'s statement remains puzzling.

We need not, and probably should not, assume that the *HB* used a now-lost set of British annals, whence came its references to Ambrosius, Vortigern, Vitalinus, and 'Guoloph'. That these entries and the other information I have postulated do not appear in any extant text of Prosper's *Chronicle* or Victorius' *Cursus* does not compel us to envisage a separate source. Late antique and early medieval texts did not have 'correct' or canonical forms. Prosper's and Victorius' work circulated in numerous manuscripts, many of which contained additions and insertions relating to local events, sometimes drawn from other surviving sources such as Rufinus of Aquileia's *Ecclesiastical History*. Between their composition and the *HB*-author's use of them, there were 350 years for scribes to add entries to these texts. This was absolutely typical for writers in this period. This is also ample time for a manuscript to enter Britain with various additions made, be copied, and for the copyist to misunderstand the insertions, and for that process to be repeated more than once.

As a result of these perambulations, we can draw some important conclusions. Where we can identify the *HB*'s lost sources for the period before about 600 these are almost entirely legendary. If the *HB*'s statements about fifth-century chronology came from one of these there would be no reason to assume that they were trustworthy. We need not assume that they came from a lost chronicle; they could derive from comments in the manuscript of his identifiable, surviving sources. If this is so there is, again, no compelling reason to suppose that such entries were more reliable than the legends about Maximus, Vortigern, Emrys, Germanus, or Patrick. The entry about Decius and Valerian might originate in a fifth-century source but need by no means be British. There were over 300 years during which the entry about Ambrosius, Vitalinus, and 'Guoloph' could have been inserted into a manuscript of Prosper or Victorius. The dates assigned to Vortigern and to the *adventus saxonum* are the *HB*-author's own calculations. Overall, there is no reason to place any trust in the *HB*'s chronology for fifth-century Britain.

'Great the greatest' and 'the highest ruler': misremembering Maximus and Vortigern

In *HB* 31 is contained the following passage:

> After the end of the above-mentioned war, that is the one between the Britons and the Romans, in which the leaders of those people were killed, and the killing of the tyrant Maximus, and the ending of the *imperium* of the Romans in Britain, it happened that for forty years they were in fear. Vortigern reigned in Britain and when he reigned in Britain he was troubled by fear of the Picts and the Scots, and of an attack from the Romans, and by fear of Ambrosius.

Yet another of the *HB*'s mysterious statements, supposed to draw on 'lost annals', this has been the basis of many theories about early fifth-century British history. Vortigern, a successor of Maximus, was worried that the Romans would reconquer Britain as well as by Scottish and Pictish raids and by his rivalry with Ambrosius, assumed to be Gildas' Ambrosius Aurelianus. This seems plausible enough, although the passage's style resembles the legendary stories about Vortigern, Emrys, and Germanus. We should, however, remember that there is one indubitably historical person who is said, by unimpeachable contemporary sources, to have reigned in Britain, to have fought against raids by Picts and Scots, to have had reason to fear an attack by the 'Romans', and to have had a conflict with an Ambrosius. That person is Magnus Maximus. The *Gallic Chronicle of 452* mentions his wars against the Picts and Scots. He clearly feared a counter-attack by the armies of Valentinian II or Theodosius I and he had a showdown with St Ambrose, whose name, as it happens, was Aurelius Ambrosius. The saint was sent to Maximus as Valentinian II's ambassador and he describes his railings against the usurper more than once.

If we accept this, we can return to the curious statement that there were twelve years from the *imperium* of Vortigern to the discord (*discordia*) between Ambrosius and Vitalinus, 'which is Gualoppum, that is Catguoloph [the battle of Guoloph]' (*HB 66*). This presents several possibilities, though none is more than that. St Ambrose squabbled (*discordia* in Rufinus' *Ecclesiastical History*) with Empress Justina, Valentinian II's mother, who wanted a basilica turned over to Arian Christian worship for herself, her court, and her Gothic soldiers. Could *Iustina* or *Valentinianus* have been corrupted to *guitolini*? It seems unlikely. However, in 393, Ambrose left Milan, by then occupied by the usurper Eugenius, and helped to 'discover' and re-inter the relics of the martyrs Vitalis (San Vitale) and Agricola in Bologna, with his customary tact desecrating a Jewish cemetery in the process. Coincidentally, some of the relics were sent to Bishop Victricius of Rouen, who visited Britain in the 390s. In September 394, twelve years after Maximus' usurpation by antique reckoning, Eugenius was defeated and killed by Theodosius I's largely Gothic eastern Roman army. The decisive encounter is nowadays called the battle of the river Frigidus but contemporary sources rarely referred to it as such. Orosius just describes it as in the Alps. The Alps were occasionally referred to as the *vallum alpium* (by St Ambrose for example) and, as the *HB* says, *vallum* is *gwawl* in the British tongue. Now *vallum alpium* starts to look as though it could be corrupted to *Guoloppum*.[4] The period 392–4 certainly contains an Ambrose, a Vitalis, and more than enough *discordia*.

This might justifiably be regarded as a bit contrived. It nevertheless warns us against assuming that the *HB*'s mention of Vortigern, his troubles, and the 'battle of Wallop' must refer to British events or that these references were introduced into the *HB*'s sources in the British Isles. Even leaving Ambrosius, 'Vitalinus', and 'Guoloppum' aside, this reading of *HB* 31 permits the suggestion that, in ideas about British history, Magnus Maximus had become confused with Vortigern. An assumption that the (Aurelius) Ambrosius mentioned in some sources was the Ambrosius (Aurelianus) discussed by Gildas might have added to the confusion. Events initially associated with Maximus could thus have been transferred to the controversial Vortigern of Welsh politics.

Vortigern certainly was controversial. From ninth-century Welsh sources we can trace different versions of his story. The *HB* itself provides most of our leads, giving for example three accounts of Vortigern's death. It claims authority for the first version it presents (where heavenly fire consumes Vortigern) by saying it was found in 'the book of the blessed Germanus', whatever that might have been. In the other accounts Vortigern died lonely and heart-broken, hated by all, or he was swallowed up by the earth when his fortress was burnt down.

---

[4] I cannot resist saying that the western army was walloped at this battle.

However, it was not all bad. The son whom the *HB* says Vortigern fathered on his own daughter grew up to be the saintly bishop Faustus of Riez (certainly British by birth)—a curious association for a uniformly wicked king. The *HB* also records the genealogy of the rulers of Builth and Gwerthrynion (a name derived from Vortigern), starting with 'Vortigern the Thin, son of Vitalis, son of Vitalinus, son of Gliou'. This Gliou had four sons and built Gloucester, we are told. Vitalis may or may not be the Vitalis whose discord with Ambrosius is mentioned, if that is a genuine tradition. Although making Vortigern's descendants rulers of such small territories might have been a slight, other rulers claimed Vortigern as a founding ancestor. This would be unlikely if he was universally seen as bad. In Powys, on the Pillar of Eliseg, kings claimed descent from Vortigern's son Brittu. In this version, Vortigern is interestingly Magnus Maximus' (Macsen's) son-in-law and Brittu is blessed by Germanus. Brittu, seems (from *HB* 10) to be an equivalent of Brutus, an eponymous ancestor of the Britons.

By the time the genealogies appended to the *Welsh Annals* were compiled (called 'the Harleian genealogies'), Vortigern's bad reputation had led to his being expunged from these lists. Several lines reach back to individuals recorded as his sons in the *HB* or on the Pillar: Brittu, Pascent, and Cattegirn. Vortigern's deliberate omission is confirmed by the fact that in a different collection of genealogies (in Jesus College, Oxford), he retains his position at the head of those lists.

The apparent confusion of these sources is worth underlining. The *HB* says Cattegirn and Pascent were (with Vortimer and Faustus) Vortigern's sons, but Cattegirn is Pascent's father in the Harleian genealogies and his grandfather in the Jesus College set. This conversion of brothers into ancestors is common in genealogical traditions. In the Harleian genealogies, Cattegirn becomes Cadell's son, but in the Jesus College collection Cadell is the son of Cattegirn. In another Harleian genealogy, Brittu (Vortigern's son on the pillar of Eliseg) becomes another son of Cattegirn, son of Cadell.

Cadell—Cadell Ddyrnllug ('Gleaming-Hilt')—features in the *HB* (chs. 32–5) as a servant of the tyrant Benlli, raised to the kingship by St Germanus after Benlli and his fortress are consumed by divine fire. Germanus fasted and prayed against Benlli for several days and nights (two or three; the exact number is not clear) before he, his fort, and all who were with him were destroyed by fire. This is pretty much the same story as that recorded elsewhere in the *HB* (ch. 47) concerning Vortigern's death; St Germanus fasts and prays for three days before his fortress. Evidently a story circulated about how Germanus destroyed a wicked tyrant's fortress. In one version the tyrant was one Benlli (whom it is tempting to see as the Beli Mawr claimed as the ultimate founder of several Welsh dynasties) and he was replaced by a king blessed by Germanus. In another, it was Vortigern (founder of other dynasties). In *that* version his descendants, via his son Pascent, became kings, not of Powys but of two small regions around Builth. In this version Cadell Ddyrnllug is omitted from the genealogy entirely. In some stories (as in the Jesus College genealogies) Cadell was Vortigern's son; in others, Brittu was the son of Vortigern, blessed by Germanus, who became the rightful king of Powys.

From all this it is clear that legends were manipulated for political purposes, with the protagonists' names changed accordingly. Ancestral figures, like Beli/Benlli and Brittu/Britto/Brutus, otherwise mentioned as living in the remote past, were transposed to more recent history, regardless of any chronological discrepancies. Only St Germanus, the ultimate legitimator, remains constant.

We can now, perhaps, see the argument presented in Chapter 4 about the wars in Kent as even more convincing. There it was suggested that one variant of the story made the Britons under Vortimer the victors and the other had Hengist and the Jutes as the winners. The stock legend had the hero's brother, Hengist's brother Horsa or Vortimer's brother Pascent (whom we've just encountered washing up as an ancestor of the kings of Powys) killed in battle near a monument (the inscribed stone; Horsa's monument). Vortimer, unlike any of the *HB*'s other characters, is unknown in the genealogies and Vortigern does not appear in the stories that feature him except in linking sentences at the beginning and the end. Pascent, conversely, is variously recorded as Vortigern's son, grandson, or even great-grandson. Given how genealogical traditions play with relationships, I suggest that Vortimer is a doublet of Vortigern, with Pascent made into his brother.

In the *HB*'s figure of Vortimer I propose that we have a trace of an otherwise lost tradition about a 'good Vortigern', who fought and defeated the Saxons. Indeed, in the version of the four-battle Kentish war on which the *Anglo-Saxon Chronicle* drew, Vortigern commanded the Britons at the second battle (at '*Æglesthrep*', in '455'), where Horsa was killed. The *HB* or its source has altered his name to iron out the confusion that would otherwise have ensued. This 'good Vortigern' would be claimed as an ancestor by the kings of Powys—a Vortigern associated by marriage with Magnus Maximus, whose progeny was blessed by St Germanus. In this body of tradition another son, Cadell, was also blessed by the saint, and the king destroyed by divine fire was Benlli, probably the figure who, in the Jesus College genealogies, stands at the head of the Gwynedd royal genealogy. The war in Kent featured Vortigern as a hero. We can call this the Pagensian (Powys) tradition.

Powys's enemies had a rival version. In this story Vortigern, the kings of Powys's ancestor, was a *bad* king, cursed and pursued by Germanus. It was *this* Vortigern whose fortress was destroyed by heavenly fire at the saint's command. Furthermore, this Vortigern, far from fighting heroically against the Saxons, invited them in and granted them Kent and other territories in the first place. Let us name this the Venedotian (Gwynedd) tradition.

If you accept this reasoning, Vortigern of Powys need no more have been a real fifth-century historical figure than his counterpart Benlli/ Beli Mawr. Like the latter, he could have been transposed from much older traditions. The direct, if frequently hostile, seventh-century relationships between Northumbria and Gwynedd might explain how the Venedotian version was that which was transmitted to Bede. Bede unsurprisingly assumed that it was this Vortigern to whom Gildas referred in his story of the 'Proud Tyrant'. This suggests that the 'Bad Vortigern' story had existed for at least a century before the *HB*'s composition. It is interesting to ponder how our view of the fifth century might have differed if 'the father of English history' had learned about the Pagensian 'Good Vortigern' instead. It might also have been Bede who first merged this information with the Hengist and Horsa story, by his day associated with Kent, although, as we have seen, Hengist featured in legends elsewhere. In the century after Bede, his and other versions of English tradition, such as the Anglo-Saxon genealogies used by the *HB*, were transmitted to Wales and found their way into the *HB*'s account. This importantly shows how written sources and other traditions travelled back and forth across the cultural 'frontier', regardless of how some of our sources wanted us to view this period as a constant war between the English and the Welsh.

A series of propositions can conclude this discussion:

1. The 'Proud Tyrant' detested by Gildas was Magnus Maximus.

2. The *HB*'s dates for the *adventus Saxonum* are early ninth-century calculations, not traces of lost sources. Placed alongside the similar conclusions about Bede's dates, the written evidence for a fifth-century event lying behind the traditional story of the *adventus* evaporates.

3. Whether or not he really existed, the figure of Vortigern, legendary founder of the Powys royal dynasty, has clearly been manipulated by rival political traditions by the time of his appearance in eighth- and ninth-century sources. A genuine connection with the introduction of Saxon troops into Britain cannot be relied upon.

4. There are grounds to suspect that Vortigern and Magnus Maximus were confused by the ninth century at least.

Overall, the written or excavated evidence that the event described by Gildas took place in the fifth century is not probative. An alternative scenario is that a fourth-century settlement of some Saxon troops by Magnus Maximus later evolved into the story of the dramatic mid-fifth-century *adventus saxonum*. As a result of Maximus' generally positive image, Gildas' vagueness, and later Welsh politics, in some stories the blame for the *adventus saxonum* got shifted, some time before 700, onto the figure of Vortigern.

Maximus' reforms of the defence of Britain

Maximus' employment of a Saxon mercenary contingent, which Gildas thought was where everything started going wrong, may have been part of a wider scheme of defensive reforms. These were doubtless intended only to be temporary, whilst he took the pick of the garrison across the Channel to support his attempt to gain the imperial throne. However, Maximus' bid failed. His surviving British troops were apparently not returned to Britain after defeats by Theodosius' armies, and the temporary measures ended up being permanent. I suggest three key elements to these reforms.

The first was the recruitment of barbarian *foederati*. This was perhaps a very new expedient in 383. The first *foederati* of a new kind were recruited by Maximus' former associate Theodosius I in 382. These were regiments raised from barbarians, rather than allied barbarian contingents, which was what *foederati* had been hitherto and was indeed the technically accurate meaning of the term ('those bound by treaty'). Gildas discusses a specific incident, which *he* saw as where things went wrong. It was not necessarily the first arrival of 'Saxon' mercenaries in Britain, and has no necessary relationship with other immigration from the North Sea littoral. That could have taken place independently through similar or quite different mechanisms, before and after. Bede, reading Gildas 200 years later, decided that this was *the* coming of the English, crystallized as in AD 449 by the *Anglo-Saxon Chronicle.*

Where such Saxon troops were settled is unclear. Gildas is vague and by Bede's day the kings of Kent had appropriated the story. The earliest 'Anglo-Saxon' material cultural traces with clear links to the German North Sea coast are found in East Anglia. Maximus might have stationed his new recruits there, rather than further south, defending the east coast from further Saxon attacks but safely away from the lines of communication between Britain and the mainland. On the other hand, stationing them in Kent might have secured those lines of communication once Maximus had crossed to Gaul. Neither written nor archaeological evidence allows us to be prescriptive.

There is an intriguing seeming contradiction in late Romano-British archaeology. Late fourth-century material culture indicative of the presence of the imperial army—its distinctive belt-sets and brooches—is hardly found at all along the line of Hadrian's Wall (Figure 9.5). Yet, recent excavations, not just along the Wall itself but also in its northern English hinterland, have increasingly detected continuing occupation, lasting into the post-imperial period. By the sixth century some forts—most famously Birdoswald on the Wall—had acquired many characteristics of 'high-status' sites (see Chapter 6). The hypothesis currently advocated sees the Wall garrisons gradually evolving into local warlords and their retinues. This is very plausible. However, the absence of official metalwork is very significant and argues strongly that this evolution might have begun rather earlier than usually envisaged, and in a more official manner. One can find military metalwork where the Roman army was not stationed (like the North Sea coastal areas of Germany) but it is very unusual not to find such material in areas where it *was* located. This kind of material is found in various regional forms along other western Roman frontiers, especially the Rhine *limes*, so the idea that its absence merely signifies a material cultural difference between *limitanei* (border troops) and *comitatenses*

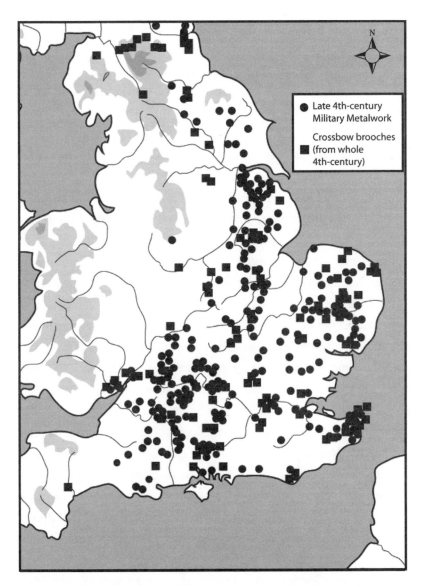

Figure 9.5 The distribution of official imeperial metalwork in fourth-century Britain. After Laycock (2008), figs 45 and 48.

(higher-status field army units) is unconvincing. Significant too is the identification of locally produced copies of such metalwork. Across the Rhine frontier, Alamannic chieftains also produced imitation badges of office to distribute to their followers. The Roman Empire's official insignia carried great social and cultural weight, and where one could not acquire such items one made copies. Such was the colossal dominance of Roman ideas of how power was symbolized, outside the imperial frontiers as well as within. The absence of official metalwork on the old Wall frontier is thus very important.

I hypothesize that when Maximus raised an army to support his attempt on the throne, units were withdrawn from the proportionately heavily manned Hadrian's Wall line. Before launching his usurpation he had campaigned among the Picts; this may have aimed at quietening that frontier. Such detachments as remained were, I propose, given control over their surrounding areas as a sort of local paramilitary 'police', but the 'official' border retreated to the south, to a line roughly from York to Gloucester—possibly along the old, first-century Fosse Way frontier between the civil and military zones. Military metalwork is found commonly to the south and east of this line, which is roughly the villa-zone. As an arable region, it is also where stray finds of metalwork are most common (through metal-detecting for example), and the latter are known from all sorts of contexts, making a precise delineation of any frontier difficult. There was probably no formal frontier. As before, Roman units were billeted across a wide area but based administratively on particular *civitates* and their capitals or small towns. Some of the latter, along the main roads, acquired fortifications in the fourth century. Some units stationed in the area in the later fourth century could have been withdrawn from Hadrian's Wall to replace better-quality *comitatenses* (field-army troops) taken abroad; others could have been Maximus' Saxon *foederati*. I will shortly return to this possibility.

In the north, the hypothesized 'paramilitaries' would certainly not have regarded themselves as 'non-Roman'. The opposite is suggested by their copying of old rank-badges. But they seem no longer to have had regular official contact with the Empire. A final possible element of Maximus' reforms is the settlement of Irish *foederati* on the west coast. This proposal comes largely from a reading of later Irish traditions of dubious worth but it makes much sense in the context of the other reforms that Maximus can be argued to have carried out. Relations between Ireland and the Empire were increasingly important at this time.

None of the evidence I have adduced is very conclusive. That must be admitted. Taken in total, however, it suggests wide-ranging reforms by Maximus in advance of his attack on Gratian in 383. Almost certainly, none was intended to be permanent. Had his campaign in the West succeeded, the British defences would doubtless have been returned to their former state. But the attempt failed and as far as we know the units did not return.

This had two, presumably unintended but vitally important, results. In the absence of a restored regular military presence the northern and western 'paramilitary' forces became the foci for new political units, eventually kingdoms. Thus Maximus became a figure of great importance in British politics, as Macsen Gwledig, legendary founder of several Welsh dynasties. The other result was the introduction of Saxon units into the island—perhaps stationed far inland—with close links to their relatives beyond the North Sea. These were placed in a very strong position, militarily, with the departure of other Roman units, only emphasized with Constantine 'III's' usurpation. In the socio-political stress that emerged in the early fifth century, presumably, as Gildas said, leading to the breakdown of these units' supply and pay, what would happen? This, I propose, was the historical context from which emerged the various contradictory traditions of Maximus, Macsen, and Vortigern.

East to west? (2)

If there is one thing that our written sources allow us to say for certain about the Anglo-Saxon migration to Britain, other than that there was one, it is that its earliest stages involved Saxon troops. The most reliable, if cryptic, description—Gildas'—states that this settlement took place to respond to attacks by barbarians. If these other barbarians were Saxons too, then an east coast settlement is plausible. Archaeology appears to reveal Roman troops in the south-east into the early fifth century, although such troops could of course be Saxon. If, however, Gildas' implication that the Saxons' role was to defend against Picts is correct, it is most unlikely that the first Saxons were stationed on the coast, whether in Kent or East Anglia. Indeed, in Gildas' account it was the subsequent arrivals who seized the east coast. Other traditions—English and Welsh—place early Saxon settlements in the north, by the Wall. It is perfectly possible that Maximus stationed his Saxons on the British land frontier. That might mean that they were along the Wall, which might also account for the lack of the usual military finds there, as well as for the later traditions. It might also mean that the *foederati* were garrisoned around the edge of the villa-zone. Either way, the possibility is opened of very early English settlements far inland. The implications of this are further explored at the end of the next chapter.

10

Rethinking the Anglo-Saxon Migration and Settlement (2)

The Nature and Scale of the Migration

ॐ

Having concluded that the date of the Saxons' arrival is much vaguer than often supposed, and that this was a more complex event, we can return to the other questions posed at the start of Chapter 9 about the relationship between migration and change.

Crisis around the North Sea

We have seen the profound crisis in lowland Britain around 400, with settlements abandoned and severe economic recession. The same thing can be observed in northern Gaul. In the far north of that region the extent of collapse is much the same as in Britain, but the further south one progresses the better the Roman system weathered the crisis. Nevertheless even there, by the mid-fifth century villas had been abandoned and towns had contracted to shadows of their former selves. The pottery industry might have survived better than in Britain but nevertheless it went into a severe decline around 450. So restricted are the forms produced that only hard, technical work by archaeologists and the fortuitous presence of items in occasional coin-dated burials, such as are absent from Britain, have allowed a chronology to be established. Like Britain's, the regional economy generally ceased to rely on coinage.

The North Sea coastal regions of modern Germany, which I refer to as the 'Saxon homelands', were almost as closely bound into the Roman imperial system as the north-western Roman provinces. Large cremation cemeteries had been the norm for some centuries, suggesting a fairly stable population. The archaeology of rural settlements shows gradually increasing social complexity. By the late fourth century, for example, probably the area's best-known archaeologically excavated settlement, Feddersen Wierde, reveals the establishment of a large homestead. The excavators called this the 'Herrenhof' ('Lord's Farm'). It is difficult to see this entirely plausibly other than in terms of increasing social stratification. Simultaneously, the settlement appears to have been subject to some sort of central organization or planning; buildings radiate out from its centre. Similar tendencies can be seen in Denmark at Vorbasse, whose population might have reached about 200 by the end of the fourth century. So had that of another orderly and well-known excavated settlement, Wijster, in the Netherlands. Throughout the region, clusters of buildings show signs of being fenced off from their neighbours, hinting at an enhanced idea of private property. Close relationships with the Roman Empire are attested by the number of items of Roman metalwork in cremations. The many official Roman belt-sets and brooches demonstrate how position and prestige within barbarian society was bound up with imperial service. There seemed no better way of making a man's importance manifest than by laying his ashes to rest with his old uniform. Indeed the area reveals a huge number of imports from the Roman Empire (particularly northern Gaul), in terms both of artefacts and of cultural ideas and influences. This crucial point must be remembered.

Yet, as in England and northern Gaul, this picture ended abruptly in the fifth century. Around 400, settlements across the region, including Feddersen Wierde and another site at Flögeln, lost the orderly and planned nature of their fourth-century predecessors. Feddersen Wierde's 'Herrenhof' was abandoned. Buildings changed too, with traditional *Wohnstallhäuser* (long-houses with cattle byres at one end and human habitation at the other) being replaced by smaller post-built houses for humans only. By the second quarter of the fifth century, like the villas of Britain and northern Gaul, settlements such as Feddersen Wierde had been abandoned. Palaeobotany (the archaeological study of plant remains, often from soil cores sampled across large areas) suggests a retreat of cultivated land and a spread of forest.

In the mid-fifth century, many cemeteries ceased to be used. Slightly earlier, around 400, inhumation with grave-goods appeared. Men were typically buried with weaponry and women in a costume revealed by the use of quite elaborate jewellery. This custom had begun to appear slightly earlier in northern Gaul and starts to be attested in the British lowlands at about the same time: the early fifth century. We will examine the reasons for its appearance later. For now, we can anticipate that discussion by saying that it seems to be another symptom of a deep early fifth-century crisis in the Saxon homelands.

This and the changes in the Saxon archaeological record have traditionally been explained as stemming from the historically (and linguistically) attested migration to Britain. Any counter-debate has, as mentioned, largely been concerned with questioning the reality of that population movement. There is no doubt that this migration occurred or that the changes visible in the Saxon homelands are related to it. That said, this must still be examined more closely and critically.

The archaeology of Anglo-Saxon migration has tended to be restricted to the study of the two geographical areas involved—the starting point in north-western Germany, the Netherlands, and southern Denmark, and the end point in the lowlands of what is now England. Older generations thought this sufficient but it renders many important questions of causation impossible to resolve adequately. As younger generations of archaeologists have questioned the scale and even the reality of migration, their awareness of *any* mainland European archaeology has, with some notable exceptions, diminished correspondingly. Yet, as might have become clear, one cannot understand this migration outside its broader European context. One absolutely vital problem that arises from looking only at northern Germany and eastern England is that the dense relationships between Roman Gaul and the Saxon homelands and their immense importance are utterly obscured.

The crisis in the 'Saxon homelands' belongs to pretty much the same time as the crises equally visible in lowland Britain and northern Gaul. Furthermore, many symptoms of change are the same: the desertion of long-occupied settlements, the abandonment of cemeteries, the introduction of furnished inhumation (burial with grave-goods). Palaeobotanic study shows the abandonment of areas and the regrowth of scrub and forest.

Therefore two (perhaps three) related questions demand our attention. Does the evidence in the Saxon homelands necessarily imply mass emigration to Britain? If the changes *are* related to Saxon emigration does migration *explain* the changes, either in the Saxon homelands or in England, and, if it doesn't, what does? Overall, the issue is whether migration is the cause or the consequence of the social changes revealed archaeologically. The misguided debates on the existence of the migration and on the detection of what we might call binary ethnicity (Saxons versus Britons) have prevented this crucial question from being posed.

The first question can speedily be answered in the negative. Similar changes observable in the archaeology of other regions at this time are not explained by mass emigration. This is not to say that there is no connection between change and emigration in Saxony; just that the latter is not *necessary* to explain the former. It is not a *sufficient* explanation either. In detail, however, it becomes clear that movement across the North Sea or along its coasts must have *some* relationship to the precise forms of material culture seen in the regions that border it. Changes in the English archaeological and linguistic record relating precisely to the movement of people from the North Sea regions of northern Germany, the Netherlands, and Denmark have already been set out. Another set of archaeological changes has much more problematic links with migration than is usually admitted, which does not imply that no relationship existed.

In Chapter 6 we briefly considered the debate on the origins of early Anglo-Saxon settlement forms and architecture. As we saw there, the arguments against a continental Saxon origin for the 'halls' and other aspects of these post-imperial British settlements have not been entirely convincing and are not widely accepted. Nevertheless, other arguments deployed to support the linkage between the houses of the Saxon homelands and those of lowland Britain are far less persuasive. Most importantly these 'migrationist' arguments make no sense of the changes in Gaul. There are differences in detail but—overall—a very similar range of cultural features appears at the same time (indeed they begin rather earlier) in Gaul. There was no Saxon settlement there, and little or no relationship between these forms and those of the homelands of the barbarians who *did* settle there, the Franks. Indeed forms of semi-excavated hut are now being revealed archaeologically right across the western Empire in the late and post-imperial era. Many are very different from Anglo-Saxon *Grubenhäuser* but it is important to see this as part of a widespread architectural response to socio-economic change. These architectural forms could arise in the Roman provinces without being introduced from *barbaricum*. The main problem concerns the role of migration in explaining the change.

The use of 'migration theory' by those keen on retaining Anglo-Saxon migration as an explanation for cultural change has been limited to showing how migration could have happened rather than in more subtle fashion. The argument thus remains a less crude variant of the 'migration hypothesis': the idea that material cultural changes relate directly to a change in people. However, 'migration theory' is far more useful than that. One of its insights is that movement during migrations is rarely one-way. People return home, sometimes permanently, as well as staying in the land of destination. The flow of information is therefore *two-way*. This is crucial and indeed finds support in the sketchy sources for contemporary Europe, which refer to movements back to the mainland or back to *barbaricum*.

It is clear archaeologically that trade from the Roman Empire reached far into northern *Germania* and Scandinavia. Furthermore, Saxons had long served in the Roman army, especially, judging from the design of the metalwork they took home with them, in northern Gaul. Germanic-speaking barbarians had also long been stationed in Roman Britain. These too might well have included Saxons. Certainly, the Saxons knew Britain from fourth-century raids but it is important to repeat my suggestion that an official settlement of Saxon *foederati* took place in the early 380s under Magnus Maximus. This means that there were many contacts across the North Sea in both directions by *c.*400. That in turn implies that cultural exchange could have taken place in *both* directions. This network allows us to explain the similarities not just between the developments in north-western coastal Germany and the Netherlands and those in England, but also—crucially—between these and the analogous changes in northern Gaul. The traditional, 'migrationist' or 'Germanist' arguments require us to believe that two *different* kinds of barbarian (Franks and

Saxons), whose respective homelands show quite *different* archaeology, migrated to separate parts of the Empire (Gaul and Britain), where they suddenly started using more or less the *same* material cultural forms in burials and settlements. This culture, moreover, was in some cases quite different from that of either of their homelands and in others was only appearing there at this time. This is hardly plausible without the invocation of nineteenth-century ideas of the cultural unity of all 'Germans'. It is far simpler to see this pattern in the light of the enormous cultural influence that the Empire, and northern Gaul in particular, had over *barbaricum* and of the archaeologically well-attested fact of movement from Gaul back to Saxony. In this light we would view these cultural changes as deriving their inspiration at least partly from the transformations and responses to crisis that took place in Gaul north of the Seine, where the changes began earliest. Without the historical narrative of Anglo-Saxon migration to force our preconceptions about the directions and routes of influence and population movement into an interpretative straitjacket, this would doubtless be how an archaeologist would read these changes around the North Sea. The transformations in Britain and in Gaul seem to be analogous responses to the collapse of a villa system. We must start thinking of the North Sea as an interconnected 'cultural province', much as it is treated in later eras of history, rather than seeing it as separating two different, opposed worlds.

The observed range of architectural forms seems to merge influences from the north-western provinces of the Roman Empire with those from *barbaricum*. That these might arise in areas with cultural and political contacts during a period when all these areas suffered deep socio-economic crisis seems most plausible. This flexible argument appears to offer the best explanation of the archaeologically revealed developments without, on the one hand, either minimizing migration or its role in change or, on the other, deploying a crude and, overall, equally unconvincing explanation, simply seeing all changes as a sign of the presence of newcomers. Sadly those positions coincide with the two positions adopted in the current debate over Anglo-Saxon migration. It is time for more subtlety.

This is especially true in discussion of the other key material cultural change: the introduction of furnished inhumation. In Anglo-Saxon archaeological discussions this is still more or less universally accepted as an element introduced from northern Germany. Yet, unlike the house-types, this evidence provides no very convincing empirical basis for the assumption. The ancestral burial ritual in the Saxon homelands was cremation, the rite the Saxons definitely brought with them to Britain. By the fifth century, inhumation had long been usual in the Roman Empire. The custom had tended to lack grave-goods but from the late fourth century these began to be reintroduced. The custom of more lavishly furnished burial first appears in the northern Gallic provinces in the last quarter or so of the fourth century. It must be pointed out straight away that the ritual has in itself nothing to do with paganism. This has long been demonstrated; the Church never outlawed such burial and well-furnished graves under churches are known from written and excavated sources. These graves have usually been interpreted as those of incoming Franks or other 'Germanic' barbarians. This reading is still probably the most common one, especially amongst French and German archaeologists. However, a strictly archaeological interpretation shows that there is nothing un-Roman about these graves. The ritual is essentially Roman and the material deposited almost exclusively originates in the Empire's northern provinces. What changed was the deceased's burial in a more elaborate and archaeologically visible costume than had hitherto been the case, with additional objects placed around the body. Typically these graves yield jewellery in women's burials and items of weaponry in those of men.

Why had this change happened? It is important to look at the broader context of northern Gallic archaeology. These graves appear at the point of crisis, with severe economic decline, the abandonment of villas, and the dramatic contraction of towns. Earlier, I linked that crisis to the imperial court's withdrawal to Italy and the end of effective governance north of the Loire. Seen thus, the precise nature of the objects in these burials makes additional sense. They claim an elite status whose bases are entirely Roman and traditional. Official metalwork (male cloak brooches and belt-sets) suggests legitimate authority linked to imperial service. The weapons either mark a connection with the army or a role in hunting (a traditional late Roman aristocratic pastime); hunting scenes are also depicted on some of the vessels deposited in the burials. The elaborate female costume is probably related to the manifestation of the deceased's standing as an honourable daughter, mother, or spouse. For this symbolism to be meaningful an audience had to be present at the funeral. This was a transient display to neighbours: members of the local community. The deaths of these individuals, especially, but not exclusively, the mature adult male heads of households, caused a crisis in their family's local status. This had to be smoothed over with a public ritual display of their status and their heirs' ability to bury them with full honour. Food offerings and vessels in the graves suggest that feasting around the grave took place, a classic location for the cementing of late antique social relations. These burials are thus symptomatic of a crisis in local power and are surely what we would expect when the local elite was being compelled to abandon its villas. Indeed, if we look at the sixth century, when the custom had become general across communities, the distribution of cemeteries with grave-goods tends to match the distribution of late Roman villas in northern Gaul very closely. Many such cemeteries are indeed found right by the old villas. Furnished inhumation is frequently a symptom of the breakdown of the stable social hierarchy that was earlier manifest in the villas.

In the late fourth century some barbarians in the far north of Germany, neighbouring the Saxon homelands, started to inhume their dead, albeit generally without grave-goods. It is generally agreed that this custom was copied from the Romans, yet another manifestation of how the barbarian aristocracy demonstrated its status and distinction through Roman culture. Again we can see the movement of cultural information *from* the Roman provinces *to* northern Germany (entirely unsurprising in that *Germania* was very much the economic hinterland of northern Gaul). When the Saxon homelands entered their crisis period around 400 the furnished burial custom appeared. Given the many similarities in the ritual and material deployed, it seems reasonable to see it as an analogous response to situations similar to those in Gaul. Further, the close cultural links between the areas and the clear service of locals in the Roman army there make it entirely plausible to trace the inspiration for this burial ritual to contemporary northern Gaulish aristocratic practices. All of this supports the notion that ideas about houses moved in the same direction.

It should therefore be absolutely clear that, contrary to usual Anglo-Saxon archaeological practice, the early fifth-century appearance of furnished inhumation in England *cannot* be read simply as another mark of Saxon immigration. It can be seen as the same response to the same sorts of crisis. As in Gaul, the distribution of grave-goods cemeteries covers approximately the same area as that of Roman villas (Figure 10.1). There are differences at the overall level and on a local scale. The villas spread further west, for instance, and the cemeteries further north. Furthermore the cemeteries do not overlie the villas in the clear fashion observable in the Gaulish and upper Danubian frontier provinces, but can be more marginal. Yet villas and cemeteries show many of the same general clusters and blanks (in the Chilterns for example). This immediately discounts one commonly proposed idea, that gaps in the distribution of grave-goods cemeteries mark out British political units. Furnished inhumation does not spread westwards very much over this period, in the

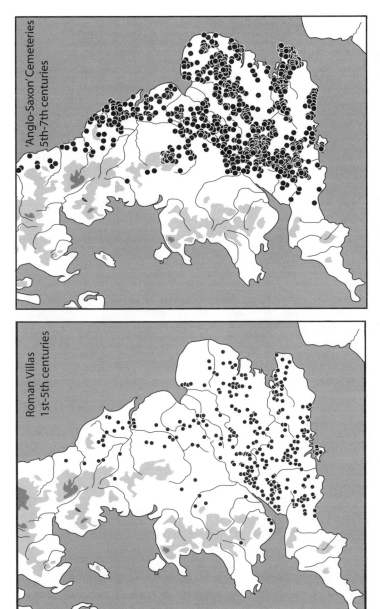

Figure 10.1 A comparison of the general distribution of Roman villas and 'Anglo-Saxon' cemeteries (distributions as they stood in the mid-1980s).

way that one might expect if it was a mark of Saxon settlement. A line drawn from Whitby on the Yorkshire coast through the mouth of the Severn to the Dorset coast would leave almost all 'Anglo-Saxon' cemeteries to its east, whether in the fifth century or the seventh (Figure 10.2). The westward limit of 'Anglo-Saxon' cemeteries is only (at most) about sixty miles further west in the seventh century than it was in the early fifth. Nor does this distribution correspond to the areas occupied by kingdoms during the period of the cemeteries' use. Much of Mercia, for example, has no such cemeteries. A similar

Figure 10.2 The expansion of 'Anglo-Saxon' cemeteries in lowland Britain, *c.*400–*c.*700. After Dark (1994).

growth in the number of furnished inhumation cemeteries occurred in seventh-century northern Gaul (Figure 10.3), with new sites filling in many gaps in the distribution of earlier sites. This cannot be explained as revealing later phases of Frankish conquest. Furnished inhumations, in England as elsewhere, are found where arable farming was common and where a particular form of landowning and social organization had predominated, manifested by the villas. They are a clear manifestation of socio-economic crisis.

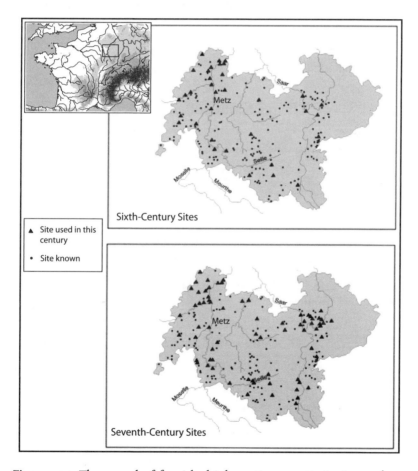

Figure 10.3 The spread of furnished inhumation cemeteries in northern Gaul, *c*.500–*c*.700

This does not necessarily imply that those buried in these graves were not incoming Saxon barbarians. The flow of information around the North Sea region meant that Saxon immigrants and Roman provincials were familiar with this form of interment. The occupants of such burials could thus be of Romano-British or continental Saxon birth; they could have claimed all sorts of ethnic identities. The artefacts in them sometimes originate in northern Germany, and sometimes have other origins and designs. What seems certain is that the people thus laid to rest were members of families of local prestige whose pre-eminence was called into question by their death. That is the important thing. These graves are thus best discussed in terms of *why* they appeared rather than of *who* was buried in them.

The push and pull of politics

Locating migration within a broader context of crisis and two-way communication across the North Sea enables us to pursue the discussion of an early federate settlement of Saxons and resolve some of its problems. Such soldiers could act as a conduit for information back to the Saxon homelands. They could also act as 'scouts' for further migration into Britain. Studies of migrations suggest that such early settlers are a very common feature of population movements. They provide information about the new lands and a settled community into which newcomers from the old country can fit. Saxon *foederati* would have needed recruits to replace those who grew old and retired or were lost in action. Continuing contacts would explain why, when the Saxons of Britain made their non-Roman identity visible in their material culture, around 430, the material used was from contemporary northern Germany. They did not dig out old artefacts from up to fifty years previously. Given the way in which barbarian settlers generally disappeared into the host culture of the Roman Empire it is unlikely that such material would have been retained.

Late fourth- and early fifth-century relationships between Britannia and the Saxon homelands are difficult to unravel. One problem is the assumption which we have already encountered, that artefactual similarities and influences must come from *barbaricum* to *Britannia*, following the historically recorded population movement, although such a conclusion is not always warranted. Another is that Britain and northern Gaul—and the army in particular—shared a wide range of material culture, especially metalwork. Thus, while objects found in *Germania* could well have arrived there as trade from Gaul, or with Saxon and other troops returning home after serving in the Gallic army, it is also possible that they were brought by men returning from service in Britain. There is enough to suggest that contacts between late Roman Britain and the north of Germany were regular. 'Romano-Saxon' pottery's influence on the design of northern German cremation urns underlines this point.

The difference in the distributions of material between Gaul and *Germania* on the one hand and Britain and *Germania* on the other might match diverging relationships between barbarian settlers and the Roman Empire. A formal Saxon federate settlement in *Britannia* could have led to a higher degree of permanent settlement and a greater status for Saxons in provincial British society. Service in the regular army in northern Gaul might conversely only have perpetuated traditional patterns of 'career migration': movement to a new area to follow a profession, with a later return home. It is possible that, unlike Saxon soldiers in the Gallic army, successful *foederati* in Britain did not return home to Saxony to claim status in society there.

Why did the Saxons declare their identity in Britain in the 430s? The political crises around the North Sea shed further light on the migration. We have already seen the tension and stress caused in Roman Britain and northern Gaul when effective imperial government withdrew to Italy. One result was competition for local authority in what rapidly became something of a power vacuum. Appeals to outsiders were not uncommon in trying to resolve these. Furthermore, the Saxon troops in the island could provide muscle for particular contenders' claims to authority. Studies of migration have discussed the mixture of 'push' (from the homelands) and 'pull' (into the new country) factors involved. Political instability was an important 'pull' factor, drawing people from across the North Sea into lowland Britain.

There were equally significant 'push' factors. All too frequently the causes for migration are hardly considered. The two usually suggested, to the exclusion of all others, are climate change and a somehow natural barbarian desire to attack and conquer the Roman Empire. A rise in sea levels occurred from the third century onwards, making some areas of the North Sea littoral less easy to inhabit, but this is unsatisfactory as a real cause of migration. This situation had existed for some time so it does not account for the change of the 430s. It also fails to explain why the people of the North Sea coast should undertake the perilous voyage to Britain, where similar changes were taking place, rather than simply moving further inland. It has correctly been pointed out that moving inland would require learning a whole new way of life, as the ecology and economy were different. This would apply even more to a move to Britain.

Barbarians were long used to raiding the Roman provinces for their wealth but one must remember that the Empire was also a source of prestige and career advancement. Its destruction and conquest cannot seriously have been the aim of even the most bellicose Saxon war-leader. More importantly, the barbarians often wanted to settle within the Empire. The collapse of the frontier could have been a spur to this. With communication across the North Sea, it cannot have taken long for the news to get home that society and economy, wealth and prospects in the imperial provinces were very much not what they had been, but the greater opportunities for war-leaders there were probably also made known. These factors were surely significant but whether they account for the migration's scale is questionable. So is whether they constitute a 'push' rather than a 'pull'.

A more plausible 'push' factor is the socio-economic crisis that we have discussed in the Saxon homelands. We've seen that the Empire was a source of prestige and status in the north of *Germania*. One strategy for bolstering political power was by limiting access to prestigious Roman goods, which could be used as important gifts to buy support. Taking these by raiding was important but risky; acquiring them as diplomatic gifts was better, having the added kudos of implying a direct, personal relationship with mighty Rome. When the Empire entered its period of acute crisis, from 395 onwards, when the government in Italy took its eye off the north-west, its long and successful policies of frontier management ended. Apart from the kings on the frontier itself, who may have been bolstered by large subsidies, the complex relationships which maintained balance among the barbarian polities were thrown into chaos. Any rulers in the hinterland of *barbaricum* whose status relied on a certain relationship with the Empire will have found their position questioned. Another means by which barbarian leaders acquired the prestigious Roman goods with which they purchased support was through trade. In the crisis afflicting the north-western provinces around 400, manufacture and trade of these items ceased. All this must have caused deep political crisis in the Saxon homelands.

The name Saxon appears during the third century, and the Romans called all barbarians from the North Sea coastal areas by this ethnic designation. It appeared at the same time as the coalescence of other great barbarian confederacies (the Franks, the Alamans, and the Goths, not to mention the Picts) and the disappearance from the written sources of names used earlier, such as Angles (English), Jutes, and Frisians. This permits the plausible supposition that the Saxons were another new barbarian confederacy. An interesting feature of the post-imperial period is the reappearance of those old names at this time. Procopius refers to *Angiloi* (Angles) and *Phrisioi* (Frisians), while a sixth-century Frankish source mentions the *Eucii*, probably the Jutes. It is reasonable to propose that the crisis detectable in the northern German archaeological record, which we have connected with the Roman Empire's troubles around 400, led to the fracture of the Saxon confederacy. Groups hitherto subsumed within it reasserted their identity. Simultaneously, the fifth-century Elbe valley, one of the most important trade routes from the Empire, and the central and eastern Mediterranean in particular, came under the control of a new confederacy: the Thuringians. As the period wore on, other pressures exerted themselves. By the early sixth century the Franks were pressing from the south. By the middle of the century they had destroyed the Thuringian kingdom, bringing its remnants under Frankish overlordship, and allegedly reduced the Saxons to tributary status. At the same time a new people seems to have emerged to the north, the Danes (first mentioned in an account of a raid on northern Francia *c.*520). Artefacts with Danish, Thuringian, and Frankish associations are found in Saxon graves, suggesting that different factions associated themselves with one or other of these outside groups, to secure their backing.

Such political fragmentation and competition had, since Julius Caesar's time at least, led to losing factions migrating into the Roman Empire. With the information coming to the region from Saxons in Britain, it might have been even more attractive to those losing out in political struggles in *barbaricum* to try their hand in those in *Britannia*. This seems like a more convincing 'push' factor in explaining migration to Britain than either climate change or a somehow innate barbarian desire to invade Rome.

Counting keels

The last issue to concern us is the debate about the size of the Anglo-Saxon migration. Chapter 6 laid out the arguments in favour of a minimal scale of migration; they have not, on the whole, been very sophisticated. Sometimes they have been based upon a selective reading of the written sources that dismisses most of their accounts but retains, for no very good reason, the legendary traditions about the Saxons' arrival in three keels. Otherwise they have been constructed around flimsy attempts to dismiss the northern German origins or significance of the material culture that appears in England from the 430s, and equally insubstantial claims that the whole idea of a mass migration is based upon an agenda driven by the written sources.

The traditions about the migration make very little reference to numbers beyond the three to five keels in which the founders of kingdoms supposedly arrived. This might imply small numbers, although whether such obviously legendary tales and their folkloric elements had any such implications to their contemporary audiences is very much a moot point. On the other hand, Bede says that Angeln, the homeland of the Angles, was deserted in his day because of their movement to Britain. Archaeology reveals him to have been mistaken about this. Although a 'gap' (of debated significance) in Saxon settlement archaeology has been seized upon as 'proving' Bede's statement and supporting the idea of mass migration, this 'gap' spans the fifth to later seventh centuries. By the time Bede was writing (the 730s) it had been closed. That point, however, is less important than the fact that Bede *thought* there was a large-scale movement. There are also references to the initial settlers (later on, to Hengist) receiving numerous reinforcements from *Germania*. On the whole, though, the documents say little very clearly about the size of the migration one way or the other. Given what was said in Chapter 4 about the written evidence's value, there would be scant reason to believe them even if they did.

Something that people *did* think by Bede's time was that the Anglo-Saxons had either slaughtered the Britons or driven them west into the Cornish, Welsh, or Cumbrian highlands. If any early medieval notion gave rise to the idea of mass migration then it is probably this one. Yet it is quite clear why Bede and his fellows thought this. In their day the majority of people living in the English (Anglo-Saxon) kingdoms, especially the politically dominant classes, were indeed English. Bede knew that the islands had been occupied by the Britons before, so to him their absence from the eighth-century British lowlands allowed only one interpretation: the English had killed them all or driven them away. It was an understandable conclusion. Four years before Bede finished his *Ecclesiastical History*, an anonymous author in northern Gaul, or *Francia* as it had come to be known, wrote the *Book of the History of the Franks*. He (or it might have been she) faced a similar problem. Everyone knew that the Romans and Gauls used to live in northern Gaul, yet now there were only Franks. Thus the Franks must have exterminated the Gallo-Romans, although someone added a marginal comment to the work clarifying that before they did so the Franks got the Gallo-Romans to teach them Latin first! That was an additional difficulty that Bede did not face. The Franks spoke a dialect descended from Latin; at least the English spoke English. Eighth-century writers, obviously, were not social anthropologists; they did not study ethnic change, although fortunately for us some of their predecessors described it. Later on we will see how at least some Britons became Anglo-Saxons, just as the Gauls had become Franks.

The arguments against the minimalist interpretation of Anglo-Saxon migration have, however, rarely been less crude than those proposing it. They have often based themselves on fairly unsophisticated arguments about the material culture that can be shown to derive, in whole or part, from northern Germany, which we have already encountered. They assume, simply enough, that where such archaeological evidence is found, there were Anglo-Saxon migrants, and that all the people using this culture were migrants or their descendants. Arguments which nuance (as with building-types) or even deny (as with furnished burial) an a priori link between other types of evidence and the barbarian homelands are ignored. The claimed links between men buried with weapons and Anglo-Saxon immigrants, and between those without such objects and the Britons, are belied by numerous circular arguments. There are in any case many other factors that could account for the biological differences. Nonetheless, a connection between weapon burial and Anglo-Saxon identity should not be ruled out—just as long as we are clear about what we understand by such an identity.

Chapter 6 outlined strong arguments in favour of linguistic change supporting large-scale migration from northern Germany. However, there is one key problem with them all. That is the assumption, still more or less universal, that the people the Anglo-Saxon migrants encountered in lowland Britain spoke British (or Brythonic as it is sometimes called). This is very rarely questioned but it is more than a little problematic, being based upon absolutely no evidence. It is likely that the highland regions of Britain were little affected by the Romans in terms of their overall language, but this cannot be said of the lowland villa-zone. Here Roman influence was profound. 'Roman' material culture predominates, even on 'native' settlement sites. This culture introduced new culinary forms and doubtless new vocabulary to match. In northern Gaul, a region whose archaeology matches that of lowland Britain in many ways throughout the period from the fourth century to the seventh, it is clear that (outside Brittany) the local Celtic language was replaced by low Latin. After 400 years of Roman rule the same was probably true in Britain. It is worth pointing out that all Romano-British written material (curse tablets, graffiti, and so on) is in Latin. Unlike in early Roman Gaul, there is no writing in a Celtic language. If the inhabitants of lowland Roman Britain spoke a local form of low Latin then the Anglo-Saxons' lack of contact with British-speakers would be entirely unsurprising. If we look for Latin loan-words in Old English, we find hundreds: about as many as there are in Old Welsh. It is usually claimed that these words were introduced during the Anglo-Saxons' conversion to Christianity, yet that argument is itself founded ultimately on two presuppositions. One is the idea that because the Britons spoke British this would have been the earliest moment at which such Latin loan-words could have been introduced. The other is that Christianity died out entirely in lowland Britain before Augustine's mission. Neither assumption is secure. This does not preclude the linguistic evidence from showing a large-scale migration, by any means, but it does force us to think about it more carefully.

The employment of modern DNA to study the Anglo-Saxon migration is a deeply problematic and indeed—I would argue—dangerous line of argument. The problems lie not so much in the scientific analysis of the DNA itself—on which I am not qualified to comment—but in the movement from such analysis to interpretative conclusions about the early Middle Ages. There the approach becomes decidedly unscientific. European DNA has been inextricably mixed since prehistoric times. The distribution of particular DNA traits reveals very broad areas with these similarities. The self-same maps have thus been argued to reveal the spread of Indo-European language and the Anglo-Saxon migration some millennia later, as well as an alleged migration of Germanic-speakers into Britain in the first century BC. This in turn reveals a further problem: when these patterns became similar cannot convincingly be dated. If, for example, a DNA pattern very similar to that of modern inhabitants of Saxony was reported for dwellers in a southern English town, need that result from a fifth- or sixth-century migration, or from sexual encounters with a unit of the King's German Legion (largely from Hanover) stationed there during the Napoleonic Wars? Or from sexual encounters between troops from that town and northern German women after 1945? A DNA similarity will not tell you the direction of population movement. A Saxon soldier could return home from the Roman army with his British wife and have a family there; Saxon raiders could take British slaves and sire children on them. And so on. Movement back and forth around the North Sea was an important feature of late Roman history. The rate at which DNA chains change has also been debated: the introduction of new genetic components, currently placed in our period, might have occurred much earlier. Even arguments using DNA to support the idea of a mass Anglo-Saxon migration place that movement over ten generations. That might be as much as 300 years. If the rate of change was slower than currently assumed, the period in question could be even longer.

Genetic similarities can spread without any major movement of people, as the result of a chain of local marriages. If two people on a border meet and produce children, those children (with genes from both parents) can then meet and marry people from slightly further into the two different territories. Their children in turn might have children with partners from slightly further inland, and so on. Genetic traits might thus move across a territory without any great migration.

Another difficulty concerns the method used. Samples have been drawn with particular hypotheses in mind: that there was a migration from northern Germany. They are not taken from areas that would not fit this problem. It is hardly surprising that DNA from modern English and German urban populations should show more similarities with each other than with samples from highland, rural North Wales or Norway, where social and cultural mixing is, and has been, far less. Finally, it has been possible for the same researchers, at various times, to present diametrically opposing interpretations of the same results.

Moving beyond methodology, further problems arise concerning the analyses' assumptions. One is that migration happens in discrete periods. Thus, for example, the fifth and sixth centuries are often known as the period of *the* migrations. Therefore, in this view, demonstrable population-mixing can be dated to specific blocks of time.

Yet migration is a constant of human existence. People were moving from *barbaricum* east of the Rhine into the Roman Empire for centuries before 400. People moved, *within* the Empire, on a large scale too. And of course people have continued to move and to marry the inhabitants of other areas ever since. The similarities between English and German DNA might result from late antique migration from Germany but it might equally stem from such movement at many other times and, indeed, from movement in the opposite direction, or a series of such movements in one DNA chain. Movement from the Empire to *barbaricum*, amply demonstrated in the archaeological record, is excluded from reasoning because it does not fit a model derived from problematic written sources. Thus this use (or misuse) of DNA is driven by a particular, crude, reading of history and its results chosen to fit this story rather than to examine it.

Better prospects are likely for the analysis of ancient DNA, now thought capable of producing good-quality evidence. Such analyses have already yielded interesting results in the study of mainland European cemetery populations. Similar benefits might accrue from studies in England. However large numbers of samples are needed before significant conclusions can be proposed, conclusions which might only serve to underline what Bede and other sources told us in any case. There are much better and more interesting uses to which costly genetic analyses can be put than the simple demonstration of migration.

Even with these data, an even more serious problem concerns the move from DNA to conclusions about ethnic or political identity. Ethnic identity is multi-layered. It is deployed (or not) in particular situations as the occasion demands, and it can be changed. DNA cannot give you a sense of all of the layers of that person's ethnicity, or of which she thought the most important, or even if she generally used a completely different one, or of when and where such identities were stressed or concealed. A male Saxon immigrant into the

Empire in, say, the fourth century, would—one assumes—have DNA revealing the area where he grew up, but he would probably increasingly see himself, and act, as a Roman. Saxon origins would have little part in his social, cultural, or political life, and even less for his children, if they stayed in the Empire. If he returned home with the cachet of his imperial service, it might have been his *Roman* identity that gave him local status. He might even have called himself a Roman. However, if a distant male relative moved into Britain 150 years later, his DNA might be very similar but, in complete distinction, he might make a very big deal of his Saxon origins. They would, or could, propel him to the upper echelons of society. DNA tells us nothing about any of this. What is pernicious about this use of genetic data is its *essentialism*. It views a person's identity as one-dimensional, unchanging, and as entirely derived from that person's biological and geographical origins. In short, it reduces identity to something similar to nineteenth-century nationalist ideas of race. Everyone sane knows that people moved from northern Germany to Britain in the fifth and sixth centuries. In that sense, these expensive analyses tell us nothing we did not know already. In their implicit reduction of identity to a form of race, masking all the other contingent and interesting aspects of cultural interaction and identity-change, they risk setting back the understanding of this period by more than a century. Moreover, they provide pseudo-historical and pseudo-scientific ammunition for present-day nationalists, xenophobes, and racists. Before leaving recent DNA analyses, we should flag up that the historical sources cited to show racial segregation are used very uncritically and rarely say what they are claimed to. Many of the same general points can be levelled at other analyses of such things as the isotopes from teeth, which are far less exclusive in the geographical zones revealed than one might hope—again, the part of the map chosen is often determined by the historical story the analyst wants to tell.

As frequently in this chapter, my attitude to current academic archaeological debate resembles that of Mercutio in *Romeo and Juliet*: 'a plague on both your houses'. I should like to highlight three factors which have not been given due importance but which might help us steer a middle course. One is that the extent of cultural change produced by migration is not determined only by the strength of the incoming culture but also by that of the indigenous one. So overwhelmingly dominant was Roman identity during the first four centuries that the sizeable immigration from *barbaricum* left almost no trace. On the other hand, Roman society, economy, and culture went into meltdown before 430. This must have seriously undermined the social value attached to a traditional Roman identity. In northern Gaul, where a similar meltdown can be identified, linguistic change also occurred in the far north of the region and similarly, by about 600, everyone who was anyone claimed to be a Frank. Further south, Roman culture and social structures survived far better and the change to non-Roman culture was that much less. The collapse was, if anything, worse in Britain. This must be important in explaining the scale of the shift from Roman to 'Anglo-Saxon' in the British lowlands, rendering the numbers or scale of migration less of a determining factor.

The second factor is time. The North Sea was an important route of communication and movement before the fifth century. It remained so afterwards. Cultural contacts between England and areas like Scandinavia persisted until at least the seventh century. People thus continued to move from what had been *barbaricum*, throughout the early Anglo-Saxon period. They moved from Britain back to the mainland too, as seventh- and eighth-century Frisian traders did. The history of the Saxon homelands remained turbulent, with repeated Frankish attacks, and could have produced further waves of migration. This means that the scale of migration should not be seen solely in terms of the numbers of immigrants alive at one time—envisaging a mass of people swamping the locals (note, as with my use of the word 'wave' above, the watery similes so popular in migration studies). The actual numbers of immigrant Saxons could have been small at any one time, but a constant stream of migration would be vital in topping up the strength and importance of the English element in the population. Even the arguments for mass immigration using modern DNA analyses place such a movement over a 250–300-year period.

The third point responds to minimalist arguments. There were key differences between the Anglo-Saxon migration and the movements of mainland European barbarians. The reasons for the Anglo-Saxon migration, the general push and pull factors and their relationship to political crises in the Empire, are very much like those behind a number of other movements. This is especially true of other migrations from what we might call the 'middle band' of barbarian groups, behind those bordering immediately on the Roman frontier. The Vandals and Lombards also moved a long way. The initial phase of settlement, with Saxons employed as a Roman force, also has parallels on the mainland, clearest perhaps with the Gothic settlement in Aquitaine in 418/19. But there the similarities end. Whether one sees them traditionally, as a people on the move or, with greater probability, as military forces of increasingly diverse origin, clustered around particular generals, the arrival of most mainland groups was a one-off event. More to the point, perhaps, the Gothic warriors who descended upon Aquitaine in 419 or the Vandals who took Carthage in 439 had grown up inside the Roman Empire; many had been born there. A large number will have had Roman mothers. The Anglo-Saxon migration was a longer-term process, the duration of which cannot now be established but which surely lasted in excess of a century. It involved movement directly from *barbaricum*. The only parallels here would be the drift across the frontier of border peoples like the Franks and Alamans, which had some analogous results. What is more, the arrival of 'peoples' like the Goths was often governed by formal treaties or agreements, or in other cases like that of the Vandals, by the rapid military occupation of an area. The British situation involved, as far as we know, no such neat, short-term formalizations. The subsequent history of most mainland barbarian groups tended to be driven by relationships with the imperial government in Ravenna and with regional Roman aristocracies. This in turn revolved around factional competition for control of the centre of imperial government. It is a very strong likelihood that the Saxons in Britain became similarly embroiled in local political fighting, in alliance with factions of the Romano-British aristocracy. After all, Celtic names appear in the earlier reaches of many Anglo-Saxon royal genealogies. Some names might have been chosen to appeal to speakers of both languages. The alleged founder of King Alfred's dynasty in Wessex was called Cerdic, a British name. His supposed son and successor, Cynric, has an English name but one which sounds quite similar to a British or Irish name like Cunorix. This might be a process similar to that which we will encounter in the next chapter, in Gaul, with Count Lupus and his son Romulf. Yet, this increasingly took place beyond the effective limits of imperial politics and with no direct linkage to the policies or courts of the emperors in Ravenna. Finally, although there were some similarities with certain parts of mainland Europe, particularly northern Gaul, the social, economic, and political situation of post-imperial Britain had many important specifics, not least the extent of collapse in the lowlands and the presence of formidable highland polities. All these things make it risky to draw simple parallels between Anglo-Saxon and other better-documented migrations, and to claim that, like them, it was essentially a small-scale, elite military movement, even if we can trace general structural resemblances. None of this implies any sort of binary ethnic structure or struggle.

What is important about the Anglo-Saxon migration is not its size, which is impossible to determine, but the social and political changes of which it became a focus. On balance, it seems that more people migrated from the Saxon homelands than from other parts of *barbaricum*, but this movement lasted a long time. If we think of it as a mass migration this term must be qualified as implying the total movement of people over a long period, not a huge wave flooding over the lowlands in one rush. At any one moment there may have been no more, or indeed fewer, new arrivals from *Germania* in Britain than, say, arrived with the 'Great Invasion' in Spain in 409. Steady reinforcement over many decades, combined with the weakening of indigenous Roman identity, meant that this migration produced dramatic effects regardless of the numbers involved.

East to west? (3)

At this point we can return to the question of whether the traditional picture of steady, east-to-west Anglo-Saxon expansion is necessarily entirely apt. In Chapter 8 it was pointed out that barbarian territories in the Roman Empire rarely developed simply through spreading out from the old frontier. It was admitted that most migrations were unlike that of the Anglo-Saxons, so the settlement of the *Britanniae* could well have happened differently. However, the closest analogy to Anglo-Saxon settlement, that of the Franks in northern Gaul, worked not only on the 'moving front' model but spread back towards the frontier from military bases, in Roman service, on the Loire. The leaders controlling this latter movement were those who eventually dominated all of the Franks. Chapter 9 added the suggestion that our only reliable written information about the earliest Saxon settlement allows us to postulate Saxon bases well into the interior of Britain, whether on Hadrian's Wall or along the frontier between highland and lowland zones.

Now we can build further on this, employing 'migration theory'. One of its most important insights is that migration does not 'flood' over territories on a wide front but follows particular routes. We have seen that migrations tend to involve scouts returning to the homeland with information about the new country, and that established communities are usually the initial destination for later arrivals. Thus it must be entirely plausible that some of the earliest Saxon communities were established far inland. Like the Franks on the Loire, they would be focused on military forces in Roman service—the initial federate groups. This does not make the idea of other groups settling on the coast and spreading their authority inland any less plausible. Let's be clear about that. It simply adds another element to the equation.

Over twenty years ago, Barbara Yorke pointed out that the West Saxon traditions that contributed to the *Anglo-Saxon Chronicle* seem to have involved one that saw the kingdom emerging inland, in the upper Thames valley. In traditional interpretations, some of the earliest 'Saxon' cemeteries are in that sort of area, as at Dorchester on Thames. The name of Mercia, intriguingly, means 'border dwellers' and that of Deira, the southern half of Northumbria, derives from Deur, a British form. The king at the head of the West Saxon genealogy, Cerdic, has a British name and so too, possibly, does Penda, the first Mercian king we know about. The cores of these realms, Wessex, Mercia, and Deira, all lie on the border between the lowland and highland zones, in that prosperous band of late Roman Britain. They were, moreover, the most powerful Anglo-Saxon kingdoms. This continuity between late Roman socio-economic stability and prosperity and Anglo-Saxon political power has been obscured by the traditional division of scholars into 'Romanists' and 'Anglo-Saxonists' and by the concentration on binary ethnic opposition between Britons and Saxons. It deserves closer scrutiny. The stability of social organization would explain why 'Saxon' archaeological traces are comparatively few in this band of territory. One is entitled to ask whether the Frankish model applies (Figure 10.4). Like the Merovingians', did these kingdoms owe their success to a typical

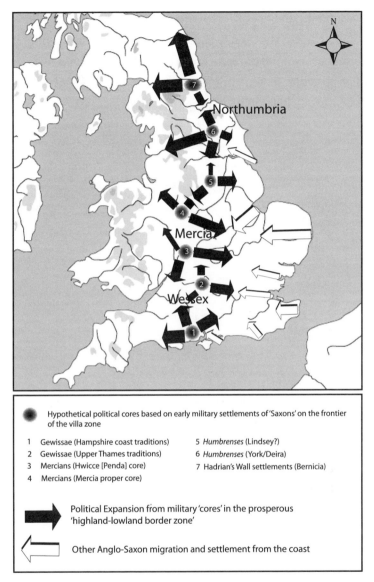

Figure 10.4 The Anglo-Saxon political takeover of *Britannia*: a hypothetical alternative

fifth-century Romano-Barbarian alliance? Did provincial Roman wealth pay for and give the edge to 'barbarian' forces originating in the last Roman armies? And is that, then, what enabled the kings of the lowland–highland border to expand their power from the interior of Britain towards the 'Saxon Shore'? This model of Saxon migration and conquest is quite different from the one we are used to, but it is entirely possible. How it might fit into the dynamics of fifth- and sixth-century British politics is explored in the next chapter.

II

Fifth- and Sixth-Century Politics in *Britannia*

☙❦❧

A ny Saxon warlord and his followers would have encountered an increasingly turbulent political situation in fifth-century *Britannia*. In principle, Rome's authority remained. In 428, an appeal to the mainland to resolve a religious dispute produced the first visit of St Germanus of Auxerre. As it happened, in that year Aëtius, Master of the Soldiers, was campaigning against the Franks in northern Gaul. If Germanus made a second visit, it also took place when the imperial government was attempting to restore its authority in the regions bordering on the Channel. The appeal to Aëtius mentioned by Gildas ought to have been made between 445 and 453 when he could be called 'thrice consul'. A plausible context would be 448 when Aëtius was again campaigning in northern Gaul. The inhabitants of Britain—or some of them—had not abandoned the idea that the Empire might return. However, on the mainland some of their contemporaries felt that the island was lost. A short source, called *The Narrative of the Valentinianic and Theodosian Houses* and written on the mainland in the 440s, says that Britain was lost during Honorius' reign (395–423).

The socio-economic meltdown of the fifth century's first decades has already been described, as has the crisis that it evidently caused for provincial aristocrats. Other problems faced any attempt to govern fifth-century Britain. One was the lack of real legitimacy in the Empire's absence, especially after 455. Another was the unavailability of any decisive coercive force, most—though doubtless not all—of the army having been withdrawn. Yet another was the inability of any one faction to garner the social and economic resources necessary to dominate their rivals. The Romano-British aristocracy was not especially wealthy and the removal of imperial government had called their very social position into serious question. Perhaps most seriously of all, other powers could provide military backing for their opponents.

Effective imperial power was retreating but no one knew they were living through 'the End of the Roman Empire'. Before about 470, nobody could be sure that the Empire would not recover. It had lasted for over four centuries and bounced back from innumerable past crises and civil wars, as in the third century. Nevertheless by the 430s many—perhaps most—of those active in British politics would have had no real memory of effective imperial governance. With time, official Roman military operations north of the area between the Loire and the Seine became fewer and fewer. After 451 they ceased altogether. This must have meant a steady diminution in the effectiveness of claims to rule based on a connection with the fading Empire.

For the political rivals or opponents of those who adopted this strategy, alternatives closer to hand might have seemed more immediately effective. One was the 'Saxons'. In the context we are discussing, any government might have found it difficult to collect taxes and other resources to pay armed forces. It is thus probably not surprising that by about 430 the Saxons living north of the Thames, which might have been where the Saxon *foederati* described by Gildas had initially been settled, should have started to proclaim their non-Roman identity. This might very well have been associated with an outright rebellion, the one mentioned by Gildas as occurring when the Britons withheld supplies and pay. One of the Saxons' advantages, of course, was their military role, which might, as Gildas seems to say, have given them an early superiority. It must be repeated, though, that *all* of Gildas' stories follow the pattern of an initial setback before a rally and victory under righteous leaders, and finally degeneration into sin. This must make us pause before assuming any factual reality behind his rhetorical pronouncements.

By the 430s too, with memories of effective imperial rule fading fast, a consciously 'non-' or even 'anti-Roman' identity might have been less problematic to rally behind against one's enemies. The Roman army had been adopting barbarian identities for much of the fourth century without abandoning claims to legitimate Roman-ness. So even followers of the 'Saxons' could have seen themselves as participating in what by then had become traditional Roman politics. This is yet a further reason why fifth-century politics should not be seen as a 'binary' struggle between Romans and barbarians.

Another alternative might have been provided by the rulers of the highland kingdoms, to whom we will return to consider in more detail. The archaeological evidence from the lowlands seems to suggest at least two different, rival groupings using metalwork of a Roman tradition, one south of the Thames and one around the Severn estuary. There were doubtless others. The excavated data reveal that the material proclaiming a Saxon origin lies north of the Thames. It is difficult to trace the clear east/west opposition required by the traditional views of a moving front line between Britons and Saxons. The archaeological record shows movement into Britain from the Saxon homelands and—actually much more importantly—the fact that such movement was of social and political importance. Nevertheless, seen on its own terms this evidence does not easily fit the models within which it is usually employed. Those models are ultimately based on a picture derived from the written sources discussed in Chapter 4, one entirely without value for the 'World of Arthur'. That ought to make the lack of fit between model and evidence less surprising. By now it should really force us to abandon the former. We must build our interpretative frameworks around the archaeological evidence itself and a broader, European understanding of the western Empire's collapse.

A wider perspective reveals that conflict between Romano-barbarian factions within the old structures of Roman politics was far more common than war between invading barbarians and defending Romans. Archaeological evidence equally suggests that the latter model is inappropriate for an understanding of post-imperial Britain. So we might return to the passage of Gildas' *De Excidio* about Mount Badon, discussed in Chapter 8. I suggested that Gildas' Latin could be understood to mean that, after Ambrosius Aurelianus' defeat of the Saxons, the war which lasted for forty-three years and a month until the siege of Mount Badon was not between Britons and Saxons but between different factions in a civil war. Gildas called the two sides *cives* (citizens) and *hostes* (enemies) or *furciferes* (rascals; scoundrels). This would be entirely consistent with Roman political vocabulary for a war between those claiming political legitimacy and those they considered to be rebels.

It is often said that Gildas refers to a forty-year peace with the Saxons after Badon. He does not. That claim comes partly from the long sentence about the 'forty-forth year' having elapsed since Badon and partly from reading the next sentence to mean that after Mount Badon foreign wars ceased. Neither component of the argument is solid. On balance Gildas seems to have said what Bede thought he had said: that Mount Badon came forty-four years *after* the war against the Saxons won by Ambrosius. The succeeding sentence is also crucially misread. It says nothing about a forty-year peace with Saxons. It simply says that, 'foreign having ceased but not civil [wars]' (this kind of sub-clause is called the ablative absolute in Latin), the cities are not populated as they once were. *That* is Gildas' main point. We saw in Chapter 8 that this can be seen quite easily as a commentary on the war referred to in the 'Mount Badon' sentence, lasting forty-three years and a month up to that battle, after Ambrosius' defeat of the Saxons. Civil war is something that worried Gildas far more than Saxon invasion. He was even more worried about religious malpractice and doctrinal backsliding. This would be entirely in line with the fifth- and sixth-century western European history and with Gildas' contemporaries' reactions to it.

Another feature of the fifth century was *emigration*. A strange tale told by Procopius recounts a sizeable migration of Saxons back to what is now Germany. Other Saxons are described fighting on the Loire in the 460s and 470s, whilst others still had, by the late sixth century, washed up around Bayeux in Normandy, where many place-names bear witness to their settlement. More significantly in the long run, Britons also migrated to the western peninsula of Aremorica, which as a result came to be called 'Lesser Britain' and, in time, Brittany. This migration is far shadier than the Anglo-Saxon, leaving little or no archaeological trace. The extent to which Breton language or the place-names shared between Brittany and south-west England derive from it remains a matter of heated debate. Such Britons as left, however, could have been motivated by an entirely analogous mix of push and pull factors as drove the Saxons to Britain. Britain was in social and economic crisis with long-established bases of power and authority under threat. Rivalry for political control was fierce. In northern Gaul a similar situation existed, offering opportunities for an adventurous warlord, as did the presence of the Empire, even as it gradually withered. There was also the long tradition, from Constantine I onwards, of British armed forces moving to the Continent to attempt to win power within the Empire. The Britons (and Saxons) who moved to Gaul might well have been, like the continental Saxons I suggested earlier, losers in political conflict who decided to make a play for a better result on the mainland.

Ethnic and political groupings and identities...and how to change them

In Chapter 6 I described the debate on ethnicity and the fact that ethnic identity is now more usually understood as flexible and mutable; essentially a state of mind. This means that ethnicity can be adopted by people with no geographical or genetic origins in common. It does not, however, imply that anyone can claim whatever identity they like and nor does it imply that ethnic change is a swift process of a one-for-one swap. People have several layers of identity that might be thought of as ethnic. In late antiquity, imperial citizens saw themselves not only as Romans, but as from a particular region (say Gaul or Britain) and from a specific *civitas* (city-district). It was not unusual for aristocrats at least to claim to belong to a number of *civitates* according to the links of their maternal and paternal kin. Local identifications within the *civitates*, based around smaller towns or *pagi* (country districts), might also have existed. Service in the army could provide a claim to other ethnic identities. A sixth-century Egyptian papyrus reveals, for example, that members of a particular regiment were still known as 'Franks'. These cannot possibly have come from the Frankish regions of *barbaricum*; their unit was raised a couple of centuries previously. They must themselves have been Egyptian by birth. In the fourth-century Saxon confederacy, as well as his general Saxon identity it is likely that a barbarian male from the region also saw himself as a Frisian, Angle, or Jute (the ethnic identities currently subsumed, as far as the Romans cared, beneath the confederate ethnicity). He might very well have also had a loyalty to his more local region or village. These points are important in assessing the 'failed state' idea as they do not suggest incomplete 'Romanization' or the maintenance of age-old rivalries.

Ethnic change involved taking another layer of ethnicity and, over time, reordering the importance which particular layers were accorded until an adopted identity became the principal one. Children might then be raised to regard this as their most important ethnicity. Ethnic change was thus a more subtle process than is sometimes imagined by those supporting the idea of mutable ethnicity, or than it is painted as being by those who retain old ideas of more fixed ethnic identity. It also took about a generation—at least—to work through. The shift from Roman to barbarian ethnicity, although very important, was also far from the only manifestation of the changes of identity during this era. Loyalty to one's *civitas* was enhanced in various parts of the West and it has been plausibly suggested that post-imperial British politics might have been played out within maintained earlier *civitas* boundaries. Many early medieval British kingdoms possibly preserve the boundaries of the *civitates*: Essex those of the Trinovantes, for example, and Kent those of the *Cantii* (whose name it also preserves). It is also vital to stress that non-Roman ethnicities other than Germanic ones became important. Here the obvious case is 'Briton'. Last and certainly not least was change in religious identity. The shift from Roman to Christian ways of dividing up the world was as important as the move from Roman to barbarian identity at high political levels. Gildas' kings used Christian forms of legitimization and the fifth- and sixth-century Anglo-Saxon kings, uniquely in the post-imperial West, stressed their paganism.

How and why did one change identity? One obvious reason was to join a more successful political grouping, one that could back up claims to local leadership. In sixth-century northern Gaul, being a Frank seems to have brought tax privileges, higher legal status, and the right to participate in the army: the political assembly. Small wonder that by about 600 all those of the free population who could had become Franks. It is easy to imagine similar processes in the Anglo-Saxon realms. Traces of it seem to exist in the English law-codes that begin to survive from the early seventh century. If we had sixth-century Anglo-Saxon codes the process would doubtless be clearer. Ways by which one changed ethnicity, well attested on the European mainland, included the adoption of a new, Germanic name. Others involved taking up the other group's ritual or legal practices as a good means of making public one's claim to be, and acceptance as, a member. In Britain, this could have included adopting Saxon paganism and crucially there was also the new language, to which we must return. Finally there was material culture: hairstyles, clothing, and ornament.

After these preliminary points about identity and cultural change, we can return to the regional groupings of metalwork and other artefacts, and to the understanding of furnished burial. Initially, three groupings of metalwork concern us. Although there are naturally overlaps, the distribution of these groups is interestingly distinct. One is found principally south of the Thames and in Essex, with outliers a little north of the upper Thames in the west Midlands (Figure 11.1). This metalwork is called 'Quoit Brooch Style'. Originally thought to be Jutish because of the Kentish aspect to its distribution and therefore called 'Jutish Style A', it now seems fairly clear that it is an insular British development from late Roman official metalwork. It features animals, rendered in fairly naturalistic style (even if the animals themselves are quite mythical) around the edges of objects, the centres of which can be filled with geometric and spiral decoration (Figure 11.2). 'Quoit Brooch Style' is characteristic of the fifth century's middle quarters. It appears at roughly the time that the 'Saxon' material culture begins to occur and might be a different response to the political crisis referred to earlier. Its stylistic origins proclaim a political identity based upon a claimed connection with the Empire. It is still described by some archaeologists as 'Germanic'

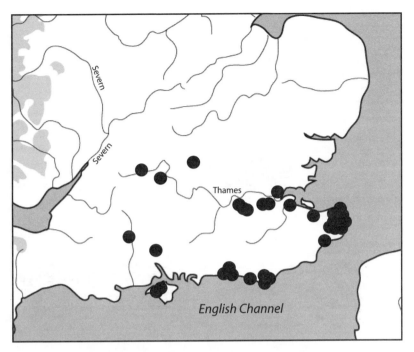

Figure 11.1 The distribution of 'Quoit Brooch Style' metalwork. After Böhme (1986), fig. 47.

or as influenced by 'Germanic' style, but this interpretation lacks clear foundations.

The 'Saxon' material just alluded to hardly overlaps at all with 'Quoit Brooch Style'. It is found north of the Thames in eastern England: East Anglia, Lincolnshire and the east Midlands, and Yorkshire (Figure 11.3). It is technically referred to as 'Saxon Relief Style'. Its immediate origins are to be found in the German North Sea regions, where are located the cremation cemeteries whose rite is imported into broadly the same parts of Britain. That said, like much 'Germanic' material, it owes its inspiration ultimately to Roman models, again imperial metalwork. At this stage it too primarily features geometric designs: rosettes, palmettes, running spirals, and face-masks. In spite of its roots, it seems clear that this style makes a link with the non-Roman polities of northern Germany.

Figure 11.2 'Quoit Brooch Style' animals (not to scale). After Suzuki (2000).

The third grouping has emerged more recently and is less easy to date, being found less frequently in furnished burials. It is focused around the Severn estuary and identified more from the form of objects like brooches and buckles than the decoration of their surfaces. It seems most likely that the manufacture and use of this style was associated with one of the 'border-zone' British kingdoms. Perhaps their political identity was based on a different claim to Roman-ness, possibly a Brito-Roman (rather than Romano-British) identity. Later fourth- and early fifth-century 'Dobunnic' metalwork (the Dobunni were the tribe of the region) has a similar distribution. The group represented by the later metalwork may well be a continuation of that producing the earlier material.

These dress adornments might have proclaimed particular identities, associations with one of the competing groups within

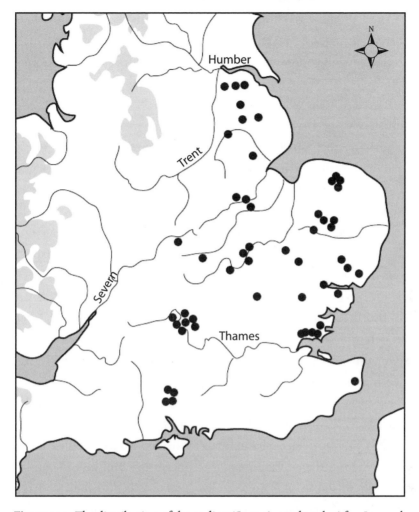

Figure 11.3 The distribution of the earliest 'Saxon' metalwork. After Laycock (2000), fig. 74.

post-imperial *Britannia*. When deployed in the public burial ritual, such claims to political identity were made to an audience of neighbours and (perhaps) rivals. They showed a link with political power. On female costume, these objects doubtless also proclaimed status as a good, honourable wife and mother, but this was the case far more often in the 'Saxon' area than in the 'Quoit Brooch' area.

If the premiss given at the start of the preceding paragraph is correct, it might be taken alongside the distinct groupings of such artefacts to suggest areas where particular political identities dominated. There are obvious limits to this method. It is, for instance, restricted to areas where the social structure was—or had become— sufficiently open to competition for the deployment of such symbols in burials. Areas which had always lain outside the villa-based social system (the hills north and west of London, for example, or the highland zones) will not show this type of evidence, so vague political groupings cannot be suggested even as tentatively as this.

Nonetheless interesting points may be proposed. One is the complete lack of a meaningful east–west divide, such as one might expect were the traditional bipartite picture of invading Saxons versus defending Britons correct. One of the clearest fifth-century divisions is actually north–south, along the line of the Thames, between 'Quoit Brooch' and 'Saxon Relief' styles. Abandoning the search for two old-style ethnic-political groups according to artefacts and burial forms also makes sense of what have traditionally looked like anomalies. These include the fact that the only chance finds of metalwork in the supposedly 'British' fort at South Cadbury were 'Anglo-Saxon'. This fact has hitherto been explained in terms of loot taken from the enemy, but perhaps such explanations are unnecessary and indeed fundamentally mistaken. A similar point surely applies to the quest for Britons and Anglo-Saxons in cemeteries. Furnished inhumation does not have any straightforward link with the Saxon homelands. Some families might have competed for leadership within a community by the use of this ritual; others might either not even have been in the running or, perhaps, were of a social level that was sufficiently well recognized not to need to take part, even if the ranks below were open to fierce competition. It is also worth stating that, as in northern Gaul, only in the sixth century do whole communities appear to partake in furnished inhumation. Another significant point concerns the quite large size of the areas within which these objects are found. This questions the most commonly accepted model about the size of immediately post-imperial political groupings in Britain, seeing them as very small. We will return to this after looking at the events of the 470s.

Riothamus and the end of the western Roman Empire

The most famous, or infamous, refugee from the complex fifth-century British politics was one Riothamus. Little is known about this character except that he arrived in Gaul, with an army of Britons, apparently from Britain. It is less plausible, but still possible, that he and his men moved from Aremorica/Brittany. Here he received a letter from the famous Gallic senator and letter-writer Sidonius Apollinaris, complaining about his troops' behaviour. Riothamus' army was defeated at the battle of Bourg-de-Déols by the Goths of Toulouse, often called Visigoths by historians although they never referred to themselves by this name, and driven into refuge among the Burgundians. That is all we know about Riothamus.

Riothamus would have remained a historical footnote were it not for the fact one crazy Arthurian hypothesis makes him into 'King Arthur' himself. This suggestion is based on four things. First, Riothamus, rather than a personal name, might be a title (like Vortigern), meaning great king (Rigo-tamos). Who, other than Arthur, could be a great king? Second, Riothamus contains some of the same letters as Artorius, a suggested Latin form of Arthur. If Artorius had a medallion or seal with his name written around the edge then someone like Sidonius might have started at the wrong letter and ended up with Riothamus instead. Third, the legendary King Arthur fought wars across the sea in Gaul. This, runs the argument, was a 'dim memory' of Riothamus' Gallic expedition. Fourth, Riothamus is last heard of in France and there is a town in France called Avallon. The fact that Arthur's association with the

Isle (not town) of Avalon only appears 700 years later, in Geoffrey of Monmouth's work, does not get in the way of the theory. No source associates Riothamus with Avallon (known then as Abalo). His last recorded location is Bourg-de-Déols, 200 km away from Avallon, but he did flee to the Burgundians and Avallon is in Burgundy.... It is difficult to represent this argument without sarcasm and its flaws are probably glaringly obvious even to a novice in post-imperial history. Doubtless it earns points for creativity and imagination.

Riothamus' career tells us far more interesting and important things than whether (with little or no likelihood) he *was* or (with overwhelming probability) was *not* Arthur. Riothamus' appearance is difficult to date but recent analyses suggest that his campaign on the Loire should be dated to about 471 rather than a couple of years earlier, as was previously suggested. This allows us to associate his actions with a campaign launched against the Toulouse Goths by Emperor Anthemius (467–72). Riothamus could thus be incorporated in a faction, possibly also including the Burgundians, allied with the imperial court. Had the campaign been successful, Riothamus and his Britons might have replaced Euric and his Goths as the principal military force in south-western and central Gaul, with an imperially sanctioned command. As it happened, the Goths defeated Anthemius' army and that of Riothamus, who disappears from history. Nevertheless, this reconstruction of Riothamus' intentions seems plausible and lies well within what had become the standard outlines of late Roman politics.

As well as the attractions offered by a career in Gaul, Riothamus' actions might have been motivated by defeat in British politics. By 470 or so it surely seemed most unlikely that the Empire would ever re-establish itself in Britain. Its forces had not approached the Channel for nearly a generation; very few people alive in Britain would have any memory at all of imperial government. The strategy of basing political identity and claims to power on a claimed link with the Empire must have started to lose whatever effectiveness it had left. From about the time of the failure of Anthemius' Gothic campaign, and his murder shortly afterwards, mainland contemporaries appear to have realized that the Empire had effectively collapsed. With this in mind it is perhaps not surprising that the imperially derived 'Quoit Brooch Style' died out at about this time. This cannot be pinpointed exactly but a date in the 470s seems broadly accurate. Its symbolic content must have become more or less meaningless. If Riothamus' political strategy had also been based around a link with the Empire then the period's political events might similarly have undermined his claims to power in Britain and led to his move to Gaul and attempt to establish a position in the imperial hierarchy.

Changes in the decorative styles employed on metalwork in Britain took place at about the time of the western Empire's demise. 'Quoit Brooch Style's' disappearance has just been mentioned. Archaeologists refer to its principal successor as Salin's Style I (after the Swedish archaeologist Bernhard Salin, who originally classified it), Animal Style I, or just plain Style I (Figure 11.4). The important thing about 'Style I' is that it is of clearly northern Germanic and Scandinavian origin, although, like its predecessors, its stylistic genealogy ultimately reaches back to imperial metalwork. It thus had specifically non-Roman symbolic content. Its appearance at the time of the Empire's final collapse cannot be coincidental. Across the Channel in northern Gaul, a new polychrome metalwork appears at roughly the same time. One must acknowledge that dates for the appearance or disappearance of artistic styles must always be given a certain leeway; to be facetious, no one rang a bell on 1 January 475, whereupon everyone threw away their 'Quoit Brooch' metalwork and put on new 'Style I' brooches. The date of *c*.475 for the appearance of 'Style I' is called a 'conventional date'. Nevertheless, even within looser

Figure 11.4 Style I animals. After G. Haseloft, *Germanische Tierornamentik der Völkerwanderungszeit* (3 vols; Berlin, 1981).

brackets, the disappearance of 'Quoit Brooch Style' and the appearance of 'Style I' is surely linked to the demise of the western Empire and the way that that compelled people to rethink the bases of political authority. People knew the Empire had 'fallen' and that new ways of representing authority were needed.

In spite of the change in the form of objects, some basic geographical groupings remained. The Thames remained an important dividing line; numerous forms of artefact are notably more common to the north or south of this line. Reservations and caveats are always necessary about archaeological distribution maps. Gaps might relate to ecology or geology, the relative visibility of archaeological remains, or even the extent to which people have been interested in looking for them. Many blanks south of the Thames are there essentially because of the great Wealden forest, generally unsettled at this time. The same is true north of the Thames in the heavy-soiled areas north of London, not generally settled until the later Middle Ages, or around the fens. Many object-types are found right across lowland England and, on the other hand, other divisions exist, for instance between the areas either side of the rivers flowing into the Wash. Nonetheless the Thames seems frequently to show up as a dividing line within lowland material culture in the later fifth and sixth centuries. In this sense it might perpetuate the border that appeared earlier, between 'Quoit Brooch Style' and 'Saxon Relief Style'.

It is, perhaps, interesting that, as has long been known, this conforms roughly to the division that existed in Bede's day between the Anglian kingdoms and those of the Saxons and Jutes, even if the correlation was earlier pinned too crudely on a difference between the settlers' origins. It is entirely plausible, given the way that migration works, with newcomers going to areas where they know networks of people of a similar origin exist, that immigrants from particular parts of *barbaricum* did tend to settle in the same areas of Britain as their compatriots. But the division between Saxon and Anglian could, as more subtle commentators on this period have suggested before, have arisen within fifth-century Britain. It possibly owed something to the nature of the politics and rivalries in the Saxon homeland, suggested earlier. The Saxon polities might have emerged from the unit in the far south whose existence is suggested by 'Quoit Brooch Style'. With the identity crisis produced by the end of the Empire it could be that this unit adopted a new identity based around that of its military forces. Saxon was the Romans' generic name for North Sea coast barbarians. In a post-imperial Roman state in the south, it might have been a more acceptable non-Roman identity.

The scale and nature of fifth- and sixth-century lowland kingdoms

Chapter 6 discussed 'The FA Cup Model'. This model, it must be stressed, is grounded in thorough and scholarly study of a wide array of evidence from across the disciplines concerned with early Anglo-Saxon England. It should also be pointed out that many of its conclusions are entirely reasonable and solidly based. The discussion of cemeteries and settlements and the lack of a secure social hierarchy, for example, tallies entirely with my interpretation of the breakdown of the villa system in the north-western imperial provinces. The small geographical territories identified through place-name and charter study also seem to be real. Yet, the move from those solid points to the argument that kingdoms were necessarily small or that kingship did not exist is problematic. Some difficulties have been alluded to already; others will emerge later on.

The most important problem is insularity. The evidence from the other side of the English Channel reveals the model's shortcomings. The archaeology of Roman collapse and of the responses to it in Gaul, in terms of settlement forms and burial rites, is very similar to that in England. Analyses of cemeteries show, similarly, a society where age and gender were the most important structuring principles. The known rural settlements are ephemeral. As in England, their traces do not become significant until the later sixth or seventh century and only then do they reveal differentiation in the size or elaboration of buildings. The *Tribal Hidage* shows most units in the area where grave-goods were used, and if we had such a document from Merovingian Gaul around 700 it is likely that it would show the same characteristics. Whereas the Roman *civitas* (city district) remained the principal administrative unit in the south, the smaller *pagus* had replaced it by then in the grave-goods-burying north. Study of place-names and charters would reveal smaller territorial units. If political history was only known after *c*.600 we would see something like the gradual elimination of rival territories culminating in the creation of a large, unified Frankish kingdom—eventually empire—under Charlemagne. And so on.

Yet, because we have reliable written sources for fifth- and, especially, sixth-century Gaul, we know that this evidence does not reveal a society with no kingship or only small kingdoms. By 535 at the latest, northern Gaul was the heartland of the largest and most enduring of all post-imperial realms, that of the Merovingian Franks. But, in its northern French and Rhineland heartland it left few traces. Apart from the spectacular grave of Childeric I (d. *c.* 480), discovered by chance in Tournai in the 1650s, the great fifth- and sixth-century Merovingian kings thus far remain archaeologically invisible, a point of considerable interest. Thanks to writings from south of the Loire, notably by Gregory of Tours, we know that their kingdoms taxed and used many Roman forms of government, not least a literate bureaucracy. We learn of letters routinely sent out to local counts and other officers, of tax lists, and even registers of those liable for military service. Pretty much none of this survives, especially from north of the Loire, which is almost as great a documentary 'blank' as lowland Britain. The evidential 'signature' of the Frankish north is very similar to that of post-imperial Britain. This must give us serious pause for thought when considering the nature of fifth-century British kingdoms.

We have already touched on reasons why local instability and competition need not be incompatible with large-scale kingdoms. As an effective strategy in local politics, rivals for authority 'bought into' the authority of successful military leaders, receiving vital back-up in communal politics in return for governing that locality for the leader—or king. Kings like the Merovingians could and did withdraw support and bestow it upon other competitors for local power. This made small-scale leaders into their officers, wholly beholden to kingly favour. Royal power was thus sucked down into local societies by rivalry for communal leadership. Nevertheless the study of the post-imperial European mainland also shows that such kingship, though it could be extensive, was very fragile. Military setbacks could undermine all the value that supporting a king had in local politics. A communal leader could find that his rivals had backed the winning side, whose backing was now considerably more effective. For these reasons dramatic haemorrhages of political power followed defeat in the fifth and sixth centuries. To weather these crises, kings strove to create other ideological underpinnings for their power and claims to be the sole source of political legitimacy. The Merovingians were uniquely successful in this. Overall, then, the fifth- and sixth-century lowland British evidence is by no means incompatible with sizeable kingdoms and fully-fledged, effective kingship.

Another aspect of Merovingian history, and indeed that of the rest of fifth and sixth-century Europe, is that kingship and kingdoms do not develop in neat straight lines, from simple to complex or from small to large. At Chlothar I's death (561), the Merovingian realm encompassed all of France except for Brittany and the area around Narbonne, and the Rhineland, including modern Belgium and parts of the Netherlands; Frankish overlordship reached well to the east of the Rhine. The kings were all-powerful within their realm. A hundred and fifty years later, the kingdom was more or less permanently divided into two, hegemony beyond the Rhine was in tatters, and parts of southern Gaul were to all intents and purposes independent. The ability to enforce royal writ, even in the heartland of their kingdom, had been seriously eroded. There is no reason to suppose that English kingdoms had to develop steadily from small to large. Kingdoms grow, they fragment, and they get put back together, sometimes as different types of kingdom. More to the point, perhaps, the political history of England between *c*.600 and the ninth century reveals a remarkable and fascinating stability in the number and size of kingdoms. Another problem with the 'FA Cup Model' is how these small, valley-sized kingdoms could have held off the larger, powerful highland kingdoms that Gildas tells us about and which the archaeological evidence also suggests.

There is no reason to doubt the reality of the small English units revealed by charters and place-names, or those listed in the *Tribal Hidage*. Whether they were kingdoms rather than other administrative or landholding regions seems less plausible. There are nevertheless kings listed as governing smaller areas in Anglo-Saxon England. The rulers of the *Hwicce* of Gloucestershire and Worcestershire are well attested in charters, for instance. Terms like *subregulus* (usually translated as 'sub-king' although it actually means 'less-than-a-little-king') and *regalis* ('minor royal') are encountered in narratives and other sources. The 'Grande Armée' that King Penda of Mercia led unsuccessfully against Northumbria in 655 allegedly included thirty *duces regii* (royal leaders). This implies a hierarchy of kingship and therefore maybe different sizes of kingdom that might fit the 'FA Cup Model'. We should not, however, invest the word 'king' with too many ideas from later history, equating 'king' with 'sovereign'. Dozens of petty kings existed in early medieval Ireland, for example, none of whom was ever in any sense sovereign. Similarly, many Anglo-Saxon 'kings' or 'under-kings' never seem to have been other than subordinate, even if their title and jurisdiction might have been hereditary. Medieval kings habitually carved out 'kingdoms' for sons or junior branches of their families without intending these to be independent. Finally, all Merovingian royal males were 'kings', even if their fathers were alive and even if they were given nowhere to rule. Words like 'prince' had not yet come to mean 'royal son' so precise technical terms for royal males were lacking, especially in Latin. Across the former Empire kingship was itself a new, fifth-century institution. Its rules were only slowly being invented in the different areas of western Europe.

We should not expect it to have all the connotations of later medieval sovereignty.

Before we get carried away with the Gallic comparison some important caveats must be made. Even if the evidence suggests *large* (or *larger*) realms it would imply nothing about dynastic *stability*. Furthermore, the extent of post-imperial collapse in Gaul, though similar—and more or less analogous in the far north of the region— was generally less than in Britain. Towns contracted dramatically (one or two seem to have been abandoned) but they continued to be political and administrative *foci* and yield evidence—ephemeral but nevertheless clearer than that in Britain—of continued occupation as higher-order settlements. One key reason for this was the continued presence of the Church in towns. Bishops were important for urban survival. Northern Gallic economic collapse, though serious and dramatic, was less than on the English side of the Channel. Although, like Britain, northern Gaul lacked proper coinage before the late sixth century, the Rhenish glass industry persisted and the Roman pottery tradition of the area continued to exist and to exchange its wares. That said, some recent studies suggest that some late Romano-British pottery industries continued in similarly attenuated form, particularly in the north and west (this geographical distribution is important), and glass was also manufactured. As in England, sixth-century northern Gaul reveals far less evidence than seventh- of craft specialization. Nevertheless, northern Gaul *was* clearly different in interesting and significant ways. Most importantly it had, through military domination of the area, close links with the south (Aquitaine, Burgundy, and Provence), where post-imperial survival was much greater. Indeed Roman structures probably survived better and for longer in Aquitaine than anywhere else in western Europe.

When I say that kingdoms could have been large, how large is large? Clearly no definitive answer is possible. One plausible suggestion has been that kingdoms could have emerged within *civitas*-sized units, as mentioned, but there is no reason why they could not have been bigger. The distribution of types of metalwork, if we accept their hypothetical association with political identities, would indicate polities extending across several *civitates*. Post-imperial British kingdoms might have been of the same order of size as the 'middle Saxon' (c.600–c.800) realms and even, however briefly, bigger still. This view, I should stress, would not currently find many supporters in the field of early Anglo-Saxon history and archaeology. Nevertheless I hope to have shown that the evidence upon which the dominant model is based does not really support its conclusions.

Pursuing the argument that post-imperial British kingdoms shared features with their mainland contemporaries, other suggestions become possible, which find some support in the English archaeological evidence. One concerns what might be called 'functional ethnicity'. Throughout the post-imperial West a common division existed, with late Roman origins, into 'barbarian' soldiers and 'Roman' taxpayers. This is most clearly seen in Ostrogothic Italy but it evidently existed in Visigothic Spain, Frankish Gaul, and Vandal Africa. It possibly pertained among the Vandals' neighbours, the Moors, as well. With the late Roman army's 'barbarizing' nature and especially with the presence of Saxon *foederati* in Britain, possibly from the late fourth century if I am right about the date of that settlement, it is easy to see how an equation could have emerged between the military and Saxon (or other northern Germanic) identity. In the late Empire, status as a soldier was hereditary. The army had its own courts and special laws. Soldiers not only had specific tax exemptions but were coming to be paid significantly in drafts of tax revenues, which they extracted (whether collectively or individually is unclear) from designated taxpayers. This could easily have evolved into the armies of landowners which we encounter across the post-imperial West, whose service related to a specific ethnic identity and tenure of particular types of land, with legal privilege and tax exemptions. Anglo-Saxon military service, when it becomes visible in the seventh century, is similar to that among the neighbouring Franks, suggesting that it moved through similar stages to that point.

If we return to the lowland furnished inhumation cemeteries we can revive the linkage, discussed above, between weapon burials and 'Saxon' identity. Perhaps males buried with weaponry were indeed members of families which claimed, or had acquired, Saxon ethnicity (remembering that such things cannot be proven from skeletal data). In the circumstances of the burial ritual this would be a suitable way of demonstrating that identity's basis and the social privileges and status it entailed. Note, though, that this does not imply anything about these families' geographical origins. They might have migrated from across the North Sea; they might have been Roman Britons who adopted a Saxon identity. A similar argument can be made that northern Gallic weapon burials are those of Franks. The difference between the burials of Anglo-Saxon and Frankish male children, mentioned in Chapter 6, might imply that this ethnic identity or the potential to acquire it was seen as more hereditary in England than in Gaul. Given the burial ritual's nature, however, it could be that the deposition of weapons related more to a demonstration of the *father's* status than the son's. The main point is that the burial evidence suggests a similar social and military organization in England to that found across the West. This should not surprise us.

Viewing Britain in broader European context permits further suggestions about the government of its kingdoms. It is usually assumed that the Anglo-Saxon kingdoms did not tax and were illiterate, writing only being introduced by St Augustine's mission. There is no secure basis for either assumption, other than the silence of the record, a silence so uniform on almost *every* topic that little significance can be accorded it. No written sources survive, to be sure, but, as mentioned, almost no written sources survive from the highly literate administration of contemporaneous Merovingian Gaul. The Anglo-Saxons were familiar with an alphabet, the runic 'futhark', based on the same principles as the Latin alphabet. Runic letters, however, seem to have been imbued with religious significance. More importantly, literacy clearly survived and possibly flourished in the hitherto less Romanized highlands. Why should it have entirely died out in the villa-zone? Further, Æthelberht of Kent must have had some means of communicating with the Pope in 596–7 and may have done so by letter. When negotiating with the Franks for his Merovingian bride, Bertha, letters might have been exchanged. Æthelberht's law-code was issued within a few years of Augustine's arrival. To me, this suggests some literacy existing prior to the mission, rather than that the small group of Italian monks took time off from establishing an organized church to create a bureaucracy literate, according to usual assumptions, not only in Latin but also in the Anglo-Saxon vernacular. Finally, there is the suggestion that Bede's list of kings with *imperium* was based upon some sort of document recording lordship over Kent. This ought, according to the argument set out in Chapter 4, to reach back into the last third or quarter of the sixth century.

That leads us to taxation. Mainland European taxation survived up to around 600, when it died out as the late antique state withered. It is difficult to know how it operated in places like northern Gaul, which, like Britain, lacked coinage. Perhaps old coins were used as bullion; perhaps taxation was essentially in kind; and perhaps few of the proceeds made it to the royal centre, functioning principally as a reward for royal officers in the localities. This would further boost the attractions of royal patronage. We do not know. But function it did, and it could have done so in England. Across the Channel one reason that taxation died out seems to have been that it was granted away or otherwise converted into local dues collected by aristocratic lords from their estates. A similar process was possibly part of the emergence of the smaller kingdoms that we hear of from around 600.

Another area of general similarity but specific difference concerns religion. The non-Roman rulers of fifth- and sixth-century realms tended to follow different religious credos from their Roman subjects. On the mainland, among the Goths, Burgundians, and at least some Lombards, as well as—possibly, and briefly—the Franks, this took the form of adherence to a moderate version of the Arian heresy. However, in Britain—uniquely in the post-imperial world—the new kings were pagans. Their gods were analogous to those of the Vikings: Woden (Odin), Thunor (Thor), and the rest. Some identifiable scenes from Scandinavian mythology are found on metalwork circulating in the lowlands. Other gods are less well known, like Seaxnet, whom the East Saxon kings claimed as their ancestor and who is attested among the continental Saxons. It seems reasonable, nevertheless, to suppose that like their Arian contemporaries the Anglo-Saxon kings used their religion politically, to underline the differences between their followers (probably the military elite) and the bulk of the population. If Woden was a war-god, this might have been especially relevant. If the analogy with the mainland is correctly drawn from the weapon burials and the similarities between Anglo-Saxon and Frankish law, the Romano-British population might well have had to pay tax instead of performing military service. Religious practice would be a means of reinforcing this difference, especially through ritual performance in things like burial and marriage ceremonies, important public gatherings like law-courts, and particularly the army, the political focus of the realm and the main assembly of 'Saxons'.

Roman Britain had been significantly Christianized. The archaeological traces of this are usually nebulous and ambiguous but some are clear and the general process seems beyond doubt. After all, by Gildas' and St Patrick's time, the rulers of the western highlands were Christians, and paganism, as a problem to tempt his British audience, does not figure in Gildas' railings, unlike heresy. Thus it seems most unlikely that the lowland villa-zone, tied more closely into the Christian Empire, had not been largely Christianized as well. But, from the accounts of the seventh-century mission to the Anglo-Saxons, the lowlanders were pagans. Bede and other writers had good reasons to oversimplify the situation. Bede wanted his people, chosen by God to be the scourge of the sinful Britons, to convert directly from unsullied paganism to the pristine light of Roman Christianity. Any muddying of the waters by involvement with the British Church (which by Bede's day held views on the date of Easter that were held to be heretical) was undesirable. We can, plausibly enough, postulate that whatever Bede thought or said, some—perhaps many—of the Anglo-Saxon kings' subjects were Christians. There is nothing pagan about burial with grave-goods, and even the Church's opposition to cremation only really crystallized after it had ceased to be practised in Anglo-Saxon England. The pagan kings need only have refused to allow the consecration of bishops for an organized lowland Church to have gradually withered away. If one envisages a large number of nominally Christian subjects of pagan Saxon kings, living without formal church structures, the huge numbers seeking baptism soon after Augustine's arrival—as the new bishop himself reported back to Pope Gregory—seems slightly less of a miracle.

Yet there is no reason to discount the general thrust of the conversion narrative, that many, perhaps the bulk, of the Anglo-Saxon inhabitants of Britain were pagans. This need not imply a huge migration of pagans, though it clearly shows that there *was* a migration. In the social structure I have outlined we can see how pagan religion could have radiated out from the royal core of the kingdom in directly analogous fashion to the way in which Christianity spread through the Roman Empire. The social instability and competition for power following the villa system's collapse has already been described. So has the way this rivalry could lead to subscription to larger political units, through the search for patronage and military backing. This is one important means by which Anglo-Saxon identity spread. Obtaining the support of the Saxon kings, however, probably also meant adopting their religion, which I have already suggested was vital in underpinning Saxon identity and claiming the privileges that accompanied it. Thus conversion to paganism could be drawn along the arteries of royal patronage, from the heart of the kingdoms into the many rural communities.

The Anglo-Saxon conversion to Christianity illustrates how post-imperial Britain should not be considered aside from the rest of fifth- and sixth-century Europe. By the late sixth century, Saxon identity had doubtless spread far and wide among the lowlands' inhabitants. The old distinction between 'Saxons' and 'Romans', or 'Britons', was perhaps no longer enforceable or necessary. In northern Gaul by this date, those Romans who had been unable to adopt a Frankish identity appear to have become a semi-free legal sub-stratum dependent upon Franks. Similar changes had occurred elsewhere and we can see that the distinctions that the kings tried to enforce in the fifth and sixth centuries were being abandoned. At the 589 Council of Toledo, King Reccared of the Goths formally abandoned Arianism and adopted Catholicism. Less than ten years later, King Æthelberht of Kent decided to invite a Christian mission from Rome.

Previous writing about post-imperial British kingdoms has tended to suffer from a lack of awareness of the European mainland. Contrasts and comparisons have generally been made with a Europe assumed to be typified by Theodoric the Ostrogoth's Italy or the Aquitaine of Gregory of Tours. The Roman system endured to an unusual degree in these fairly well-known and thoroughly docu-mented regions (until the mid-sixth century in Italy; rather longer in Aquitaine). This means that arguments for *similarity* have been forced to hypothesize an unsustainable degree of post-imperial continuity in Britain, while theories based around *difference* are founded on too crude an opposition with the mainland. Once we appreciate the diversity of the nature of, and responses to, the end of the Empire across western Europe, we can make some important points. One is that Britain does not have to be *either* the same as everywhere else *or* following a unique, distinctive path. Variety and difference characterize this period, across the former Empire and beyond, as well as structural analogies at different levels. What happened in Britain shows similarities, in some areas, with what occurred in certain regions and resemblances to different zones in others, as well as its own regional specifics. A spectrum of post-imperial continuity existed, which could be argued, crudely, to run from the very Roman societies of Italy and Aquitaine at one end through to areas like the far north of the Frankish kingdom, where there was more or less complete collapse of the imperial system, at the other. Seen thus, Britain can be seen simply as an extension of this spectrum. My argument is that Britain does not stand outside the currents of fifth- and sixth-century western European history; it was fully a part of them. This allows us to see a region with distinctive responses and developments, to be sure, but also one where those changes and adaptations were not so different from ones taking place elsewhere. It also permits a better way of explaining those responses and developments.

Kent and the Frankish connection

Kent occupies a special place in early Anglo-Saxon archaeology. Its material culture is quite distinctive and includes a significant amount of Frankish material. The burials of the region are unusually well furnished with grave-goods. This engenders some important ideas. One is Kent's wealth in this era, founded on the lavish burials just mentioned, and the suggestion that this was based to some extent on trade with the Frankish kingdoms. Some have suggested that the people buried with these artefacts were actual Frankish settlers. The idea of Frankish leadership of the Anglo-Saxon 'invasions' has for many reasons never been accepted, but a not dissimilar, and more plausible, suggestion is Merovingian overlordship. A reconsideration of Kent's wealth leads to further discussion of the Frankish connection.

Although widely held, the argument projecting wealth from the lavishness of grave-furnishings is seriously problematic. As has been argued, grave-goods tend to imply instability and competition within local social structures, rather than just reflecting the wealth of particular families. The idea that the furnishing of burials simply mirrors actual social structures has, in any case, long been rejected. What's more, while impressive by Anglo-Saxon standards, the riches deposited in Kentish graves are not enormous. A mainland European comparison is again instructive. The most lavishly furnished graves in Europe at this time are found in south-western Germany, in the area occupied by the Alamans. Against these, the Kentish graves pale into absolute insignificance. Horses, suits of armour, helmets, elaborate suites of weaponry, and all sorts of other artefacts were frequently buried with men, while women were interred accompanied by lavish displays of jewellery and other adornments. Yet it cannot seriously be argued that Alamannia was the wealthiest (or militarily the best-equipped) area within the Merovingian hegemony. It was peripheral, off the major communication and exchange routes, dominated by its Frankish neighbours. Conversely, the Merovingian kings' enormous wealth has left almost no trace and Aquitaine, the most prosperous area of sixth-century Gaul, has almost no grave-goods at all.

It is time to reassess Kent's 'wealth'. The furnishing of Kentish graves probably indicates the extent of this area's social instability, a sign that the crisis of the end of the Empire and its socio-economic structures was particularly acute here. Further, in the fifth and most of the sixth centuries, Kent might, like Alamannia, have been rather peripheral. The most prosperous, powerful, and stable areas of post-imperial Britain were probably those in the western and northern highlands and along the border between this area and the former villa-zone. The south-east could be seen as peripheral to this 'core'. This might have been accentuated by the fact that, from the early sixth century, it lay on the periphery of the greatest polity of the post-imperial West, the Merovingian kingdom.

Sources for the northern frontiers of the sixth-century Frankish realm are scanty. Our best source, Gregory of Tours, says next to nothing about them and refers to Britain only twice. We know, nevertheless, that during the sixth century the Franks exercised a fluctuating but more or less effective hegemony over the peoples beyond the Rhine: Saxons, Thuringians, Alamans, and Bavarians. It would be odd, perhaps, if they were uninterested in events across the Channel. A couple of sources suggest such an interest. The earliest Frankish law-code, the *Compact of Salic Law* (*c.*511), which initially applied between the Loire and the Ardennes, envisages Frankish power to recover freemen illegally sold into slavery 'across the sea'. The simplest explanation is that this meant some sort of ability to project authority across the Channel to Kent and/or the rest of the English south coast. Another indication comes from a confrontational letter written by the Frankish king Theudebert I to Emperor Justinian I (527–65) in which Theudebert lists the peoples over whom he has authority. These include the *Eucii*, most plausibly the Jutes and more likely the Jutes of Kent and the English south coast than those of Jutland. Without written descriptions, quite what Frankish domination meant is anybody's guess. It might well have been no more than ritual subservience, simultaneously giving the subordinate king the appearance of the Franks' powerful backing and providing evidence for Merovingian claims to widespread overlordship (as in Theudebert's letter). Both sides benefited without anything changing very much in practice. Tribute might have been exacted when it was possible and allowed to lapse when it wasn't. There could have been more regular, significant interference from across the Channel. We do not know but archaeology permits some insights.

Æthelberht of Kent's marriage to Bertha, a Frankish princess, did not represent a political alliance between equal partners. Bertha was the daughter of the discarded wife of a dead king—some way down the list of eligible Merovingian princesses. The first time that Gregory of Tours mentions the marriage he refers to Æthelberht simply as 'a man in Kent', and later only as 'a son of a king'. Gregory might have had as much difficulty in acknowledging the existence of kingship in Kent as he did among his troublesome neighbours the Bretons, whose rulers, he said, were 'called counts and not kings' (the opposite was almost certainly true). This could imply Frankish overlordship. Bertha herself arrived with a Frankish bishop, Liudhard, in tow. Some sort of nominal Kentish dependence on the Franks seems more than likely. If Kent was planning to break free of dominance by Sussex or the Gewissae (Wessex)—see below—seeking Frankish backing might have been part of the plan. Some Frankish hegemony might however have been of considerably longer standing, as the laws and Theudebert's letter suggest. In this connection it is surely much more than coincidence that when Æthelberht asked Pope Gregory for a bishop (remember he already had a Frankish bishop, although Liudhard might have died) he did so after the death of Childebert II of Austrasia (596), precisely the point when, for the first time ever, all three Frankish 'partition-kingdoms' were ruled by children. This was surely a move to shake off Frankish domination as well as to cement his primacy among the English kingdoms. It may have been short-lived in the immediate instance. In 614, when the Frankish realms were reunited under a single, powerful king, Chlothar II, and the Merovingian ruler summoned a council of his bishops at Paris, we find the bishops of Canterbury and Dorchester meekly in attendance.

The presence of Frankish objects in Kentish graves now takes on a slightly different significance. Burial with grave-goods represents a public ritual in the context of claims for local standing. Objects placed with the dead made symbolic statements about the deceased and his or her family. The Frankish objects might in this sense represent a claim to a Frankish identity, provided that we are clear about what this meant: a political ethnicity similar to others we have discussed, rather than necessarily familial, genetic origins in the Frankish kingdom. As mentioned, though, even if the objects related to Frankish birth or descent some reason why it was important to demonstrate such an identity in the burial ritual must have existed. Following this line of thought we could make the less restrictive suggestion that Frankish artefacts are analogous to the Roman goods in fourth-century northern German burials, representing claims to status based upon association with a powerful political entity. The Frankish realms, only twenty-odd miles away across the Channel, were the most powerful in the West and it is easy to see how they might have played a similar role in Kentish local politics. An association with the Franks, whatever its nature or reality, could have been considerably valuable in the social dynamics of Kentish communities. It might have been a political identity played off against others, perhaps based around Jutish and Scandinavian origin myths, seen not only in the surviving written sources but also on some Kentish metalwork, in this peripheral but interesting realm.

Wolf-hounds? The British kingdoms

Thus far we have concentrated upon the obscure lowland politics. We must now explore the kingdoms to the north and west, railed against by Gildas. In Chapter 8 I argued that in the late fourth century, as a temporary measure by Maximus, the effective frontier of the British provinces might have been withdrawn to a line extending from the Severn Estuary to the East Yorkshire Wolds. Beyond that line governance seems to have passed to military leaders, perhaps with some form of official imperial backing, possibly the former commanders of local army units. Later traditions assign particular importance to 'Macsen Gwledig' in the formation of Welsh royal dynasties. Other figures from genealogies have suggestive features such as names derived from official titles. A memorial stone from South Wales erected to one Vortiporius (possibly the king of that name mentioned by Gildas; possibly not) refers to him by the Roman title 'protector'. The highland chieftains—or kings—might thus have been military powers to reckon with for any vestigial quasi-imperial authorities in the south.

The region's archaeology supports this contention. Highland high-status sites were discussed in Chapters 3 and 6. The trade links revealed tied them into a network reaching as far as the Levant. Across the post-imperial west, the key to understanding socio-political developments is the shrinkage of political horizons. Yet, on the British shore of the Irish Sea horizons *expanded* in the fifth and sixth centuries. Near Penmachno, in the heart of Snowdonia, the carver of a sixth-century tombstone knew the name of the last western consul and the fact that he had been the last. Other high-status sites include the probable chief-tain's residence occupying the former baths-basilica in the old town of Wroxeter, and some of the forts of Hadrian's Wall. The lowlands show no high-status sites anything like this before the seventh century. In the fifth and sixth centuries the balance of power, perhaps uniquely in British history, lay with the rulers of what is now Cornwall and Wales.

These included the 'tyrants' railed against by Gildas: Constantine of Dumnonia (Devon), Cuneglassus, Maglocunus (often—albeit insecurely—associated with Maelgwn of Gwynedd), Vortiporius, who seems to have ruled South Wales, and Aurelius Caninus, possi-bly one of Ambrosius Aurelianus' grandchildren. These kings seem to have ruled extensive territories and to have created their own means of legitimizing power. Gildas' account contains the earliest reference to the early medieval use of the Old Testament rite of anointing with oil. The use of Christian forms of legitimization in addition to Roman titles is very interesting. So is the fact that the ceremony presumably used North African olive oil brought in the amphorae mentioned. What more obvious display of power and wealth than the conspicuous, seemingly wasteful usage of, in Britain, an expensive and rare commodity?

Names were important markers of identity in the post-imperial world. Those of Gildas' kings allow some speculation. Note the repetition of canine imagery in their names. The *cuno* element in Cuneglassus and Maglocunus means 'dog' or (perhaps better) 'hound': their names are 'Grey Hound' and 'King Hound' respectively. Conmail, mentioned by the *Anglo-Saxon Chronicle* as one of those defeated at Dyrham, bears the same name as Maglocunus but with the elements reversed: Cunomaglos. Aurelius Caninus has a canine epithet. *Cuno* is apparently one of the most common Celtic name elements. One wonders whether Aurelius' epithet translates a second, Celtic name or was chosen for its resonance with Celtic highland names. In this period on the European mainland, we know of numerous individuals with two names, one Germanic and one Latin: 'Avius who was also Vedast' appears in Gregory of Tours's *Histories*. This was part of the shifting ethnic identities discussed earlier. Another aspect of that shift was the adoption of composite Latin–Germanic names or of names translated from one language to another. Illustrative here are two generations of Frankish magnates. The name of Lupus, duke of Champagne, means 'wolf' in Latin, wolf being a common element in Germanic names, in Francia usually taking the form *-ulf* as the second element: e.g. Radulf. His son was called Romulf, a Germanic name meaning 'Rome-wolf'; 'Rome-wolf' in a sense equals the Latin *lupus*. It seems plausible that Aurelius *caninus* might have been similarly shifting his family's names from Latin to Brythonic. We saw something possibly analogous in Cerdic and Cynric in the last chapter.

Other possibilities related to these 'dog-names' are impossible to push even as far as the ideas just outlined, because of these names' sheer popularity within the Celtic name-pool. One concerns the popularity of wolf-names among the Anglo-Saxons (e.g. Æthelwulf—'Noble Wolf'—or Wulfhere—'Wolf-Army'). Wolf-names are apparently unknown in Celtic languages, the prowling wolf being a hated, possibly despised beast. The other Germanic word for wolf—*wearg*—has the same 'outlaw' overtones. Instead, the Britons seem to have gone for its domesticated opponent, the loyal hunting hound. Cuneglassus—Grey Dog—might actually mean 'wolf' in more cryptic fashion; if it did perhaps he stands as a British equivalent of Duke Lupus? One wonders idly whether in Gildas' day the choice of 'dog-names' had acquired an added frisson. Perhaps British kings saw themselves as wolf-hounds, hunters of 'wolves'. Perhaps Aurelius, with his Latin name, felt obliged to add his canine epithet. Another speculation goes in a quite different direction and relates to the ways in which names could be used, as mentioned earlier, in processes of political and cultural interaction and change. Perhaps the *cuno*-element's value lay in its resonance with the common *cyn*- element in Anglo-Saxon names. This element relates to the modern words 'kin' and 'king' via one of the Old English words for king—*cyning*—the head of a kindred. Again, Cynric springs to mind. As stated, though, *cuno*- names are so common that neither of these ideas can ever be more than very tentative suggestions.

The surviving fifth- and sixth-century British written sources—the works of Gildas and (probably) St Patrick—have western connections. That their authors expected to be read and heeded by the secular elite implies the existence of literacy. Gildas certainly had access to books for all that he claimed learning was in retreat. The British Church was capable of involvement in and understanding of ecclesiastical disputes on the mainland and the writings they engendered. Gildas' reference to military manuals left behind after the second Roman rescue of the Britons might imply the survival in Britain of manuscripts of classical Roman military treatises, perhaps even that of Vegetius. It has been plausibly suggested that our period was the zenith of Roman learning and literary culture in the British highlands. It seems likely that in the crisis of the villa-zone and its aristocracy— surely fatal for any schools in the region—many of the learned elite packed such books as they could and sought the patronage of the more powerful highland rulers.

It is odd that these powerful war-kings did not swallow up the economically weak and socially unstable lowland realms, especially if these were as ephemeral as currently fashionable views of early Anglo-Saxon kingdoms suggest. Perhaps they did. The traditions behind the *Historia Brittonum*'s image of a highland king ('Vortigern') lording it over lesser rulers as far as the Channel might have been more than mere fancy. In the previous chapter, though, I suggested that the links between Vortigern and Kentish history are purely legendary. But powerful highland rulers need not have wanted to absorb smaller lowland kingdoms. It is entirely plausible that an over-king's prestige was manifested by having a swathe of tributary rulers, as later in early medieval Britain, rather than by a huge tract under his immediate authority.

East to west? (4)

Another reason why the highland kings did not swallow up the lowlands, though, is that the rulers along the lowlands' western and northern edges were also powerful. Here we return to our alternative scenario, where Anglo-Saxon dominance over the lowlands spreads not simply westwards from the coast but also, and perhaps more importantly, eastwards from early military settlements far inland. In the preceding chapters I have built up a picture, using continental parallels, some elements of the British sources, and 'migration theory', to suggest that powerful Saxon forces might have been located along the frontier between the villa-zone and the highlands. We've seen that it is here that the cores of Wessex, Mercia, and Deira were located.

Alliances between the wealthier Romano-British aristocrats and Saxon army officers in this zone could have produced formidable polities, as it did with the Merovingians in Gaul. It the early, shadowy days of the Merovingians' rise to power, it is clear that their forces were commanded sometimes by Roman and sometimes by Frankish leaders: Aegidius and his son Syagrius, and Childeric and Clovis, his son, respectively. The latter won out in the end. We've noticed the British elements in the early reaches of West Saxon, Mercian, and Deiran traditions, as well as, in Cynric's case, a possibly hybrid stage. This might reflect a similar stage in their histories. As well as making brothers into fathers and sons, genealogical traditions can smooth out difficulties by having rivals succeed each other as members of the same family.

The dominance of these areas within the lowlands could, therefore, reach back well into the fifth century. The socio-economic stress produced by the Empire's effective absence was greatest further to the south and east. We've noted how this sort of vacuum could have sucked in warlords and their followers from across the North Sea. It could easily, too, have enabled the expansion of more powerful polities based along the lowland–highland frontier. Saxons settling on the east coast could have found themselves defending their territories against other Saxons from more inland kingdoms. The political unit that, on the basis of 'Quoit Brooch Style', I have suggested existed south of the Thames might have spent much of its time countering rivals further to the west, rather than in fighting off Saxon raiders on the coasts. If the disappearance of 'Quoit Brooch Style' equates with a shift in ideology in the area and, possibly, the adoption of a Saxon identity, that ethnicity might have been taken up to distinguish the region from others to the north. It might equally, however, have been based on Saxon soldiers originally stationed in the west of the region, the later heartland of Wessex, rather than brought in by invaders from the southern and eastern shores. This would tally with Barbara Yorke's suggestion about the West Saxon foundation story subsumed within the *Chronicle*.

Whilst all this must remain hypothetical, it is no more hypothetical than the steady westward-drifting 'moving front' model of Anglo-Saxon expansion. It permits one further intriguing possibility: an alternative view of language change. The villa-zone's western fringe, the border between the arable lowlands and the pastoral highlands, was quite likely a linguistic frontier too. Low-Latin-speakers from the former villa estates might have come into contact with British-speakers from the uplands. While there were doubtless many who were bilingual to one extent or another, the introduction of a Germanic-speaking military elite might have led, in the context of the fifth-century changes, to Old English becoming a lingua franca for British- and Latin-speaking inhabitants, especially those wanting to adopt the English identity. These borderland polities' military dominance over the lowlands could have been crucial in making English the dominant language there.

Northern Britain

The idea of early, powerful and predatory Romano-Saxon polities along the borders of the villa-zone allows a different light to be shed on the north of *Britannia*, the regions around, and north of, Hadrian's Wall. The Picts have frequently been mentioned threatening this northern frontier. It was to defend against their depredations, Gildas implies, that the Saxons were hired. However, in traditional thinking about the north of Britain, it is often envisaged that the Picts lived far north of Hadrian's Wall, beyond the Firth of Forth. Between their realms and the Wall lived various 'British' peoples, like the Votadini. These groups are mentioned in early Roman geographical sources and reappear in the post-imperial era, the Votadini becoming the Gododdin and so on. This view of political geography is, however, based ultimately upon the seventh- and eighth-century state of affairs, when written sources begin to describe the history of this part of the world. Whether it applied in the late Roman period is questionable.

Late Roman sources describe two Pictish confederacies, the Dicalydones and the Verturiones. The Verturiones appear to have lived north of the Mounth, according to later references to people with the same name. The Dicalydones, probably some sort of continuation of the earlier Caledonii, have left traces in place-names north and west of the Forth estuary. This would support the traditional view. Yet, whenever peoples north of the Wall are mentioned by the Romans, they are called Picts, *Picti*. This, admittedly, simply means 'painted men', but there is no differentiation made between these people and 'Britons' living immediately north of the Wall. We have two options. The Picts, as understood by the Romans, lived right up to the frontier; after all it is on the frontier that most of the new barbarian confederacies of the late Roman period emerged. Alternatively, whenever a Pictish raid or invasion, or an imperial expedition against the Picts, is referred to, our sources describe a long march (in one direction or the other) across a large, uniformly peaceful stretch of territory between the Hadrianic and Antonine Walls. The former alternative seems the more plausible.

If the Dicalydones were the southernmost Pictish confederacy, it seems that, while their own territory, the lands of the 'Dicalydones proper' if you like, was located north of the Forth, their political overlordship extended as far as Hadrian's Wall, encompassing people like the Votadini, the Selgovae, and so on. At the start of Chapter 10 I discussed how the early fifth-century crisis might have led to the break-up of the Saxon confederacy and the reappearance of the Angles, Frisians, and Jutes. Like the Votadini, these tribes are attested in the early Roman period but then disappear from the record until the post-imperial era. We might be seeing similar events north of the Wall. In Chapter 7 I mentioned the re-emergence of the Maetae as the Miathi named by Adomnán's *Life of Columba* in reference to a battle of *c*.600.

The reforms that I suggest Maximus introduced before leaving for his Gaulish campaign might have been the trigger. Like that beyond the Rhine, this area shows good evidence of trade with the Empire. Access to Roman goods might, as beyond the Rhine, have been a means of ensuring political dominance. There is evidence to suggest that, in distributing prestigious goods, late Roman authorities in Britain targeted particular political centres north of the Wall. The removal of effective Roman presence to the south, with the highlands occupied by 'paramilitary' groups who gradually evolved into local rulers, would cut these Picts off from such relationships. An attempt to shore up intramural-zone leaders around 400 is suggested by the Traprain Law hoard, a collection of silver which might well have originated as a Roman diplomatic payment. At about this time, too, the Traprain Law fort had its defences refurbished. Possibly, for a while, attempts by Maximus and perhaps Constantine 'III' to secure the northern frontier whilst they campaigned on the mainland led to some southern Pictish leaders acquiring impressive authority.

This was short-lived. Shortly afterwards, Traprain was abandoned. Thereafter the archaeology suggests a less stable situation. Some changes may be visible archaeologically in the inhumation cemeteries now found throughout the intramural region and north of the Forth. The most important change in burial practice seems to be the shift towards communal burial—or at least more communal than hitherto. This took place against a background of ephemeral settlement archae-ology, described as a late third- to fifth-century 'gap'. The new ceme-teries were possibly used by several different settlements, providing a shared ritual focus. This would be similar to the sixth-century northern Gaulish situation, where cemeteries also appear against a backdrop of scattered, ephemeral settlement evidence. This hypothesis could suggest that burial became a more public, communal occasion than had earlier been the case. A wider audience participated in the funeral process, now apparently including some sort of procession from the household to the cemetery. The cemeteries' frequent organization into rough rows of graves suggests that a grave's location and arrangement was to some extent governed by factors other than a desire to place members of the same family near each other. This might in turn mean that funerals 'spoke' to each other, ritually, in quite direct and distinctive ways. The funeral could thus have been the occasion for statements about the deceased, his or her family, inheritance, and so on. This 'dialogue' between different families, using rituals connected with the life cycle to demonstrate, enhance, or cement local standing, suggests that politics had retreated to very local, small-scale arenas. This would be a classic sign of increasing instability. Especially in Fife and Angus but to some extent also in Midlothian the patchy data suggest that it was younger and female subjects that tended to be buried in these sites. In the light of local, inter-familial alliances and the stress within them that a death could bring, this cemetery evidence can be read as suggesting, as in sixth-century Gaul and lowland Britain, a level of competition for authority. This was nevertheless expressed rather differently and probably in a more muted way than it was in contemporary northern Gaul or England.

Inscriptions are also found between the Walls. These too can be incorporated into the schema of local competition. Permanent inscribed monuments tend to be associated with a more established local elite than is implied by competitive, temporary ritual displays. Their appearance at this point in time is instructive. So is the fact that this, essentially, is a Roman means of commemoration.

Thus, we can propose that political competition was played out using different ethnic/political identities based on the old Pictish confederacies, the lower-level tribes, or perhaps even claimed links with the departing or departed Empire. Such, doubtless often violent, competition surely encompassed whatever military leaders now controlled the Wall and its hinterland. In this context it becomes easier to understand why the Picts made so little difference to post-imperial Britain south of the Wall. The Rhineland Franks and Alamans, and the Anglo-Saxons across the North Sea, had provinces into which they were drawn by social stress and competition. By contrast, the southern 'Picts' were barred from the former villa-zone by evidently quite effective military leaders in the erstwhile military zone. In my reconstruction, they were also crucially weakened by internal turmoil, caused by the late fourth-century southwards retreat of Roman authority.

Indeed, in a situation diametrically opposed to that on the Rhine, the 'British' powers on the Wall were possibly drawn north into *barbaricum* by crisis and political competition there. In this connection it is further to be expected that 'British' political identities would surface and spread. Something that cannot be overlooked in thinking about post-imperial northern Britain is the so-called Anglian takeover. This is all too rarely considered in subtle terms, usually just being viewed as a violent process of conquest and domination by an exogenous group. It would be rash to remove those elements from the equation but it is timely to think more closely about what Anglian takeover might have involved.

Two or three features of the 'Anglian takeover' feature most prominently in the literature; the appearance of allegedly Anglo-Saxon cemeteries (furnished inhumations) and that of the equally supposedly diagnostic *Grubenhaus*, to which we can add changes in the organization and planning of some high-status hill-top sites that emerge at the end of our period. That at Yeavering, eventually becoming an Anglo-Saxon royal palace, is the most famous example but others have been added in recent decades, such as Doon Hill and Sprouston.

All these elements need critical revaluation. We have already seen that that there is nothing at all inherently 'Germanic' about furnished inhumation. These graves are rather different from the region's usual burials, and the material deposited in this public ritual probably makes a link with political identities we would think of as Anglian, in the same way as we saw objects in Kentish graves making a link with the Frankish kingdom. By the time these burials begin to appear, however, it is worth saying that such a link would be with polities further south in Britain, not with Saxon territories across the North Sea, except perhaps in myth. Once again, we must think of the appearance of these graves as indicative of local competition. Artefacts reveal, perhaps, the political use of ethnic identities, but to see them as simply demarcating the inexorable march of the English across the landscape would be too unsubtle an interpretation. Such graves as do exist are usually few in number and not especially lavishly furnished. This is important in determining how one reads the precise political circumstances and degree of stress. Comparison with furnished burial elsewhere in western Europe suggests that it was quite limited, which would fit with the more or less contemporary development of high-status settlements in the region.

The *Grubenhäuser* are crying out for more refined interpretation. Many of the problems involved in reading off an ethnic identity from these buildings have already been discussed. Furthermore, these huts are now known from sites right up the east coast of Scotland as far as the Mounth, where it would be rash indeed to see them as passive indices of English settlement. It seems more fruitful to see them as a feature of our 'North Sea Cultural Province', with movement of ideas in all directions.

The high-status settlements mentioned earlier, which begin to appear in the late sixth century, are another important feature of the Anglian takeover. There frequently seems to be a change in the nature of the site, often read as marking the change from British to English rule. The debate has again been too crude. Political ownership is again expressed, implicitly at least, in terms of biologically or genetically determined ethnic groups. More subtle readings of change and its relationship to ethnic identity are possible. They can perhaps be understood in the context of the transformations taking place across western Europe in the decades either side of 600, a period which, I suggest, is crucial for the political history of Britain, north and south, and which I will discuss more in the next chapter.

My proposition is that the southernmost Pictish confederacy underwent serious fifth-century crisis and the territories between the Roman Walls became one of competing political identities. Into this area the British warlords of Hadrian's Wall were drawn, expanding their kingdoms. Other realms in this region might have emerged from groups that had been subsumed within the Dicalydone confederacy. The best-known political group in the region are the Votadini/ Gododdin, largely due to their participation in the mysterious but evidently disastrous battle of Catraeth, lamented in Aneirin's Y *Gododdin*. Traditionally the capital of 'Manau Gododdin' has been regarded as Edinburgh, although evidence of post-imperial occupation either of the rock of Edinburgh itself or the neighbouring hillfort at Arthur's Seat has proved elusive. Were this the case, the Votadini/Gododdin would be a good example of a group formerly included in the Dicalydones, reasserting their identity in a crisis like, perhaps, the Angles and the Jutes. More recently, though, it has been argued that the Votadinian capital was Corbridge, a Roman town just behind the east of Hadrian's Wall. The evidence for this theory is not especially compelling but it has a number of attractions. If it is correct then the Gododdin would be one of the groups expanding northwards from the Wall region during the fifth-century crisis. By the time we have written evidence, the region between the Roman Walls was competed for by several groups, mostly British, but with two new groups entering the picture, to whom we will return in the next chapter. It is interesting that the Picts themselves seem conspicuous only by their absence, perhaps another index of the extent of the crisis into which their confederacy was plunged in the fifth century.

The Arthurian context?

What should have emerged by now is the idea that post-imperial politics and society in Britain are ill served by the traditional model of Romano-Britons fighting Anglo-Saxons in a gradual process of barbarian conquest. The more one looks at the material cultural record, the more that model seems completely to obfuscate the reality of the situation. Social, political, or cultural groupings do not fit with the idea of an east–west divide, with uniform groups on either side. Material culture supposedly revealing the two ethnic groups is much more complex. Politics in this period were dominated by inter-factional rivalry rather than by binary struggles between Romans and barbarians, and there are crucial indications in our British source, Gildas' *De Excidio*, that civil war rather than barbarian invasion was the norm here too. Ethnic change was a complex, subtle process based on more widespread and significant factors than birth or geographical origins. Some differences emerging in the early medieval world, between highland and lowland zones, for example, or the power of the realms that lie along the border between those zones, originate before the end of the Roman Empire. The division between Saxon polities, generally south of the Thames, and Anglian ones to the north, evident by the time our earliest written sources describe the Anglo-Saxon kingdoms, also seems to emerge in fifth-century politics and not through the differential origins of northern German settlers. Kingdoms might have been rather larger than is usually thought, and could have shared important features with contemporary realms across the Channel.

In this context, an 'Arthur' figure heading the forces of a post-imperial realm with heroic, notable, but short-lived effects looks far from implausible. The problem is that any such figure—one, say, who led 'Saxon' forces fighting for a 'Roman' state in the *south* or midlands of the island, fighting rivals to north and west, as well as to east and south—would have no place in the type of histories that were envisaged and ideologically necessary in the eighth century and later. He would not fit the model of 'Britons versus Saxons'. If he ruled a polity which in his day saw itself as Roman—in the usual complex late imperial sense—but which adopted a non-Roman identity afterwards, he would not fit *anyone's* historical agenda by the eighth century. All that might have left 'our' Arthur with nowhere to go except into legend, and it might help us understand why he did not gain much popularity before the twelfth century even there. It is more important to think *with* this 'Arthur', to think of him as a *type*. Kings like this could perfectly well have existed in fifth- or sixth-century Britain with fascinating careers, all details of which have been irretrievably lost. This is more important than whether or not any of them happened to be called Arturus or Arthur. Indeed, whether or not one of the post-imperial British kings was called Arthur is probably the *least* interesting question that one can ask about this important period.

12

The End of the 'World of Arthur'

✣

From the late sixth century, the outlines of British political history begin to be set out in more or less reliable sources of various kinds. As we have seen, these know nothing of any great Arthur, although three (admittedly rather humdrum) historical Arthurs lived at precisely this time. Be that as it may, the world revealed to us in the documents from the end of the sixth century is very different from that which has been under discussion in the previous chapters.

The archaeological record in the highlands and the lowlands reveals many changes. In Anglo-Saxon archaeology, the end of the sixth century is an important period of change in the design and form of artefacts. Around 600 or so the inhumation custom enters a phase where grave-goods are far less common or varied. This is the 'Age of Sutton Hoo', a period when very lavish inhumations are known, with the grave placed under a mound—and at Sutton Hoo Mound 1 in a ship as well. On settlement sites, we can detect the dwellings of more powerful people. One well-known such site is Cowdery's Down (Hampshire). Some large halls have not unjustly been termed palaces.

Evidence survives of an economic upsurge in the Anglo-Saxon regions with the introduction of the earliest coins—*thrymsas* (a corruption of the Latin *tremissis*, the name of the same coin in Gaul). The first signs of Anglo-Saxon trading sites—*emporia* as archaeologists call them—are located at Ipswich (Suffolk), and unsurprisingly perhaps evidence increases of long-distance trading connections with mainland Europe.

Putting all this evidence together gives a suggestive picture of increasing social stability and the power of local elites. Many archaeologists have ascribed the emergence of kingship to this period. However, there is no reason to discount the existence of such rulership in the fifth and sixth centuries. Many changes occurring around 600 in lowland Britain are (as before) analogous to ones taking place in northern Gaul at the same time. There it is clear that there was no newly emergent kingship. That had existed for a long time. What seems to be the case there is the emergence of a stronger, more established and independent nobility. It might very well be that what the changes visible in the record represent is earlier, larger-scale kingship fragmenting into the smaller kingdoms well known in the seventh to ninth centuries. We could be seeing the break-up of extensive but fragile realms into smaller but more stable entities. Like the suggestion of large fifth- and sixth-century kingdoms, this proposition would currently find few supporters among Anglo-Saxon specialists. Nevertheless, the idea of small kingdoms in the 'Arthurian' period is based on questionable assumptions and suffers from a failure to consider the European mainland. Therefore we should at least retain the possibility that what happened around 600 was the break-up of large kingdoms rather than the emergence of kingship itself.

Some evidence bolsters this hypothesis. It finds support in the way that for the next 150 years or so the kingdoms south of the Humber tended not to conquer or annex one another but to reduce defeated kingdoms to tributary status. In other words, 'Southumbrian'

Anglo-Saxon kings sought political dominance within a fairly stable political arena. They fought for *imperium* or overlordship, not to remove the other kingdoms from the competition. One reason might have been that it was easier to leave a ruler, or his family, and their systems of government in place, to produce tribute and military contingents (diverting resources to the over-king), than to try to establish a whole new administration. Another might have been dictated by Realpolitik; to eliminate a kingdom completely might create an overwhelming rebellious alliance of worried sub-kings. This began to change in the later eighth century when Offa of Mercia reduced some sub-kings to the status of *ealdormen*, simple royal officers, but the effort was short-lived and did not survive his death. Only the Vikings' political takeover of the regions north and east of Watling Street at the end of the ninth century definitively ruptured this old English political arena.

More supporting evidence might include the list of overlords in Kent to which Bede apparently had access (as mentioned in Chapter 2). The rulers of Sussex and of Wessex (or the *Gewissae*) had seemingly both ruled over Kent in the late sixth century. The *Anglo-Saxon Chronicle*'s entries for the last decade or so of the sixth century show Æthelberht of Kent defeating Ceawlin of the *Gewissae*. Æthelberht's direct appeal to Pope Gregory I for a bishop for his realm might, in addition to signalling independence from Frankish hegemony, have been a way of marking both freedom from West Saxon overlordship and the institution of his own *imperium*. The kings of East Anglia and of Essex are described as being subservient to Æthelberht until his death (616). This might have meant the fracturing of a larger Saxon kingdom in the south, whose existence is proposed in the preceding chapters. That suggested realm was based further west, growing out of early Saxon settlement on the edge of the villa-zone, possibly associated with or, alternatively, taking over the polity based on 'Quoit Brooch Style'. My alternative model would have this large polity fracturing around 600, as south-eastern areas broke away and became more powerful. To this period, therefore, the smaller kingdoms of Kent, Essex, and Sussex might owe their origins and to this period, possibly, belongs the creation of a different 'Jutish' identity in the south-east and, perhaps, appropriation by the Jutish kings of Kent of the 'origin myth' of Hengist, Horsa, and Vortigern, 'the proud tyrant'.

This led, indeed, to a brief period of dominance by the south-eastern English kingdoms (Kent to 616 and East Anglia for the next decade or so). Trade patterns changed around 600. A new long-distance exchange network, possibly connected with the changes in northern Gaul alluded to above, and called the 'continental system', replaced the 'Mediterranean system', which had dominated since the early Roman period. This meant that prestigious imports began to flow into Britain through the south-east.

This economic shift, while giving power to the south-eastern kingdoms, took it away from those of the highlands. The Irish Sea area was keyed into the continental system but it seems to have been secondary to the south coast in this. The Mediterranean system had, as we have seen, brought prestigious items into western Britain more or less to the exclusion of other regions. This might very well, as noted, have been a source of power and authority for the highland kings. This now ended and the economic balance of power swung to the south-east and to the English. Many hill-forts occupied in the 'Age of Arthur' were abandoned or became less notable. The Welsh kingdoms visible in seventh-century sources look small and might also have fragmented around 600.

With all this in mind it is perhaps not surprising that when British politics begin to be reliably documented we seem to be in a period of military dominance and conquest by the English at the British kingdoms' expense. In c.613–16 the Northumbrians won a major victory over a combined force of British kingdoms at Chester; the kingdom of Elmet, in Yorkshire, was conquered by the Northumbrians in the

620s. In 603 the Northumbrians inflicted a decisive defeat on a Scottish army at the battle of Degsastane; by the 630s they seem to have conquered Lothian and reached the environs of Stirling. In the first chapter describing the politics of his native Northumbria, Bede described Æthelfrith of Bernicia as conquering more lands from the Britons than any other king. This phase did not last very long; certainly by the 650s the situation had stabilized. Yet it lends support to those who see one of the historical Arthurs who died at this time as the prototype for the legendary warrior. He would have lived when one could say that the Britons were fighting against invading Saxons. Yet note that even during this period warfare *between* the English was at least as important as that against the Welsh. By the 630s the dominance of the kingdoms of the highland–lowland border (Wessex, Mercia, and Deira/Northumbria) was restored. The south-eastern English kingdoms had been reduced to a tributary status where they would remain until the Viking attacks.

Mention of Æthelfrith and the Bernicians allows us to return to northern Britain and especially the region between the Hadrianic and Antonine Walls. In the last chapter we discussed the 'Anglian takeover' of this area, suggesting that this might have been more complex than is often assumed. Here and in the Pictish territories north of the Forth, the decades around 600 were important. We have already mentioned the appearance of the high-status hill-forts at this time. There are also changes in burial, in Fife and Angus at least, with the introduction of above-ground monuments—cairns and barrows—from the later sixth century. This is the most commonly favoured date for the first types of Pictish symbol stone, as well.

The implication of these changes, paralleled around our 'North Sea cultural province' in lowland Britain and in Gaul, is that local elites were becoming more secure in their authority and control of resources. Traditionally these changes have been viewed as a step on the march to the creation of a kingdom of Scotland. As with the

English example, we should be cautious about accepting this. To my mind these changes are equally compatible with the establishment of smaller political units, whose rulers had more intensive authority. Such realms might have included several of the new 'players' on the political scene north of Hadrian's Wall. The Anglian kingdom of Bernicia apparently emerged at this time. Although its origin legends place the Bernicians' arrival in the 540s, the name of their great stronghold, Bamburgh, comes from that of Bebba, the wife of Æthelfrith. Bernicia itself is generally believed to take its name from an earlier Celtic 'Bryneich'. What might have happened at the end of the sixth century was that a political faction within Bryneich, based around an English identity (perhaps 'Saxon' mercenaries within the kingdom), seized power from its British rulers. In this 'factional' context, perhaps, the battle of Catraeth takes on an extra dimension, especially if one accepts the idea that the capital of the Gododdin was at Corbridge, south of Bamburgh. The commander of the Gododdin forces might himself have been English (Golistan being a corruption of Wulfstan).

A similar process might have lain behind Deira's creation. This kingdom also preserves an earlier British name: Deur. Around 600, with the economic shifts mentioned, English identity might have gained importance in political rivalries, being connected with currently important south-eastern kingdoms. English settlers and military forces could have existed a long way inside the former Britannia from the very start of our period. English and British traditions repeatedly envisaged the presence of Anglo-Saxons around the wall, fighting the Picts. English might thus have been another of the competing identities north of the Wall in the fifth and sixth centuries. The heroic struggles between the kings of Rheged and the Bernicians, described in Aneirin's poems and in the *HB*, could have been a rather more complex affair than the defence of northern Britain against Anglo-Saxon invaders.

Another new contender emerging from the sixth-century situation might have been the Scottish kingdom of Dalriada. Its origins might not have been dissimilar to those just mooted for Bernicia and Deira. Scottish migration into Argyll has been the topic of much debate, with no clear outcome other than that we know rather less about it now than we thought we did fifty years ago. Nonetheless, with the inevitably close links and contacts across the Irish Sea, it is likely that a Gaelic-speaking faction took power, with the backing of Irish kingdoms, in what had hitherto been part of a wider, looser Pictish confederacy. As with the Bernicians, it is difficult to push the Scottish kingdom's origins much earlier than the late sixth century. Against this backdrop it is less surprising that the showdown for control of the inter-mural zone was fought not between near neighbours, but between the newcomers, the Scots and the Bernicians, at the battle of Degsastane in 603. Nor is it as surprising that political and military history was played out across a huge area from the north-east of Ireland to the east coast of England. Traditions even record an Irish king besieging Bamburgh. Again, politics were acted out within very large territories. Interesting, again, is the Picts' absence from the story. It could be that new Pictish polities were themselves only emerging at about this time.

To end this chapter, though, the most important point to stress is the sheer extent of social, economic, religious, and political change in Britain (and indeed across western Europe and beyond) around 600. The world that emerged from it was very different from that of the fifth and sixth centuries. These upheavals buried the 'Age of King Arthur' for good. We will never now be able to recount the history of that Dark Age in any detail, or know whether there ever was an Arthur or what he did. What we *can* do, and what we can continue to refine our ways of doing, is think about the general social, economic, and political frameworks within which the history of that era was played out.

The old quest for King Arthur is fruitless. The documentary evidence cannot respond to those sorts of questions. More seriously, to pretend to have provided the answers sought by that romantic quest from the surviving written sources is downright dishonest. In this and the previous chapters I have argued that we can find new questions to ask, ones for which the evidence to hand might be able to provide plausible responses, even if ones always susceptible to refinement and correction. Many people will be unsatisfied by this but—in my view—it must be more interesting and exciting than chasing answers to unanswerable questions. Fact, after all, *is* stranger than fiction.

FURTHER READING

This bibliographical essay gives the sources for particular points and arguments and the publication of the archaeological sites mentioned in the text. Otherwise it aims to be indicative and useful and makes no pretence at comprehensiveness. Much fuller bibliographies are contained in the general works by authors much more specialized in the topics under discussion. I have not been able to cite everything from which I have learnt and there are doubtless many inexplicable-looking omissions. For the latter the explanation is either that they did not in the end relate precisely to the points I was making, or that I have simply forgotten them, or else that, inexplicably, I haven't actually read them.

Part I

The quote opening this Part comes from W. S. Churchill, *A History of the English Speaking Peoples*. Vol. i: *The Birth of Britain* (London, 1956), 46.

CHAPTER 1

A very good account of the development of the Arthur story can be found in Higham (2002). For the legends, see also Barber (2004). The primary sources referred to are listed, alphabetically by their author or (in the case of anonymous works) their title, in the first part of the bibliography. The chapter on King Arthur in Wood (1981: 40–61) remains a classic introductory essay on the subject, and the original inspiring TV programme on which the book was based can be seen (in admittedly grainy form) online: <http://www.youtube.com/watch?v=HJMof_P9wKU>, <http://www.youtube.com/watch?v=IMlMksg1GOo>, <hhtp://www.youtube.com/watch?v=R8dHW-

pUFWI>, <http://www.youtube.com/watch?v=BwDY_-2rh24>, <http://www.youtube.com/watch?v=klsJTMrdJsI&feature=relmfu>—all accessed 5 Apr. 2012. The book was reprinted with a new afterword in 2005.

The responses to Morris (1973) referred to are Dumville (1977a) and Campbell (1986a). Gidlow (2004) is by far the best recent 'pro-Arthurian' treatment of the period, and the only one that can responsibly be recommended. Higham (2002) is an attempt to disprove the historical existence of Arthur. By the nature of things, neither Higham's nor Gidlow's efforts are (or can be) entirely convincing but both may be studied with profit. Two recent French treatments of the general topic of this book are Gautier (2007), which includes a good discussion of the growth of Arthurian legend as well as a critical discussion of the historical background, and Galliou (2011), which is more archaeological and restricted to the post-imperial era. I have not listed the 'pseudo-histories' alluded to as none can be recommended without the reader risking being seriously misled. Moreover, they do not deserve the publicity.

CHAPTER 2

The rebellion of Constantine 'III' is best discussed in Drinkwater (1998) and Kulikowski (2000).

Translations of the primary sources referred to are listed alphabetically by their author or (in the case of anonymous works) their title in the first part of the bibliography. For presentations (of varying sobriety) of the traditional narrative told in this chapter, see Alcock (1971), Ashe (1968), Morris (1973), and Myres (1986) but there are innumerable others. Most of the modern pseudo-histories retell it in some form or other.

CHAPTER 3

For the traditional archaeology of the Anglo-Saxon settlement, see Leeds (1913); Myres (1986). A more balanced description of the state of play c.1970 can be found in Alcock (1971), which discusses the Irish, Picts, and Scots as well as the Saxons and Britons. The chapters by Alcock, Rahtz, and Ralegh Radford in Ashe (1968) further set out the ways in which the period was seen archaeologically before the major changes in the 1970s.

Useful critical accounts of the development of Anglo-Saxon archaeology can be found in Arnold (1987: 1–16), throughout Hills (1979) and (2003),

Welch (1992), Dickinson's chapter in Rahtz, Dickinson, and Watts (1980) and Lucy and Reynolds's introduction to Lucy and Reynolds (2002). Most of these focus on cemeteries. For settlement archaeology, see the first chapter of Hamerow (2002). The article by E. T. Leeds alluded to is Leeds (1912). See also Leeds (1925). Major (1978), originally published in 1913, plots the conquest of Wessex using hill-forts. Evison (1965) posited Frankish leadership of the Anglo-Saxon migration. Rejection of Myres's interpretation of Romano-Saxon Ware can be found in Gillam (1979) and Roberts (1982). For the famous site at Sutton Hoo, see Care Evans (1986); Carver (1998). The hill-fort at The Mote of Mark was published in Curle (1913–14). Alcock (1975) was the first major publication of South Cadbury.

For the development of the archaeology of Picts and Scots, see Foster (2004). The volume edited by Wainwright referred to in the text is Wainwright (1955). For Isabel Henderson's work on the symbol stones, see, classically, Henderson (1957–8) and (1967). For a thorough catalogue and description of the stones, see Fraser (2008).

All of these works will provide good descriptive accounts of the nature of the evidence, even if the interpretations of the older works can now be questioned.

Part II

The quote opening this Part is from Dumville (1977a: 188).

CHAPTER 4

Many revisions of our views of early medieval sources can be found *en passant* in general works or specialist studies of other problems. See also the introductions to the translations and editions of the sources themselves. For a general introduction to the sources for early medieval history, see Halsall (2005). Dumville (1977a) is the essential starting point for any reassessment of the 'Celtic' sources, with the baton taken up by Padel (1994). Yorke (1999) is a handy, brief overview, as is Yorke (1990: 1–9). Both focus on the Anglo-Saxons. A valuable introduction to the problems of the sources relating to Scotland is at Fraser (2009: 1–11). The discussions in older works though often, for their time, perfectly sound—as at Alcock (1971: 21–88)—cannot now be relied upon.

Major rethinking of Gildas really began with Lapidge and Dumville (1984). See especially the chapters by Dumville and Lapidge themselves. The alternative reading of the Badon passage by Ian Wood comes from his chapter in that volume. See also Kerlouégan (1989) for an exhaustive linguistic study. Wiseman's crucial rereading of the Badon passage is to be found in Wiseman (2000). An interesting and detailed analysis of the structure of the *De Excidio* and a treatment of how it might relate to fifth-century theological debates can be found in George (2009), though this has not convinced everyone. Another detailed, interesting, but controversial study is Higham (1994). See also Daniell (1994); Jones (1988); Sims-Williams (1983a); Woolf (2002).

Bede has been exhaustively studied. A huge amount of enormously important material is collected in Lapidge (1994a) and (1994b) and DeGregorio (2010). Of especial importance to the present work are Bonner (1976); Campbell (1966) and (1986c); Goffart (1988: 235–328); Higham (1995)—controversial; Kirby (1966); Miller (1975); Sims-Williams (1983b); and especially Wormald (1981). On genealogies as sources, see Davis (1992); Dumville (1976) and (1977b); Moisl (1981).

On the *Historia Brittonum* ('Nennius'), Dumville (1972–4), (1977a), and (1994); Padel (1994). The way in which the *HB* changes the image of Germanus from that in Constantius' *Vita* is dealt with in a forthcoming paper 'Writing Saint Germanus in Medieval Wales' by Alex Woolf. I am very grateful to Dr Woolf for letting me read and cite that paper in advance of publication.

The studies of the Anglo-Saxon chronicle referred to in the text are Brooks (1989) and Yorke (1989). See also Harrison (1971), with caution; Sims-Williams (1983b); Jorgensen (2010).

On the other sources, see Burgess (1990) and (2001); Jones and Casey (1988); Miller (1978); Muhlberger (1983); Thompson (1984); Wood (1984) and (1987).

CHAPTER 5

There are numerous overviews of late Roman Britain and its downfall. The best (in spite of being nearly a quarter of a century old) remains Esmonde-Cleary (1989). Johnson (1982), in spite of being only seven years older, seems to be from a very different age, but still contains much useful information. More recently a series of books dealing with the end of Roman Britain have appeared: Dark (1994) and (2002); Faulkner (2000); Higham (1992); Jones

(1996); Knight (1999), which, alone of these, discusses some of the European mainland; Laycock (2008). All have interesting ideas in places and all have interesting and reliable discussions of particular classes of data, although all are also problematic to a greater or lesser degree. The biggest problem is the lack of awareness of mainland Europe at the time. See also Fleming (2010: 1–29).

For the Saxon Shore, see Johnson (1979); Maxfield (1989); White (1961). Cotterill (1993) proposes that the forts were not built to keep out the Saxons, which may well be correct, but his argument that there was no fourth-century Saxon raiding is implausible. By the time that the poet Claudian was writing, around 400, Britain was already associated with Saxons in the Roman imagination.

The articles by Reece mentioned in the text are Reece (1980) and (1981). The most recent reliable overview of Roman Britain is Mattingly (2006). For the cemetery of Poundbury a useful summary is Sparey Green (1982), with Sparey Green (1993) for the full publication. For Wroxeter, see White and Barker (1998), for Silchester, Fulford (1993), and, for London, Milne (1993) and (1995).

On the third-century crisis, a good critical overview is Witschel (2004). For the late Roman Empire and its system of governance, see Kelly (1998) and (2004). The reference to the British grain fleet is at Ammianus Marcellinus, *Res Gestae* 18.2.3.

One of the early overviews of the archaeological evidence for a crisis in Roman Britain before the usual date given for Saxon settlement was Arnold (1984).

For more optimistic reading of the archaeology, especially the black earth, of late Roman towns, see Dark (1994) and especially (2002). The similar readings of Wroxeter are summed up in White and Barker (1998) and extrapolated across western Roman Britain in White (2007). On late antiquity, Brown (1971) is usually cited as the foundational text, although the concept is really rather older. See Garnsey and Humfress (2001) for an update. For papers discussing Britain's relationship to the 'late antique problematic', see Collins and Gerrard (2004); Halsall (2009).

The explanation of villa abandonment as a sign of a change of fashion can be read, *inter alia*, in Lewit (2003), with a not dissimilar, but variant interpretation by Bowes and Gutteridge (2005). The idea that military fashion explains the shift is expressed by Wickham (2005: 201–2, 331–2, 476–7). For the 'failed state' hypothesis, see Laycock (2008).

CHAPTER 6

Anglo-Saxons:
For descriptions of the evidence, see the readings for Chapter 3. See also Tipper (2004) for the *Grubenhaus*. For an overview of ideas about the Anglo-Saxon migration and of Anglo-Saxon archaeology around the start of the third millennium Hills (2003) is excellent. Another well-informed overview, more inclined towards a larger-scale migration, is Hamerow (2005).

For doubts about the 'imported' nature of the Anglo-Saxon hall, see James, Marshall, and Millett (1985) and Dixon (1982). The essential riposte can be found in Hamerow (1994), (1997), and especially (2003). Scull (1991) attempts to elucidate the ethnicity of the inhabitants of Yeavering according to building features.

For a minimalizing view of the role of immigration using cemetery data, see Lucy (2000) and (2002); on cremations, Williams (2002). Hodges (1989: 22–42) is a thoroughly minimalist account. Scull (1995) and (1998) sees migration as more important.

An overview discussion of ethnicity, its nature, and its use in late antiquity may be found in Halsall (2007: 35–62). For early medievalists, a crucial article was Geary (1983). See now Geary (2002). Other classics are Pohl (1998a) and (1998b). The subject is heatedly debated in Gillett (2002), and Goffart (2006). Anthropologically, the rethinking of the topic is often held to start with Barth (1969). For ethnicity and material culture, crucial case studies include Larrick (1986) and Moerman (1968). The move towards seeing furnished inhumations as the sign of Frankish lordship rather than Frankish settlement was begun by James (1979).

For migration theory, especially as applied to early Anglo-Saxon England, see Chapman and Hamerow (1997); Hamerow (1994) and (1997); Scull (1998); Gebuhr (1998); Trafford (2000) usefully describes the 'theory'.

On language change, the classic is Jackson (1953). See more recently, with differing conclusions, the papers in Bammesberger and Wollmann (1990); Gelling (1993); Parsons (2011); Schrijver (1999) and (2007); Woolf (2003), esp. 369–73. The debate over language change is technical and frequently based upon philological theories, developed since the nineteenth century, about pronunciations and the dates of phonetic shifts. Many of these are, given the evidence for this period (or rather its lack), unsusceptible of proof and some look questionable when compared with socio-linguistics in better-documented eras. Ultimately, what this means is that the reader either accepts the premises from which the argument starts, and follows it from there, judging it in accordance with those principles, or rejects those starting points and with them the possibility of arriving at usable conclusions from evidence first recorded centuries after the period in question.

On the use of DNA to detect migrants, see Weale et al. (2002). Hills (2003: 57–71) is an excellent critique. See also Evison (2000).

Social theory and cemeteries: A key publication in encouraging new ways of thinking about Anglo-Saxon cemeteries was Rahtz, Dickinson, and Watts (1980). See also Arnold (1980); Pader (1980) and (1981); Shephard (1979). Other collections of work include Southworth (1990); Kjeld Jensen and Høilund Nielsen (1997); Lucy and Reynolds (2002). For analysis of weapon burials, see Härke (1989), (1990), (1992a), and (1992b). Analysis of gender: Lucy (1995); Stoodley (1999). This is, of course, only a tiny sample of the work done.

On the origins of the Anglo-Saxon kingdoms, see, above all, Bassett (1989b); Kirby (2000); Yorke (1990). The 'FA Cup Model' is set out most clearly by Bassett (1989a). The state of play ten years later can be judged from Dickinson and Griffiths (1999). See also Arnold (1987); Charles-Edwards (2003b); Fleming (2010: 39–80); Hamerow (2005); Hines (2003); Scull (1993); Yorke (2003).

Highland Britons:

See Lowe (1999) for a survey of the regions north of Hadrian's Wall; White (2007) for an excellent overview of the archaeology of western Britain, in the highlands, and on the western fringes of the villa-zone; Dark (1994) also covers this area; Davies (1982) and Redknap (1991) for Wales proper; Pearce (1978), Rahtz (1982–3) and (1991), and Thomas (1994) for the south-west. See also the extensive overview and treatment of the north in Alcock (2003). For Rheged, see McCarthy (2002). Snyder (1998: 129–216) is a useful gazetteer covering most of these areas. For overviews of the early kingdoms, including historical and archaeological material, see Charles-Edwards (2003b); Davies (1982: 85–140) and (2005); Fleming (2010: 30–9, 80–8); Woolf (2003). Other studies of Britons, especially of British survival in Anglo-Saxon

England, are found in Laing (1977) and Higham (2007).

The fort at Birdoswald is described in Wilmott (1997) and the evidence for post-imperial use of the wall-forts as high-status sites is assembled by Dark (1992). Dinas Powys is written up in Alcock (1987), and South Cadbury in Alcock, Stevenson, and Musson (1995). For Cadbury Congresbury, see Rahtz (1992), and for Clyde Rock, Dumbarton, Alcock and Alcock (1990). Alcock (1987) covers wide thematic areas as well and is in many ways an updated version of Alcock (1971). For recent studies of Yeavering, see Frodsham and O'Brien (2005).

On the archaeology of Christianity in late and post-imperial Britain, early classics were Thomas (1971) and (1981). See also Barley and Hanson (1968); Edwards (1992); Pearce (1982); Mawer (1995); Murray (2009); and Petts (2003). For British cemeteries, see Cowley (2009); Lucy (2005); Rahtz (1968). The Catstane cemetery is discussed in Rutherford and Ritchie (1972–4) and Cowie (1977–8). For inscriptions, the CISP database is online at <http://www.ucl.ac.uk/archaeology/cisp/database/> (accessed 1 Feb. 2012). See also Forsyth (2005) and (2009); Handley (1998) and (2001); Thomas (1994). For Irish settlement see Rahtz (1976), Thomas (1973) and (1994); Woolf (2007).

On Mediterranean trade into the Irish Sea in the post-imperial era, see Campbell (1996); Dark (1996); Lane (1994); Thomas (1982).

Picts and Scots

For overviews of Pictish and Scottish archaeology, see, above all, Foster (2004). See also Laing and Laing (1993); Alcock (2003). For the Picts, see Carver (1999); Foster (1992). For the Scots see Campbell (1999). The general history of the period is most recently and interestingly surveyed in Fraser (2009).

Archaeological approaches to the development of a Pictish state are set out interestingly in Driscoll (1988a) and (1988b).

Hill-forts: The publication of Dundurn is Alcock and Alcock (1989) and that of Clatchard Craig is Close-Brooks (1986). For Dunollie, see Alcock and Alcock (1987).

The Loch Glashan crannog is published in Crone and Campbell (2005). For Pictish settlements, see Hunter (2007) for the Roman background especially; Hunter (1997), for Orkney; Ralston (1997). The Eilean Olabhat site is published in Armit, Campbell, and Dunwell (2008).

For Pictish cemeteries, in addition to good coverage in the general works, see: Alexander (2005); Ashmore (1978–80); Burt (1997); Greig, Greig, and Ashmore (2000); Proudfoot (1996); Rees (2002). Useful information on Scottish burial can be found in Meredith-Lobay (2009).

For the symbol stones, see Forsyth (1997), which proposes that the symbols represent a sort of alphabet; Henderson (1996); Laing and Laing (1984) argued for an early date for the symbol stones; Murray (1986); Samson (1992), which suggests that the symbols represent dithematic names. For the Scottish inscribed stones at Cladh a'Bhile, see Gondek (2006).

Part III

The quote is from 'What a fool believes' (K. Loggins and M. McDonald) by The Doobie Brothers (1978).

CHAPTER 7

R. G. Collingwood's discussion of Arthur and his cavalry is in Collingwood and Myres (1937: 320–4). The notion also appears in Morris (1973: 97–115). Otherwise, the only work that requires recognition is Laycock (2009), the origin of the 'Germanic Arthur' theory. On mounted warfare in this period, see Halsall (2003: 180–8).

Part IV

The quote at the opening of this Part is taken from 'It Doesn't Have to Be That Way' by The Blow Monkeys (RCA/Arista, 1987).

The evidence upon which this book is based, and the debates to which it responds, are those discussed in Chapters 2–6, and there is no need to repeat bibliography given for those chapters. Only additional references are presented and, as before, citations for precise points.

CHAPTER 8

Welch (1989), for instance, proposes zones of settlement governed by treaty, in Sussex, from the absence of 'Anglo-Saxon Cemeteries'. Dark (2002) delineates British polities from similar absences. James (2000) broke away from the English vs. Celts framework to discuss northern and southern political spheres instead. A new view of the fifth-century history, which breaks away from the 'barbarian invasions' model, without denying the importance of migration or the drama (and trauma) of the period, is presented in Halsall (2007)—use the corrected 2009 reprint. Roman attitudes to, and the military reality of, the barbarian 'threat' have been importantly re-evaluated by John Drinkwater (1996) and (1997). Teitler (1992) explicitly likens Roman aristocrats to collaborators. On chiastic style, see Howlett (1986). Karen George (2009) suggests that Gildas' *De Excidio* was written to a chiastic structure, while David Howlett has at some time suggested that almost every insular source employed it. Howlett (1998: 69) proposed the chiastic structure of the *HB*'s Arthurian Battle-List, similarly arguing that it must therefore have been initially composed in Latin. The version and conclusions I present were arrived at independently of this, which was unknown to me at the time. Howlett's extreme application of the style is critiqued by Hood (1999). The revival of Mercian dominance after 829–30 is demonstrated in Sawyer (1978: 121). On Merfyn Frych ('the Freckled') see his entry (by David Thornton) in the *New Dictionary of National Biography*. For Birka, the best place to start is in Clarke and Ambrosiani (1995: 73–6). The London 'black earth' is analysed in Watson (1998). An excellent overview of the archaeology of post-imperial British towns, rejecting 'maximalist' continuity models like that for Wroxeter, is Loseby (2000). Mattingly (2006: 529–39) presents a 'post-colonial' view of the end of Roman Britain, which I find unconvincing. Laycock (2008) sets out the 'failed state' hypothesis—equally wide of the mark in my view. Handley (2000) discusses the use of the measurement of time to define *civitas* identity. The dramatic consequences of the withdrawal of the imperial court, for northern Gaul and Britain, are argued for by Halsall (2007: 209–10, 217–19). The quote comes from Orchard (2003: 194). The 'moving front' view of Frankish settlement is most recently set out in English by Dierkens and Périn (2003) and questioned in Halsall (2010: 169–97).

CHAPTER 9

A traditional—but scholarly and knowledgeable—discussion of the dating of early Anglo-Saxon federate settlement is Welch (1993). See also Böhme (1986). My identification of Gildas' *tyrannus superbus* with Maximus was first proposed in Halsall (2007: 519–26). That argument is expanded here. Sidonius' panegyric to Majorian is no. 5 of his *Poems*, with the implicit reference to Maximus at lines 349–60. David Dumville's argument about the consulate of Valerian and Decius is presented in Dumville (1972–4). I am very grateful to Richard Burgess for discussions about chronology, minor chronicles, and fifth-century ideas about the end of the world. On the Welsh use of Germanus in their political ideology, see, again, Alex Woolf's forthcoming paper on the subject. The nature of late fourth-century *foederati* is discussed importantly by Burns (1994) and Liebeschuetz (1991). For traces of Maximus in Britain see Casey (1979b). Useful discussions and of late Roman military metalwork and its distribution can be found in Böhme (1986); Laycock (2008); and Swift (2000). Laycock (2008: 100–2) also discusses the fortification of fourth-century towns and other settlements. For the possible settlement of Irish federates in the West, see Rance (2001).

CHAPTER 10

Hamerow (2002) has excellent discussion of settlements on both sides of the North Sea. For a description of northern Gallic settlements, see Périn (2002). For the fate of northern Gallic villas, see van Ossel and Ouzoulias (2000). For discussion of the crisis in Saxony, see Dörfler (2003); Meier (2003); and Siegmund (2003). For the rejection of furnished inhumation as an index of 'Germanic' presence, see Halsall (2010: 89–167). The relationships between *barbaricum* and the fourth-century Empire, and the 'push' and 'pull' factors involved in fifth-century migrations, may be found in Halsall (2007: 138–62, 417–22, 447–54). The argument by Barbara Yorke referred to is that of Yorke (1989).

CHAPTER 11

For a fuller discussion of fifth-century identities and ethnic change, see Halsall (2007: 455–82) and the references given there. An extreme, but important, view of mutable identity was presented by Amory (1997). The equal and opposite, conservative view is that of Heather (1996). My own view lies between these two, if probably closer to Amory's. For 'Quoit Brooch Style' see Suzuki (2000); for Saxon Relief Style' see Inker (2006); and for discussion of both, see Böhme (1986). For 'Dobunnic' metalwork see Laycock (2008: 121–3); for metalwork focused on the Severn estuary, Hines (2003: 95 and refs.). Riothamus is mentioned by Sidonius Apollinaris in his *Letters*, 8.6, and in Jordanes' *Getica*, 45.237. The association of Riothamus with

Arthur is found, *inter alia*, in Du Quesnay Adams (1993). The decidedly non-linear history of Merovingian Gaul can be followed in Wood (1994). Penda's 'Grande Armée' is that described at *HE* 3.24. For 'functional ethnicity' in the post-imperial West, see Halsall (2007: 475–6 and refs). Post-imperial military organization in Britain and mainland Europe is discussed in Halsall (2003: esp. 40–70). Social analysis of Merovingian graves, with some attention drawn to implications for Anglo-Saxon England, is discussed in Halsall (2010: 199–412, with full references). For Traprain Law, see Feachem (1955–6).

CHAPTER 12

As before, the evidence upon which this chapter is based can mostly be found via the reading lists for Chapter 6. Most of the general and many of the specific studies deal with evidence across the period and so discuss the changes at the end of the sixth century. On the period of change around 600, see, most recently and interestingly, Fleming (2010: 89–119). Aspects of this period, across Britain and beyond, are also covered in Carver (1992). On change in Anglo-Saxon burial, see Geake (1997). The politics of northern Britain, emphasizing the very wide political arena fought over, are very well described in Fraser (2009: 121–74). Fraser sets out some possibilities for the Bernician takeover of southern Scotland which are not dissimilar from those presented here but which Fraser, of necessity, presents more guardedly, on 149–54. The possibility of an attack on Bamburgh by the Irish Dál Fiatach is discussed on 160–1.

BIBLIOGRAPHY

Primary Sources

Adomnán: *Adomnán of Iona: Life of St. Columba*, trans. R. Sharpe (Harmondsworth, 1995).

Ambrose, *Letters*: *Ambrose of Milan: Political Letters and Speeches*, trans. J. H. W. G. Liebschuetz (Liverpool, 2005); *St Ambrose: Letters*, trans. M. M. Beyenka, FotC 26 (Washington, DC, 1954).

Ammianus Marcellinus, *Res Gestae*: *Ammianus Marcellinus*, trans. J. C. Rolfe, 3 vols. (London, 1935–9).

Aneirin: See *Y Gododdin*.

Anglo-Saxon Chronicle: *The Anglo-Saxon Chronicle translated and with Introduction and Notes*, trans. G. N. Garmonsway (London [Everyman], 1953); *English Historical Documents*, i: *c.550–1042*, trans. D. Whitelock (2nd edn. London, 1979), doc. 1.

Annales Cambriae: *British History and the Welsh Annals*, ed. and trans. J. Morris (Chichester, 1980).

Armes Prydein: *Armes Prydein. The Prophecy of Britain from the Book of Taliesin*, ed. and trans. I. Williams (Dublin, 1982).

Bede, *Ecclesiastical History of the English People*: *Bede's Ecclesiastical History of the English People*, ed. and trans. B. Colgrave and R. A. B Mynors (Oxford, 1969).

Book of the History of the Franks: *The Liber Historiae Francorum*, trans. B. S. Bachrach (Laurence, Kan., 1973).

Canu Taliesin: See Taliesin.

Compact of Salic Law: *The Laws of the Salian Franks*, trans. K. F. Drew (Philadelphia, 1991); *The Laws of the Salian and Ripuarian Franks*, trans. T. J. Rivers (New York, 1987), 39–144.

Constantius, *Life of Germanus: Soldiers of Christ: Saints and Saints' Lives from Late Antiquity and the Early Middle Ages*, ed. T. F. X. Noble and T. Head (Pennsylvania, 1995), 75–106.

Gallic Chronicle of 452: From Roman to Merovingian Gaul, trans. A. Callander Murray (Peterborough, Ontario, 2000), 76–85.

Gildas, *On the Ruin and Conquest of Britain (De Excidio Britanniae): Gildas: The Ruin of Britain and Other Documents*, ed. and trans. M. Winterbottom (Chichester, 1978).

Geoffrey of Monmouth, *History of the Kings of Britain: The History of the Kings of Britain: An Edition and Translation of the* De Gestis Britonum (Historia Regum Britanniae), ed. and trans. M. D. Reeve and N. Wright (Woodbridge, 2009); *Geoffrey of Monmouth: The History of the Kings of Britain*, trans. L. Thorpe (Harmondsworth, 1966).

Gregory of Tours, *Histories: Gregory of Tours. The History of the Franks*, trans. L. Thorpe (Harmondsworth, 1974).

Harleian Genealogies: See 'Welsh genealogies'.

Historia Brittonum: Nennius: British History and the Welsh Annals, ed. and trans. J. Morris (Chichester, 1980)

Jesus College Genealogies: See 'Welsh genealogies'.

Jordanes, *Getica: The Gothic History of Jordanes*, trans. C. C. Mierow (New York, 1915; repr. 1966).

Marcellinus, *Chronicle: The Chronicle of Marcellinus*, ed. and trans. B. Croke (Sydney, 1995).

Muirchú, *Life of Patrick: St. Patrick. His Writings and Muirchú's Life*, ed. and trans. A. B. E. Hood (Chichester, 1978), 61–98.

Narrative of the Emperors of the Valentinianic and Theodosian Houses: MGH AA CM, 629–30.

Nennius: See *Historia Brittonum*.

Notitia Dignitatum: Notitia Dignitatum accedunt Notitia Urbis Constantinopolitanae et Latercula Provinciarum, ed. O. Seeck (Frankfurt am Main, 1876; repr. Frankfurt, 1962).

Orosius, *Seven Books of History against the Pagans: Paulus Orosius. The Seven Books of History against the Pagans*, trans. R. J. Deferrari (Washington, DC, 1964).

Pacatus: *Panegyric to the Emperor Theodosius*, trans. C. E. V. Nixon (Liverpool, 1987).

Paschale Campanum: MGH AA CM, 305–34.

Patrick, *Confession*: *St. Patrick. His Writings and Muirchú's Life*, ed. and trans. A. B. E. Hood (Chichester, 1978), 23–34, 41–55.

—— *Letter to Coroticus*: *St. Patrick. His Writings and Muirchú's Life*, ed. and trans. A. B. E. Hood (Chichester, 1978), 35–8, 55–9.

Paulinus, *Life of Ambrose*: *The Western Fathers*, trans. F. R. Hoare (London, 1954), 147–88.

Procopius, *Wars*: *Procopius*, ed. and trans. H. B. Dewing, vols. i–v (London, 1914–28).

Prosper of Aquitaine, *Chron.*: *From Roman to Merovingian Gaul*, trans. A. Callander Murray (Peterborough, Ontario, 2000), 62–76.

Rufinus of Aquileia, *Ecclesiastical History*: *The Church History of Rufinus of Aquileia, Books 10 and 11*, ed. and trans. P. R. Amidon (Oxford, 1997).

Sidonius Apollinaris, *Poems*: *Sidonius: Poems and Letters*, ed. and trans. W. B. Anderson, vol. i (London, 1936), 1–327.

—— *Letters*: *Sidonius: Poems and Letters*, ed. and trans. W. B. Anderson, vol. i (London, 1936), 329–483; *Sidonius: Poems and Letters*, ed. and trans. W. B. Anderson with E. H. Warmington, vol. ii (London, 1965).

Sulpicius Severus, *Dialogues*: *The Western Fathers*, trans. F. R. Hoare (London, 1954), 68–144.

—— *Life of Martin*: *The Western Fathers*, trans. F. R. Hoare (London, 1954), 3–44.

Taliesin: *Taliesin Poems: New Translations*, trans. M. Pennar (Llanerch, 1988).

Tribal Hidage: D. Dumville (1989). 'The Tribal Hidage: an introduction to its texts and their history', in Bassett (1989b: 225–30).

Victorius, *Cursus Paschalis Annorum DXXXII*: *MGH AA CM*, 667–735.

Welsh Annals: See *Annales Cambriae*.

Welsh genealogies: The Harleian genealogies can conveniently be found at <http://www.kmatthews.org.uk/history/harleian_genealogies/index.html>, and the Jesus College collection of genealogies at <http://www.kmatthews.org.uk/history/jesus_college_20/index.html> (both accessed 2 Feb. 2012). They are printed in *Arthurian Period Sources*, v: *Genealogies and Texts*, ed. J. Morris (Chichester, 1995), 44–55.

Y Gododdin: *The Gododdin of Aneirin: Text and Context from Dark-Age Britain*, ed. and trans. J. T. Koch (Cardiff, 1997).

Zosimus, New History: *Zosime: Histoire nouvelle*, ed. and (French) trans. F. Paschoud (Paris, 1971–89); *Zosimus. New History*, trans. R. T. Ridley (Canberra, 1982).

Secondary Works

Alcock, L. (1971). *Arthur's Britain* (Harmondsworth).

—— (1975). *'By South Cadbury is that Camelot...': The Excavation of Cadbury Castle 1966–1970* (London).

—— (1987). *Economy, Society and Warfare among the Britons and Saxons* (Cardiff).

—— (2003). *Kings and Warriors, Craftsmen and Priests in Northern Britain*, AD 550–850 (Edinburgh).

—— and Alcock, E. A (1987). 'Reconnaissance excavations on early historic fortifications and other royal sites in Scotland 1974–1984: 2: excavations at Dunollie Castle, Oban, Argyll, 1978'. *PSAS* 117: 119–47.

—— and —— (1989). 'Reconnaissance excavations on early historic fortifications and other royal sites in Scotland 1974–1984: 3: excavations at Dundurn, Strathearn, Perthshire, 1976–77'. *PSAS* 119: 189–226.

—— and —— (1990). 'Reconnaissance excavations on early historic fortifications and other royal sites in Scotland 1974–1984: 4: excavations at Alt Clut, Clyde Rock, Strathclyde, 1974–75'. *PSAS* 120: 95–149.

—— Stevenson, S. J., and Musson, C. R. (1995). *South Cadbury: The Early Medieval Archaeology* (Cardiff).

Alexander, D. (2005). 'Redcastle, Lunan Bay, Angus: the excavation of an Iron Age timber-lined souterrain and a Pictish barrow cemetery'. *PSAS* 135: 41–118.

Amory, P. (1997). *People and Identity in Ostrogothic Italy, 489–554* (Cambridge).

Armit, I., Campbell, E., and Dunwell, A. (2008). 'Excavation of an Iron Age, early historic and medieval settlement and metalworking site at Eilean Olabhat, North Uist'. *PSAS* 138: 27–104.

Arnold, C. J. (1980). 'Wealth and social status: a matter of life and death'. In Rahtz, Dickinson, and Watts (1980: 81–142).

—— (1984). *From Roman Britain to Saxon England* (London).

—— (1987). *An Archaeology of the Early Anglo-Saxon Kingdoms* (London).

Ashe, G. (ed.) (1968). *The Quest for Arthur's Britain* (London).

Ashmore, P. J. (1978–80). 'Low cairns, long cists and symbol stones'. *PSAS* 110: 346–55.

Bammesberger, A., and Wollmann, A. (eds.) (1990). *Britain, 400–600: Language and History* (Heidelberg).

Barber, R. W. (2004). *King Arthur: Hero and Legend* (Woodbridge).

Barley, M. W., and Hanson, R. P. C. (eds.) (1968). *Christianity in Britain, 300–700* (Leicester).

Barth, F. (ed.) (1969). *Ethnic Groups and Boundaries: The Social Organization of Culture Difference* (Bergen).

Bassett, S. (1989a). 'In search of the origins of Anglo-Saxon kingdoms'. In Bassett (1989b: 3–27).

—— (ed.) (1989b). *The Origins of Anglo-Saxon Kingdoms* (London).

Böhme, H. W. (1986). 'Das Ende der Römerherrschaft in Britannien und die angelsächsische Besiedlung Englands im 5. Jahrhundert'. *JRGZM* 33: 469–574.

Bonner, G. (ed.) (1976). *Famulus Christi: Essays in Commemoration of the Thirteenth Centenary of the Birth of the Venerable Bede* (London).

Bowes, K., and Gutteridge, A. (2005). 'Rethinking the later Roman landscape'. *Journal of Roman Archaeology* 18: 405–13.

Brooks, N. P. (1989). 'The creation and early structure of the kingdom of Kent'. In Bassett (1989b: 55–74).

Brown, P. R. L. (1971). *The World of Late Antiquity* (London).

Burgess, R. W. (1990). 'The Dark Ages return to fifth-century Britain: the "restored" Gallic Chronicle exploded'. *Britannia* 21: 185–96.

—— (2001). 'The Gallic Chronicle of 452: a new critical edition with a brief introduction'. In R. W. Mathisen and H. S. Sivan (eds.), *Shifting Frontiers in Late Antiquity* (Aldershot), 52–84.

Burns, T. S. (1994). *Barbarians within the Gates of Rome: A Study of Roman Military Policy and the Barbarians, ca.375–425* (Bloomington, Ind.).

Burt, J. R. F. (1997). 'Long cist cemeteries in Fife'. In Henry (1997: 64–6).

Campbell, E. (1996). 'Trade in the Dark Age West: a peripheral activity?' In Crawford (1996: 79–91).

—— (1999). *Saints and Sea-Kings: The First Kingdom of the Scots* (Edinburgh).

Campbell, J. (1966). 'Bede'. In Dorey (1966: 159–90), repr. as 'Bede I', in Campbell (1986a: 1–27).

—— (1986a). *Essays in Anglo-Saxon History* (London).

—— (1986b). 'The Age of Arthur'. In Campbell (1986a: 121–30).

—— (1986c). 'Bede II'. In Campbell (1986a: 29–48).

Care Evans, A. (1986). *The Sutton Hoo Ship Burial* (London).

Carver, M. O. H. (ed.) (1992). *The Age of Sutton Hoo: The Seventh Century in North-Western Europe* (Woodbridge).

—— (1998). *Sutton Hoo: Burial Ground of Kings?* (London).

—— (1999). *Surviving in Symbols: A Visit to the Pictish Nation* (Edinburgh).

Casey, P. J. (ed.) (1979a). *The End of Roman Britain*, BAR(B) 71 (Oxford).

—— (1979b). 'Magnus Maximus in Britain: a reappraisal'. In Casey (1979a: 66–79).

Chapman, J., and Hamerow, H. (eds.) (1997). *Migrations and Invasions in Archaeological Explanation*, BAR (I) 664 (Oxford).

Charles-Edwards, T. (ed.) (2003a). *After Rome* (Oxford).

—— (2003b). 'Nations and kingdoms: a view from above'. In Charles-Edwards (2003a: 23–58).

Clarke, H., and Ambrosiani, B. (1995). *Towns in the Viking Age* (rev. edn. London).

Close-Brooks, J. (1986). 'Excavations at Clatchard Craig, Fife'. *PSAS* 116: 117–84.

Coates, R. (2007). 'Invisible Britons: the view from linguistics'. In Higham (2007: 172–91).

Collingwood, R. G., and Myres, J. N. L. (1937). *Roman Britain and the Anglo-Saxon Settlements* (2nd edn. Oxford).

Collins, R., and Gerrard, J. (eds.) (2004). *Debating Late Antiquity in Britain*, AD 300–700 (Oxford).

Cotterill, J. (1993). 'Saxon raiding and the role of the late Roman coastal forts of Britain'. *Britannia* 24: 227–39.

Cowie, T. G. (1977–8). 'Excavations at the Catstane, Midlothian 1977'. *PSAS* 109: 166–201.

Cowley, D. C. (2009). 'Early Christian cemeteries in south-west Scotland'. In Murray (2009: 43–56).

Crawford, B. E. (ed.) (1996). *Scotland in Dark Age Britain* (St Andrews).

Crone, A., and Campbell, E. (2005). *A Crannog of the First Millennium AD: Excavations by Jack Scott at Loch Glashan, Argyll, 1960* (Edinburgh).

Curle, A. O. (1913–14). 'Report on the excavations, in September 1913, of a vitrified fort at Rockcliffe, Dalbeattie, known as the Mote of Mark'. *PSAS* 48: 125–68.

Daniell, C. (1994). 'The geographical perspective of Gildas'. *Britannia* 25: 213–17.

Dark, K. R. (1992). 'A sub-Roman re-defence of Hadrian's Wall?' *Britannia* 23: 111–20.

—— (1994). *From Civitas to Kingdom: British Political Continuity, 300–800* (Leicester).

—— (ed.) (1996). *External Contacts and the Economy of Late and Post-Roman Britain* (Woodbridge).

—— (2002). *Britain and the End of the Roman Empire* (Stroud).

Davies, W. (1982). *Wales in the Early Middle Ages* (Leicester).

—— (2005). 'The Celtic kingdoms'. In *NCMH* 1: 232–62.

Davis, C. R. (1992). 'Cultural assimilation in the Anglo-Saxon royal genealogies'. *ASE* 21: 23–36.

DeGregorio, S. (ed.) (2010). *The Cambridge Companion to Bede* (Cambridge).

Dickinson, T. M., and Griffiths, D. (eds.) (1999). *The Making of Kingdoms, Anglo-Saxon Studies in History and Archaeology* 10 (Oxford).

Dierkens, A., and Périn, P. (2003). 'The 5th-century advance of the Franks in Belgica II: history and archaeology'. In E. Taayke, J. H. Looijenga, O. H. Harsema, and H. R. Reinders (eds.), *Essays on the Early Franks* (Groningen), 165–93.

Dixon, P. (1982). 'How Saxon is the Saxon house?' In P. Drury (ed.), *Structural Reconstruction: Approaches to the Interpretation of the Excavated Remains of Buildings*, BAR(B) 110 (Oxford), 275–86.

Dorey, T. A. (ed.) (1966). *Latin Historians* (London).

Dörfler, W. (2003). 'Rural economy of the continental Saxons from the migration period to the tenth century'. In Green and Siegmund (2003: 133–48).

Drinkwater, J. F. (1996). '"The Germanic threat on the Rhine frontier": a Romano-Gallic artefact?'. In R. W. Mathisen and H. S. Sivan (eds.), *Shifting Frontiers in Late Antiquity* (Aldershot), 20–30.

—— (1997). 'Julian and the Franks and Valentinian I and the Alamanni: Ammianus on Roman–German relations'. *Francia* 24: 1–16.

—— (1998). 'The usurpers Constantine III (407–411) and Jovinus (411–413)'. *Britannia* 29: 269–98.

Driscoll, S. (1988a). 'Power and authority in early historic Scotland: Pictish symbol stones and other documents'. In J. Gledhill, B. Bender, and M. T. Larsen (eds.), *State and Society: The Emergence and Development of Social Hierarchy and Political Centralization* (London), 215–36.

—— (1988b). 'The relationship between history and archaeology: artifacts, documents and power'. In Driscoll and Nieke (1988: 162–87).

Driscoll, S. T., and Nieke, M. R. (eds.) (1988). *Power and Politics in Early Medieval Britain and Ireland* (Edinburgh).

Dumville, D. N. (1972–4). 'Some aspects of the chronology of the *Historia Brittonum*'. *BBCS* 25: 439–45.

—— (1976). 'The Anglian collection of royal genealogies and regnal lists'. *ASE* 5: 23–50.

—— (1977a). 'Sub-Roman Britain—history and legend'. *History* 62: 173–92.

—— (1977b). 'Kingship, genealogies and regnal lists'. In P. H. Sawyer, and I. N. Wood (eds.), *Early Medieval Kingship* (Leeds), 72–104.

—— (1994). *Historia Brittonum*: an insular history from the Carolingian Age'. In Scharer and Scheibelreiter (1994: 406–34).

Du Quesnay Adams, J. (1993). 'Sidonius and Riothamus'. *Arthurian Literature* 12: 157–64.

Edwards, N. (ed.) (1992). *The Early Church in Wales and the West: Recent Work in Early Christian Archaeology, History and Place-Names* (Oxford).

Esmonde-Cleary, A. S. (1989). *The Ending of Roman Britain* (London).

Evison, M. P. (2000). 'All in the genes? Evaluating the biological evidence of contact and migration'. In Hadley and Richards (2000: 277–94).

Evison, V. (1965). *The Fifth-Century Invasions South of the Thames* (London).

Faulkner, N. (2000). *The Decline of Roman Britain* (Stroud).

Feachem, R. W. (1955–6). 'The fortifications of Traprain Law'. *PSAS* 89: 284–9.

Fleming, R. (2010). *Britain after Rome: The Fall and Rise, 400 to 1070* (London).

Forsyth, K. (1997). 'Some thoughts on Pictish symbols as a formal writing system'. In Henry (1997: 85–98).

—— (2005). '*Hic memoria perpetua*: the early inscribed stones of southern Scotland in context'. In S. M. Foster and M. Cross (eds.), *Able Minds and Practised Hands: Scotland's Early Medieval Sculpture in the 21st Century* (Edinburgh), 113–34.

—— (2009). 'The Latinus Stone: Whithorn's earliest Christian Monument'. In Murray (2009: 19–41).

Foster, S. M. (1992). 'The state of Pictland in the age of Sutton Hoo'. In Carver (1992: 217–34).

—— (1997). 'The Picts: quite the darkest of the peoples of Dark Age Britain'. In Henry (1997: 5–17).

—— (2004). *Picts, Gaels and Scots* (2nd edn. Edinburgh).

Fraser, I. (2008). *The Pictish Symbol Stones of Scotland* (Edinburgh).

Fraser, J. (2009). *From Caledonia to Pictland: Scotland to 795* (Edinburgh).

Frodsham, P., and O'Brien, C. (eds.) (2005). *Yeavering: People, Power and Place* (Stroud; repr. 2009).

Fulford, M. (1993). 'Silchester: the early development of a civitas capital'. In Greep (1993: 17–33).

Galliou, P. (2011). *La Bretagne d'Arthur: Bretons et Saxons de siècles obscurs* (Clermont-Ferrand).

Garnsey, P., and Humfress, C. (2001). *The Evolution of the Late Antique World* (Cambridge).

Gautier, A. (2007). *Arthur* (Paris).

Geake, H. (1997). *The Use of Grave-Goods in Conversion-Period England, c.600–c.850*, BAR(B) 261 (Oxford).

Geary, P. J. (1983). 'Ethnic identity as a situational construct in the early Middle Ages'. *Mitteilungen der Anthropologischen Gesellschaft in Wien* 113: 15–26.

—— (2002). *The Myth of Nations: The Medieval Origins of Europe* (Princeton).

Gebuhr, M. (1998). 'Angulus Desertus?' *SzSf* 11: 43–85.

Gelling, M. (1993). 'Why aren't we speaking Welsh?' *Anglo-Saxon Studies in Archaeology and History* 6: 51–6.

George, K. (2009). *Gildas's* De Excidio Britonum *and the British Church* (Woodbridge).

Gidlow, C. (2004). *The Reign of Arthur: From History to Legend* (Stroud).

Gillam, J. (1979). 'Romano-Saxon pottery: an alternative explanation'. In Casey (1979a: 103–18).

Gillett, A. (ed.) (2002). *On Barbarian Identity: Critical Approaches to Ethnicity in the Early Middle Ages* (Turnhout).

Goetz, H.-W., Jarnut, J., and Pohl, W. (eds.) (2003). *Regna and Gentes: The Relationship between Late Antique and Early Medieval Peoples and Kingdoms in the Transformation of the Roman World* (Leiden).

Goffart, W. (1988). *The Narrators of Barbarian History, AD 550–800: Jordanes, Gregory of Tours, Bede, Paul the Deacon* (Princeton).

—— (2006). *Barbarian Tides: The Migration Age and the Later Roman Empire* (Philadelphia).

Gondek, M. M. (2006). 'Early historical sculpture and landscape: a case study of Cladh a'Bhile, Ellary, Mid-Argyll'. *PSAS* 136: 237–58.

Green, D. H., and Siegmund, F. (eds.) (2003). *The Continental Saxons from the Migration Period to the Tenth Century: An Ethnographic Perspective* (Woodbridge).

Greep, S. J. (ed.) (1993). *Roman Towns: The Wheeler Inheritance. A Review of 50 Years of Research* (York).

Greig, C., Greig, M., and Ashmore, P. (2000). 'Excavation of a cairn cemetery at Lundin Links, Fife'. *PSAS* 130: 585–636.

Hadley, D. M., and Richards, J. D. (eds.) (2000). *Cultures in Contact: Scandinavian Settlement in England in the Ninth and Tenth Centuries* (Turnhout).

Halsall, G. (2003). *Warfare and Society in the Barbarian West, 450–900* (London)

—— (2005). 'The sources and their interpretation'. *NCMH* 1: 56–90.

—— (2007). *Barbarian Migrations and the Roman West* (Cambridge).

—— (2009). 'Beyond the northern frontiers'. In P. Rousseau with J. Raithel (eds.), *A Companion to Late Antiquity* (Oxford), 409–25.

—— (2010). *Cemeteries and Society in Merovingian Gaul: Selected Studies in History and Archaeology, 1992–2009* (Leiden).

Hamerow, H. (1994). 'Migration theory and the migration period'. In *Building on the Past: Papers Celebrating 150 Years of the Royal Archaeological Institute* (London), 164–77.

—— (1997). 'Migration theory and the Anglo-Saxon "identity crisis"'. In Chapman and Hamerow (1997: 33–44).

—— (2002). *Early Medieval Settlements: The Archaeology of Rural Communities in North-West Europe 400–900* (Oxford).

—— (2005). 'The earliest Anglo-Saxon kingdoms'. *NCMH* 1: 263–88.

Handley, M. (1998). 'The early medieval inscriptions of Western Britain: function and sociology'. In J. Hill and M. Swan (eds.), *The Community, the Family and the Saint: Patterns of Power in Early Medieval Europe* (Turnhout), 339–61.

—— (2000). 'Inscribing time and identity in the kingdom of Burgundy'. In S. Mitchell and G. Greatrex (eds.), *Ethnicity and Culture in Late Antiquity* (London), 83–102.

—— (2001). 'The origins of Christian commemoration in late antique Britain'. *EME* 10: 177–99.

Härke, H. (1989). 'Early Saxon weapon burials: frequencies, distributions and weapon combinations'. In S. Chadwick-Hawkes (ed.), *Weapons and Warfare in Anglo-Saxon England* (Oxford), 49–61.

—— (1990). '"Weapon graves"? The background of the Anglo-Saxon weapon burial rite'. *P and P* 126: 22–43.

—— (1992a). *Angelsächsische Waffengräber des 5. bis 7. Jahrhunderts* (Cologne).

—— (1992b). 'Changing symbols in a changing society: the Anglo-Saxon weapon rite'. In Carver (1992: 149–65).

Harrison, K. (1971). 'Early Wessex annals in the Anglo-Saxon Chronicle'. *EHR* 86: 527–33.

Heather, P. (1996). *The Goths* (Oxford).

Henderson, I. (1957–8). 'The origin-centre of the Pictish symbol stones'. *PSAS* 91: 44–60.

—— (1967). *The Picts* (London).

—— (1996). *Pictish Monsters: Symbol, Text and Image*, M. Chadwick Memorial Lectures 7 (Cambridge).

Henry, D. (ed.) (1997). *The Worm, the Germ and the Thorn: Pictish and Related Studies Presented to Isabel Henderson* (Balgavies).

Higham, N. J. (1992). *Rome, Britain and the Anglo-Saxons* (London).

—— (1994). *The English Conquest: Gildas and Britain in the Fifth Century* (Manchester).

—— (1995). *An English Empire: Bede and the Early Anglo-Saxon Kings* (Manchester).

—— (2002). *King Arthur: Myth-Making and History* (London).

—— (ed.) (2007). *Britons in Anglo-Saxon England* (Woodbridge).

Hills, C. (1979). 'The archaeology of Anglo-Saxon England in the pagan period: a review'. *ASE* 8: 297–330.

—— (2003). *The Origins of the English* (London).

Hines, J. (2003). 'Society, community, and identity'. In Charles-Edwards (2003a: 60–102).

Hodges, R. (1989). *The Anglo-Saxon Achievement* (London).

Hood, A. B. E. (1999). 'Review article: lighten our darkness—biblical style in early medieval Britain and Ireland'. *EME* 8: 283–96.

Howlett, D. R. (1986). 'Biblical style in early insular Latin'. In P. E. Szarmach (ed.), *Sources of Anglo-Saxon Culture* (Kalamazoo, Mich.), 127–47.

—— (1998). *Cambro-Latin Compositions: Their Competence and Craftsmanship* (Dublin).

Hunter, F. (2007). *Beyond the Edge of Empire: Caledonians, Picts and Romans* (Rosemarkie).

Hunter, J. (1997). *A Persona for the Northern Picts* (Rosemarkie).

Inker, P. (2000). 'Technology as active material culture: the Quoit Brooch Style'. *Medieval Archaeology* 44: 25–52.

—— (2006). *The Saxon Relief Style*, BAR(B) 410 (Oxford).

Jackson, K. H. (1953). *Language and History in Early Britain* (Edinburgh).

James, E. F. (1979). 'Cemeteries and the problem of Frankish settlement in Gaul'. In P. H. Sawyer (ed.), *Names, Words and Graves* (Leeds), 55–89.

—— (2000). *Britain in the First Millennium* (London).

James, S., Marshall, A., and Millett, M. (1985). 'An early medieval building tradition'. *Archaeological Journal* 141: 182–215.

Johnson, S. (1979). *The Roman Forts of the Saxon Shore* (2nd edn. London).

—— (1982). *Later Roman Britain*. Rev. edn. (London).

Jones, M. E. (1988). 'The appeal to Aëtius in Gildas'. NMS 32: 141–55.

—— (1996). *The End of Roman Britain* (Ithaca, NY).

—— and Casey, P. J. (1988). 'The Gallic Chronicle restored: a chronology for the Anglo-Saxon migrations and the end of Roman Britain'. *Britannia* 19: 367–98.

Jorgensen, A. (ed.) (2010). *Reading the Anglo-Saxon Chronicle: Language, Literature, History* (Leiden).

Kelly, C. (1998). 'Emperors, government and bureaucracy'. In A. M. Cameron and P. Garnsey (eds.), *The Cambridge Ancient History*, xiii: *The Late Empire, A.D. 337–425* (Cambridge), 138–83.

—— (2004). *Ruling the Later Roman Empire* (Cambridge, Mass.).

Kerlouégan, F. (1989). *Le De Excidio Britanniae de Gildas: Les Destinées de la culture latine dans l'île de Bretagne au VIᵉ siècle* (Paris).

Kirby, D. P. (1966). 'Bede's native sources for the Historia'. *Bulletin of the John Rylands Library* 48: 341–71.

—— (2000). *The Earliest English Kings* (2nd edn. London).

Kjeld Jensen, C., and Høilund Nielsen, K. (eds.) (1997). *Burial and Society: The Chronological and Social Analysis of Archaeological Burial Data* (Aarhus).

Knight, J. (1999). *The End of Antiquity: Archaeology, Society and Religion AD 235–700* (Stroud).

Kulikowski, M. (2000). 'Barbarians in Gaul, usurpers in Britain'. *Britannia* 31: 325–45.

Laing, L. (ed.) (1977). *Studies in Celtic Survival*, BAR(B) 37 (Oxford).

—— and Laing, J. (1984). 'The date and origin of the Pictish symbols'. *PSAS* 114261–76.

—— and —— (1993). *The Picts and the Scots* (Stroud).

Lane, A. (1994). 'Trade, gifts and cultural exchange in Dark-Age western Scotland'. In B. E. Crawford (ed.), *Scotland in Dark Age Europe* (St Andrews), 103–15.

Lapidge, M. (ed.) (1994a). *Bede and his World*, i: *The Jarrow Lectures 1958–78* (London).

—— (ed.) (1994b). *Bede and his World*, ii: *The Jarrow Lectures, 1979–93* (London).

—— and Dumville, D. N. (eds.) (1984). *Gildas: New Approaches* (Woodbridge).

Larrick, R. (1986). 'Age grading and ethnicity in the style of Loikop (Samburu) spears'. *World Archaeology* 18: 269–83.

Laycock, S. (2008). *Britannia: The Failed State* (Stroud).

—— (2009). *Warlords: The Struggle for Power in Post-Roman Britain* (Stroud).

Leeds, E. T. (1912). 'The distribution of the Anglo-Saxon saucer brooch in relation to the battle of Bedford, A.D. 571'. *Archaeologia* 61: 159–202.

—— (1913). *The Archaeology of the Anglo-Saxon Settlements* (Oxford).

—— (1925). 'The West Saxon invasion and the Icknield Way'. *History* 10: 97–109.

Lewit, T. (2003). '"Vanishing villas": what happened to elite rural habitation in the West in the 5th–6th c?' *Journal of Roman Archaeology* 16: 260–74

Liebeschuetz, J. H. W. G. (1991). *Barbarians and Bishops: Army, Church and State in the Age of Arcadius and Chrysostom* (Oxford).

Little, L. K., and Rosenwein, B. H. (ed.) (1998). *Debating the Middle Ages* (Oxford).

Loseby, S. T. (2000). 'Power and towns in Late Roman Britain and early Anglo-Saxon England'. In Gisela Ripoll and Josep M. Gurt (eds.), *Sedes regiae (ann. 400–800)* (Barcelona), 319–70.

Lowe, C. (1999). *Angels, Fools and Tyrants: Britons and Anglo-Saxons in Southern Scotland* (Edinburgh).

Lucy, S. J. (1997). 'Housewives, warriors and slaves? Sex and gender in Anglo-Saxon burials'. In J. Moore and E. Scott (eds.), *Invisible People and Processes: Writing Gender and Childhood into European Archaeology* (London).

—— (2000). *The Anglo-Saxon Way of Death: Burial Rites in Early England* (Stroud).

—— (2002). 'Burial practice in early medieval eastern Britain: constructing local identities, deconstructing ethnicity'. In Lucy and Reynolds (2002: 72–87).

—— (2005). 'Early medieval burial at Yeavering: a retrospective'. In Frodsham and O'Brien (2005: 127–44).

—— and Reynolds, A. (eds.) (2002). *Burial in Early Medieval England and Wales* (London).

McCarthy, M. (2002). 'Rheged: an early historic kingdom near the Solway'. *PSAS* 132: 357–81.

Major, A. (1978). *Early Wars of Wessex* (London—illustrated reprint of 1913 edn.).

Mathisen, R. W., and Shanzer, D. (eds.) (2001). *Society and Culture in Late Roman Gaul: Revisiting the Sources* (Aldershot).

Mattingly, D. J. (2006). *An Imperial Possession: Britain in the Roman Empire* (London).

Mawer, C. F. (1995). *Evidence for Christianity in Roman Britain: The Small-Finds*, BAR(B) 243 (Oxford).

Maxfield, V. A. (ed.) (1989). *The Saxon Shore: A Handbook* (Exeter).

Meier, D. (2003). 'The North Sea coastal area: settlement history from Roman to early medieval times'. In Green and Siegmund (2003: 37–67).

Meredith-Lobay, M. (2009). *Contextual Landscape Study of the Early Christian Churches of Argyll: The Persistence of Memory*, BAR(B) 488 (Oxford).

Miller, M. (1975). 'Bede's use of Gildas'. *EHR* 305: 241–61.

—— (1978). 'The last British entry in the "Gallic Chronicles"'. *Britannia* 9: 315–18.

Milne, G. (1993). 'The rise and fall of Roman London'. In Greep (1993: 11–15).

—— (1995). *Roman London* (London).

Moerman, M. (1968). 'Being Lue: use and abuses of ethnic identification.' In J. Helm (ed.), *Essays on the Problem of Tribe Proceedings of the 1967 Annual Spring Meeting of the American Ethnological Society* (Seattle), 153–69.

Moisl, H. (1981). 'Anglo-Saxon royal genealogies and Germanic oral tradition'. *JMH* 7: 215–48.

Morris, J. (1973). *The Age of Arthur* (London).

Muhlberger, S. (1983). 'The Gallic Chronicle of 452 and its authority for British events'. *Britannia* 14: 23–33.

Murray, G. (1986). 'The declining Pictish symbol: a reappraisal'. *PSAS* 116: 223–53.

Murray, J. (ed.) (2009). *St Ninian and the Earliest Christianity in Scotland: Papers from the Conference held by the Friends of the Whithorn Trust in Whithorn on September 15th 2007*, BAR(B) 483 (Oxford).

Myres, J. N. L. (1986). *The English Settlements* (Oxford).

Okasha, E. (1996). 'The early Christian carved and inscribed stones of south-western Britain'. In Crawford (1996: 21–35).

Orchard, A. (2003). 'Latin and the vernacular languages: the creation of a bilingual textual culture'. In Charles-Edwards (2003a: 191–219).

Padel, O. J. (1994). 'The nature of Arthur'. *Cambrian Medieval Celtic Studies* 27 (Summer): 1–31.

Pader, E.-J. (1980). 'Material symbolism and social relations in mortuary studies'. In Rahtz, Dickinson, and Watts (1980: 143–59).

—— (1981). *Symbolism, Social Relations and the Interpretation of Mortuary Remains*, BAR(S) 130 (Oxford).

Parsons, D. N. (2011). 'Sabrina in the thorns: place-names as evidence for British and Latin in Roman Britain'. *Transactions of the Philological Society* 109: 113–37.

Pearce, S. M. (1978). *The Kingdom of Dumnonia: Studies in History and Tradition in South-Western Britain, AD 350–1150* (Padstow).

—— (ed.) (1982). *The Early Church in Western Britain and Ireland: Studies Presented to C. A. Ralegh Radford*, BAR(B) 102 (Oxford).

Périn, P. (2002). 'Settlements and cemeteries in Merovingian Gaul'. In K. Mitchell and I. N. Wood (eds.), *The World of Gregory of Tours* (Leiden), 67–99.

Petts, D. (2003). *Christianity in Roman Britain* (Stroud).

Pohl, W. (1998a). 'Telling the difference: signs of ethnic identity'. In Pohl and Reimitz (1998: 17–69).

—— (1998b). 'Conceptions of ethnicity in early medieval studies'. In L. K. Little and B. H. Rosenwein (eds.), *Debating the Middle Ages* (Oxford), 15–24.

—— and Reimitz, H. (eds.) (1998). *Strategies of Distinction: The Construction of Ethnic Communities, 300–800* (Leiden).

Proudfoot, E. (1996). 'Excavations at the long cist cemetery on Hollow Hill, St Andrews, Fife'. *PSAS* 126: 387–454.

Rahtz, P. A. (1968). 'Sub-Roman cemeteries in Somerset'. In Barley and Hanson (1968: 193–95).

—— (1976). 'Irish settlements in Somerset'. *Proceedings of the Royal Irish Academy* 76: 223–30.

—— (1982–3). 'Celtic society in Somerset, AD 400–700'. *BBCS* 30: 176–200.

—— (1991). 'Pagan and Christian by the Severn sea'. In L. Abrams and J. P. Carley (eds.), *The Archaeology and Early History of Glastonbury Abbey: Essays in Honour of the Ninetieth Birthday of C. A. Ralegh Radford* (Woodbridge), 3–37.

Rahtz, P. A. (ed.) (1992). *Cadbury Congresbury, 1968–73*, BAR(B) 223 (Oxford).

—— Dickinson, T. M., and Watts, L. (eds.) (1980). *Anglo-Saxon Cemeteries, 1979*, BAR(B) 82 (Oxford).

Ralston, I. (1997). 'Pictish homes'. In Henry (1997: 18–33).

Rance, P. (2001). 'Attacotti, Déisi and Magnus Maximus: the case for Irish federates in late Roman Britain'. *Britannia* 32: 243–70.

Redknap, M. (1991). *The Christian Celts: Treasures of Late Celtic Wales* (Cardiff).

Reece, R. (1980). 'Town and country: the end of Roman Britain'. *World Archaeology* 12 (1): 77–92.

—— (1981). 'The third century, crisis or change?' In A. King and M. Hennig (eds.), *The Roman West in the Third Century*, BAR(I) 109 (Oxford), 27–38.

Rees, A. R. (2002). 'A first millennium AD cemetery, rectangular Bronze Age structure and late prehistoric settlement at Thornybank, Midlothian'. *PSAS* 132: 313–55.

Roberts, W. I. (1982). *Romano-Saxon Pottery*, BAR(B) 106 (Oxford).

Rutherford, A., and Ritchie, G. (1972–4). 'The Catstane'. *PSAS* 105: 183–8.

Samson, R. (1992). 'The reinterpretation of the Pictish symbols'. *Journal of the British Archaeological Association* 145: 29–65

Sawyer, P. H. (1978). *From Roman Britain to Norman England* (London).

Scharer, A., and Scheibelreiter, G. (eds.) (1994). *Historiographie im frühen Mittelalter* (Vienna).

Schrijver, P. (1999). 'The Celtic contribution to the development of the North Sea Germanic vowel system'. *North-Western European Language Evolution* 35: 3–47.

—— (2007). 'What Britons spoke around 400'. In Higham (2007: 165–71).

Scull, C. (1991). 'Post-Roman Phase I at Yeavering: a reconsideration'. *Medieval Archaeology* 35: 51–63.

—— (1993). 'Archaeology, early Anglo-Saxon society and the origins of Anglo-Saxon kingdoms'. *Anglo-Saxon Studies in Archaeology and History* 6: 65–82.

—— (1995). 'Approaches to material culture and social dynamics of the migration period of eastern England'. In Bintliff and Hamerow (1995: 71–83).

—— (1998). 'Migration theory and early England: contexts and dynamics of cultural change'. *SzSf* 11: 177–85.

Shephard, J. (1979). 'The social identity of the individual in isolated barrows and barrow cemeteries in Anglo-Saxon England'. In R. Burnham and

J. Kingsbury (eds.), *Space, Hierarchy and Society: Interdisciplinary Studies in Social Area Analysis*, BAR(S) 59 (Oxford), 47–79.

Siegmund, F. (2003). 'Social relations among the old Saxons'. In Green and Siegmund (2003: 77–95).

Sims-Williams, P. (1983a). 'Gildas and the Anglo-Saxons'. *Cambridge Medieval Celtic Studies* 6: 1–30.

—— (1983b). 'The settlement of England in Bede and the Chronicle'. *ASE* 12: 1–42.

Snyder, C. A. (1998). *An Age of Tyrants: Britain and the Britons, AD 400–600* (Stroud).

Southworth, E. (ed.) (1990). *Anglo-Saxon Cemeteries: A Reappraisal* (Stroud).

Sparey Green, C. (1982). 'The cemetery of a Romano-British Christian community at Poundbury, Dorchester, Dorset'. In Pearce (1982: 61–76).

—— (1993). *Excavations at Poundbury, Dorchester, Dorset, 1966–1982: 2. The Cemeteries* (Dorchester).

Stoodley, N. (1999). *The Spindle and the Spear: A Critical Enquiry into the Construction and Meaning of Gender in the Early Anglo-Saxon Burial Rite*, BAR(B) 288 (Oxford).

Suzuki, S. (2000). *The Quoit Brooch Style and Anglo-Saxon Settlement* (Woodbridge).

Swift, E. (2000). *Regionality in Dress Accessories in the Late Roman West*, Monographies Instrumentum 11 (Montagnac).

Teitler, H. C. (1992). 'Un-Roman activities in late antique Gaul: the cases of Arvandus and Seronatus'. In J. F. Drinkwater and H. Elton (eds.), *Fifth-Century Gaul: A Crisis of Identity?* (Cambridge), 309–17.

Thomas, C. (1971). *The Early Christian Archaeology of North Britain* (Oxford).

—— (1973). 'Irish colonists in south-west Britain'. *World Archaeology* 5: 5–13.

—— (1981). *Christianity in Roman Britain to AD 500* (London).

—— (1982). 'East and west: Tintagel, Mediterranean imports and the early insular church'. In Pearce (1982: 17–34).

—— (1994). *And Shall These Mute Stones Speak? Post-Roman Inscriptions in Western Britain* (Cardiff).

Thompson, E. A. (1984). *Saint Germanus of Auxerre and the End of Roman Britain* (Woodbridge).

Tipper, J. (2004). *The Grubenhaus in Anglo-Saxon England: An Analysis and Interpretation of the Evidence from Anglo-Saxon England's Most Distinctive Building Type* (Yedingham).

Trafford, S. (2000). 'Ethnicity, migration theory and the historiography of the Scandinavian settlement of England'. In Hadley and Richards (2000: 17–33).

Van Dam, R. (1986). ' "Sheep in wolves' clothing": the letters of Consentius to Augustine'. *Journal of Ecclesiastical History* 37: 515–35.

—— (1993). *Saints and their Miracles in Late Antique Gaul* (Princeton).

Van Ossel, P., and Ouzoulias, P. (2000). 'Rural settlement economy in northern Gaul in the late Empire: an overview and assessment'. *JRA* 13: 133–60.

Wainwright, F. T. (ed.) (1955). *The Problem of the Picts* (London).

Watson, B., 1998. ' "Dark Earth" and urban decline in late Roman London'. In B. Watson (ed.), *Roman London: Recent Archaeological Work*, JRA Supplementary Series 24 (Portsmouth, RI), 100–6.

Weale, M. E., Weiss, D. A., Jager, R. F., Bradman, N., and Thomas, M. G. (2002). 'Y chromosome evidence for Anglo-Saxon mass-migration'. *Molecular Biology and Evolution* 197 (7): 1008–21.

Welch, M. (1989). 'The kingdom of the South Saxons: the origins'. In Bassett (1989b: 75–83).

—— (1992). *Anglo-Saxon England* (London).

—— (1993). 'The archaeological evidence for federated settlements in Britain in the fifth century'. In F. Vallet and M. Kazanski (eds.), *L'Armée romaine et les barbares, III* au VII *siècle* (Paris), 269–78.

White, D. A. (1961). *Litus Saxonicum: The British Saxon Shore in Scholarship and History* (Madison).

White, R. (2007). *Britannia Prima: The Last Roman Province* (Stroud).

—— and Barker, P. A. (1998). *Wroxeter: Life and Death of a Roman City* (Stroud).

Wickham, C. J. (2005). *Framing the Early Middle Ages: Europe and the Mediterranean 400–800* (Oxford).

Williams, H. (2002). 'Remains of pagan Saxondom? The study of Anglo-Saxon cremation rites'. In Lucy and Reynolds (2002: 47–71).

Wilmott, T. (1997). *Birdoswald: Excavations of a Roman Fort on Hadrian's Wall and its Successor Settlements: 1987–92* (London).

Wiseman, H. (2000). 'The Derivation of the Date of the Badon Entry in the *Annales Cambriae* from Bede and Gildas'. *Parergon* NS 17 (2): 1–10.

Witschel, C. (2004). 'Re-evaluating the Roman West in the 3rd century'. *JRA* 17: 251–81.

Wood, I. N. (1984). 'The end of Roman Britain: continental evidence and parallels'. In Lapidge and Dumville (1984: 1–26).

—— (1987). 'The fall of the western Empire and the end of Roman Britain'. *Britannia* 18: 251–62.

—— (1994). *The Merovingian Kingdoms, 450–751* (London).

Wood, M. (1981). *In Search of the Dark Ages* (London).

Woolf, A. (2002). 'An interpolation in the text of Gildas' *De Excidio Britanniae*'. *Peritia* 16: 161–7.

—— (2003). 'The Britons: from Romans to barbarians'. In Goetz, Jarnut, and Pohl (2003: 345–80).

—— (2007). 'The expulsion of the Irish from Dyfed'. In K. Jankulak and J. M. Wooding (eds.), *Ireland and Wales in the Middle Ages* (Dublin), 102–15.

—— (2008). 'Fire from heaven: divine providence and Iron Age hillforts in early medieval Britain'. In P. Rainbird (ed.), *Monuments in the Landscape* (Stroud), 136–43.

Wormald, C. P. (1981). 'Bede, the Bretwaldas and the origins of the *gens anglorum*'. In C. P. Wormald, D. Bullough, and R. J. H. Collins (eds.), *Ideal and Reality in Frankish and Anglo-Saxon Society* (Oxford), 99–129.

Yorke, B. A. E. (1989). 'The Jutes of Hampshire and Wight and the origins of Wessex'. In Bassett (1989b: 84–96).

—— (1990). *Kings and Kingdoms of Early Anglo-Saxon England* (London).

—— (1999). 'The origins of Anglo-Saxon kingdoms: the contribution of written sources'. In Dickinson and Griffiths (1999: 25–9).

—— (2003). 'Anglo-Saxon *gentes* and *regna*'. In Goetz, Jarnut, and Pohl (2003: 381–407).

PHOTOGRAPHIC
ACKNOWLEDGEMENTS

© David Lyons/Alamy: **4**; © The Author: **5**, **12**; © The Trustees Of The British Museum: **9**, **10**; Carmarthenshire Museums Service/photo courtesy of National Museum Cardiff: **16**; © Simon McBride/Collections: **8**; © Skyscan/Corbis: **13**; © English Heritage: **11**; © The Trustees of the National Museums of Scotland: **7**; from *Arthur and the Anglo-Saxon Wars*, by D. Nicolle, © Osprey Publishing Ltd: **2**, **6**; from *British Forts in the Age of Arthur*, by A. Konstam © Osprey Publishing Ltd: **3**, **14**, **15**; © Professor Howard Williams/Project Eliseg: **17**; from *The Story of Saxon and Norman Britain Told in Pictures*, by C. W. Airne © Sankey, Hudson & Co: **1**.

INDEX

Note: Bold entries refer to figures or illustrations.